SECONDARY ALGEBRA EDUCATION

MW01167367

Secondary Algebra Education

Revisiting Topics and Themes and Exploring the Unknown

Edited by

Paul Drijvers
Freudenthal Institute for Science and Mathematics Education,
Utrecht University, Utrecht, the Netherlands

SENSE PUBLISHERS
ROTTERDAM / BOSTON / TAIPEI

A C.I.P. record for this book is available from the Library of Congress.

ISBN 978-94-6091-333-4 (paperback)
ISBN 978-94-6091-334-1 (e-book)

Published by: Sense Publishers,
P.O. Box 21858, 3001 AW Rotterdam, The Netherlands
http://www.sensepublishers.com

A previous version of this book was published in Dutch as:

Wat *a* is, dat kun je niet weten
Een pleidooi voor betekenisvolle algebra op school

Paul Drijvers (Red.)
Utrecht: Freudenthal Institute
Editorial assistants Nathalie Kuijpers and Liesbeth Walther

Printed on acid-free paper

CONTENTS

PREFACE

Nowadays, algebra education is subject to worldwide scrutiny. Different opinions on its goals, approaches and achievements are at the heart of debates among teachers, educators, researchers and decision makers. What should the teaching of algebra in secondary school mathematics look like? Should it focus on procedural skills or on algebraic insight? Should it stress practice or integrate technology? Do we require formal proofs and notations, or do informal representations suffice? Is algebra in school an abstract subject, or does it take its relevance from application in (daily life) contexts? What should secondary school algebra education that prepares for higher education and professional practice in the twenty-first century look like?

To address these questions, the authors of this book, all affiliated with the Freudenthal Institute for Science and Mathematics Education, take different perspectives to describe the opportunities and pitfalls of today's and tomorrow's algebra education. Some authors wonder how the historical development of algebra informs its teaching and learning (Chapter 2), or what a learning trajectory from arithmetic to algebra would look like (Chapter 3). Other chapters deal with specific strands within algebra curricula, such as patterns and formulas (Chapter 4), restrictions (Chapter 5), and functions (Chapter 6). Chapter 7 makes a plea for productive practice of algebraic skills. The perspectives of technology for algebra education (Chapter 8), and the ways algebra is used in science and engineering (Chapter 9) complete the book. In spite of their different foci, the chapters in this book share a common philosophy, which acts as a – sometimes nearly invisible – backbone for the overall view on algebra education: the theory of realistic mathematics education.

By addressing this diversity of perspectives on algebra education, we hope to provide the reader with inspiring examples and points of views, not just to clarify the institute's position, but hopefully to provoke the reader's thinking, and, as its ultimate goal, to contribute to algebra education that appropriately meets students' needs.

Paul Drijvers
Utrecht, the Netherlands, June 2010

PAUL DRIJVERS, AAD GODDIJN, MARTIN KINDT

1. ALGEBRA EDUCATION: EXPLORING TOPICS AND THEMES

There is a stage in the curriculum when the introduction of algebra may make simple things hard, but not teaching algebra will soon render it impossible to make hard things simple. (Tall & Thomas, 1991, p. 128)

ALGEBRA EDUCATION UNDER SCRUTINY

Nowadays, algebra education is subject to worldwide scrutiny. Different opinions on its goals, approaches and achievements are at the heart of 'math war' debates that are taking place in many countries (Klein, 2007; Schoenfeld, 2004). Crucial to these debates is the relationship between procedural skills and conceptual understanding in teaching and learning algebra. On the one hand, computational skills are seen as a prerequisite for conceptual understanding (US Department of Education, 2007). Complaints from tertiary education focus on the lack of such procedural skills, and in several countries higher education is using entrance tests involving basic algebraic skills. Faculty members are often disappointed with students' results on such tests. Secondary school teachers, accused of being too soft on teaching skills, may in turn respond with complaints about the declining level of arithmetic skills that students acquire in primary school; as a result, they lack the elementary number sense and the factual knowledge to recognize 144 as the square of 12 or to notice that there is a relationship between 12/16 and 3/4.

On the other hand, some see the core goal of algebra education as the development of strategic problem solving and reasoning skills, symbol sense and flexibility, rather than procedural fluency. According to this point of view, future societal and professional needs will focus even more on flexible analytical reasoning skills, rather than on procedural skills. Consequently, algebra education should change its goals; it should focus on new epistemologies and aim at new types of understanding.

The relationship between procedural skills and conceptual understanding is a well-researched field. The book *Adding it up* (Kilpatrick, Swafford, & Findell, 2001) synthesizes the research on this issue as the concept of mathematical proficiency, which comprises five ingredients: conceptual understanding, procedural fluency, strategic competence, adaptive reasoning and productive disposition. Conceptual understanding is defined here as 'the comprehension of mathematical concepts, operations, and relations' (p. 116), and procedural fluency as the 'skill in carrying out procedures flexibly, accurately, efficiently, and appropriately' (ibid.). The authors

P. Drijvers (ed.), Secondary Algebra Education, 5–26.

claim that the five ingredients are interwoven and interdependent in the development of proficiency in mathematics.

The debate on procedural skills and conceptual understanding is influenced by the issue of technology in algebra education. The availability of educational technology challenges the goals of algebra education, as is expressed in the Discussion Document of the 12th ICMI (the International Commission on Mathematical Instruction) study:

> An algebra curriculum that serves its students well in the coming century may look very different from an ideal curriculum from some years ago. The increased availability of computers and calculators will change what mathematics is useful as well as changing how mathematics is done. At the same time as challenging the content of what is taught, the technological revolution is also providing rich prospects for teaching and is offering students new paths to understanding. (Stacey & Chick, 2000, p. 216)

How much procedural fluency is needed if computer tools can do the work for us? What types of skills will be needed, or will become increasingly important, due to the availability of technological tools? Technology offers opportunities for algebra education, and in that sense is not only part of the problem, but could also be part of its solution. Still, the adequate integration of technology into the teaching and learning of algebra is not a straightforward issue (Stacey, Chick & Kendal, 2004). What is adequate, of course, depends on the goals of and views on algebra education, as well as on situational factors.

All together, an important point of discussion is whether the focus of algebra education should be on procedural skills or on conceptual understanding. We agree with the US Department of Education (2007) in its aim at integration instead of polarization: a balanced equilibrium is to be preferred above an extreme position. Still, the question is how to deal with the high expectations for algebra education and with its disappointing achievements. To answer this question, various routes can be taken, each of which elicits new questions:

– Should there be more time for practicing skills? If so, should this take place separately or be integrated with other material?
– Use more educational technology? Is that old wine in new bottles, or does it really produce results?
– Should there be differentiation between students, or should there be simply as much algebra as possible for everyone? Should they all study the same algebra or preferably different algebra topics?
– Should other topics be chosen, creating a modified curriculum in which the algebra handicaps are no longer disturbing? If so, which topics, and why?

These issues can be approached from different perspectives. Three basic principles for this book can already be mentioned explicitly. The first is that algebra is an integrated part of mathematics teaching and is not an isolated piece of mathematical acrobatics.

Secondly, from the student's perspective, algebra is both a meaningful way to solve problems and a field in which challenging questions can be investigated. Thirdly, during both the teaching process and application, insight and skill go hand-in-hand.

WHAT IS ALGEBRA?

Before we continue with this exploration of algebra, it is important to clearly define what we understand as algebra. The word 'algebra' is a derivation of the Arabic al-jabr from the title of the book *Hisab al-jabr w'al-muqabala* written by Abu Ja'far Muhammad ibn Musa al-Khwarizmi. Al-Kwarizmi lived in Baghdad from about 780 to 850. Al-Khwarizmi defined al-jabr as eliminating subtractions. For example, (if the geometry of rectangles and squares is converted into contemporary notation), by applying al-jabr

$$x^2 = 40x - 4x^2$$

is reduced to
$$5x^2 = 40x$$

In this way, a very specific method for dealing with equalities later became the name for an entire field of mathematics. In Chapter 2, the historical development of algebra is addressed in more detail.

Now let us compare the above definition with a definition from a modern encyclopaedia of mathematics, which concerns the algebra of mathematics professionals.

> One use of the word 'algebra' is the abstract study of number systems and operations within them, including such advanced topics as groups, rings, invariant theory, and cohomology. This is the meaning mathematicians associate with the word 'algebra'. When there is the possibility of confusion, this field of mathematics is often referred to as abstract algebra.
> (Weisstein, http://mathworld.wolfram.com)

The above quote shows that algebra involves more than just the equalities to which the original Arabic word referred; it involves investigating number systems and their operations. However, the online encyclopaedia continues with the remark that algebra can also refer to algebra at school. This includes operating with variables, solving equations, creating formulas for problem situations (algebrafication), working with functions in terms of formulas, tables and graphs, finding derivatives, etc. Sometimes it seems that everything in mathematics in which a letter appears is called algebra. However, Freudenthal (1977) argued for not limiting algebra to working with more advanced symbols, but to see it instead as the ability to describe relations and procedures for solving problems, and the techniques that are involved in a general way:

> What is algebra? There is no Supreme Court to decide such questions. Nevertheless, 'algebra' has a meaning in everyday language just as 'chair' and 'table' have. For instance, at school algebra is solving linear and quadratic equations.

It is the kind of algebra the Babylonians started with. Was their algebra not algebra, because their symbolism was not smooth enough? Are 'length' and 'width' much worse than '*x*' and '*y*' if you can give clear recipes for solving quadratic equations in such terms? Is it not algebra if the sum of the first 10 squares is laid down in a numerical formula that allows one to extend the result to any *n*? This ability to describe relations and solving procedures, and the techniques involved in a general way, is in my view of algebra such an important feature of algebraic thinking that I am willing to extend the name 'algebra' to it, as long as no other name is proposed, and as far as I know no other name has been put forward. But what is in a name?
(Freudenthal, 1977, p. 193-194)

Clearly, there is a difference between algebra as it is used and developed by mathematicians, and algebra as it is taught in school. Although such a difference should ideally not exist, and algebra at school and abstract algebra should have as much in common as possible in terms of their method and mode of thought, it turns out that an excessively structuralist approach to algebra in secondary education overshoots the mark (Kindt, 2000). Therefore, regarding the delineation of algebra at school, let us primarily seek inspiration from Al-Kwarizmi. For the school situation, algebra is first of all a way of working, where 'working with formulas that contain letters' is important, but is not everything. Algebra at school is strongly associated with *verbs* such as solve, manipulate, generalize, formalize, structure and abstract. Although a certain amount of brain work is required for these activities, the emphasis in educational practice often lies primarily on activity.

It is unnecessary – and nearly impossible – to clearly delineate algebraic activity. *Algebraic activity* is characterized by working with numbers or number structures. The link with numbers and number structures means that the relationship between arithmetic and algebra deserves additional attention (see Chapter 3). In many cases, algebraic activity has one of more of the characteristics listed below. A mathematical activity becomes more 'algebraic' to the degree that it has more of the following characteristics:

1. Implicit or explicit generalization takes place.
2. Patterns of relationships between numbers and/or formulas are investigated.
3. Problems are solved by applying general or situation-dependent rules.
4. Logical reasoning is conducted with unknown or as yet unknown quantities.
5. Mathematical operations are conducted with variables represented with letters. Formulas are created as a result.
6. For numerical operations and relationships, special symbols are used.
7. Tables and graphs represent formulas and are used to investigate formulas.
8. Formulas and expressions are compared and transformed.
9. Formulas and expressions are used to describe situations in which units and quantities play a role.
10. Processes for solving problems contain steps that are based on calculation rules, but that do not necessarily have any meaning in the context of the problem.

This list of characteristics of algebraic activity in mathematics education – in the remainder of this book we will simply write 'algebra' when we mean 'algebra in school' – is certainly not complete. It does not have to be complete, as long as it is sufficiently effective to delineate algebraic activity. These characteristics imply that the algebraic activity does not focus exclusively on solving a concrete problem, but detaches itself somewhat from the problem. This detachment leads to the construction of a more abstract 'world of algebra', where generalization and formalization play important roles. Nevertheless, it is still important to be able to connect with the original concrete problem. Let us review some examples regarding the above characteristics:

- Calculating the answer to $123 + 56$ is arithmetic and not algebra.
- But calculating 101×99, assuming 100×100, can be seen as an algebraic activity.
- Proving that $n(n+5) - (n+2)(n+3) + 6$ is independent of n is also algebra.
- Knowing that $\sqrt{2} \approx 1.41...$ is not algebra, but understanding that $(\sqrt{2})^4 = 2^2 = 4$ is part of algebraic knowledge.
- Deriving $\sin 2x = 2\sin x \cos x$ from $\sin(a+b) = \sin a \cos b + \sin b \cos a$ is an algebraic activity.
- Proving the product rule of differential calculus involves a combination of calculus and algebra. Using the product rule with known functions is an algebraic activity.
- What about integrating x^2 over an interval? The concept of the integral as the limit of covering rectangles is not algebra. However, calculating with an antiderivative function, which is found by using the formula structure, is algebra.

These examples make it clear that algebra plays an important supporting role within other mathematical domains and within physics and chemistry. Nevertheless, the importance of algebra is discounted if it is only seen as serving other subjects; this can lead to 'target didactics' that exclude possibilities for reflection and mathematical thinking.

The description of algebra as a specific type of activity elicits two questions: how can we prevent these activities from becoming separate, independent 'tricks', and how can we ensure that they form a coherent and viable whole? In the chapter 'The algebraic language' in his book *Didactical phenomenology of mathematical structures*, Freudenthal (1983) took a step towards answering these questions. At the end of the chapter, he sketches out several important algebraic strategies that are important because they situate the micro-methods and skills in a larger context. For example, he refers to the algebraic transposition of a context or problem situation, the use of analogies between situations and the algebraic permanence principle. The latter is the idea that we, for example, determine the product of negative numbers in such a way that desired properties such as $a \cdot b = b \cdot a$ and $a \cdot (b+c) = a \cdot b + a \cdot c$ continue to apply to all combinations of positive and negative. The idea of algebraic permanence is based firmly on thinking in terms of structures with invariant properties.

In summary, algebraic activity is central to algebra education, where students work with numbers, number structures and operations. The algebraic activity is characterized by a number of the characteristics identified above. The central intention of this book is that students experience algebraic activity as a coherent, meaningful and applicable whole of concepts, techniques and proofs.

APPROACHES TO ALGEBRA

Algebra as taught in school has various aspects, which are also referred to in various ways in the relevant literature. Bednarz, Kieran and Lee (1996) distinguished several approaches to algebra: generalization, problem solving, modelling and functions. The National Council of Teachers of Mathematics (NCTM, 2009) reports the following standards for algebra education: understanding patterns, relations and functions; representing and analysing mathematical situations and structures using algebraic symbols; using mathematical models to represent and understand quantitative relationships; and analysing change in various contexts. One of the textbook series for middle school in the USA, *Mathematics in Context* (WCER & FI, 2006), splits the algebra teaching-learning trajectory into three strands: Patterns and regularities, restrictions, and graphing. For the purpose of this book, we distinguish the following strands in algebra education:
– Patterns and formulas
– Restrictions
– Functions

These three strands depict how algebra is used in mathematics and other subjects; in this book one chapter is dedicated to each of these approaches. A fourth important aspect concerns language: algebra as symbolic language. Below, we will explain these four aspects in greater detail. Of course, these four aspects of algebra are not entirely separate, and the accent often shifts from one to the other while working on a problem.

Patterns and formulas

Algebra involves researching regularity, patterns and structures: seeing a pattern in apparently different situations and recognizing a common algebraic structure (Van Reeuwijk, 2002). This may invite generalization, including generalization *across* classes of situations and generalization and transfer *to* new situations.

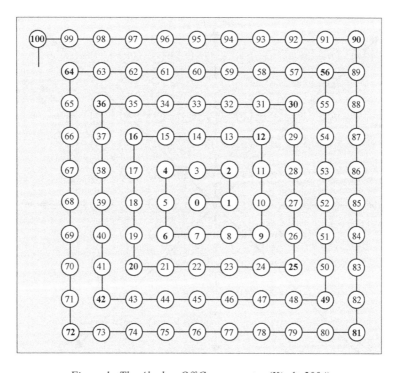

Figure 1. The Algebra Off Course poster (Kindt, 2004)

The algebra of patterns and structures can be addressed early in algebra education. For example, Figure 1 shows an intriguing number spiral (Kindt, 2004) which can give rise to interesting pattern recognition activities. The numbers in the corners, for instance, are eye-catching. The observer can quickly see that half of them are squares. This is because the differences between consecutive squares increase linearly; if 0 is seen as a square, then the sequence of differences will be: 1, 3, 5, ... The sequence of differences for the other series of corner numbers (including 0) is 2, 4, 6, ... These corner numbers – products of two consecutive numbers – are referred to as oblong numbers. A possible question to evoke students' activity might be: What would be the corner numbers if the spiral continues with two more full laps? The diagonals also reveal fascinating patterns (Figure 2). How can we be sure that a diagonal contains only even numbers or only odd numbers? Can we use formulas to prove this?

PAUL DRIJVERS, AAD GODDIJN, MARTIN KINDT

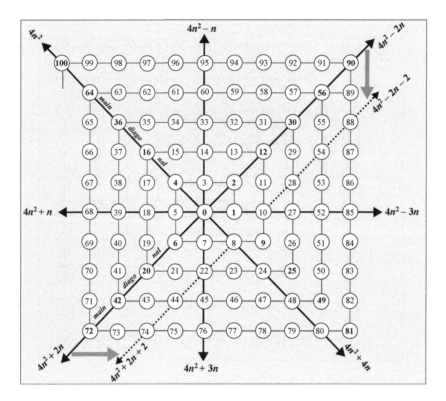

Figure 2. Diagonal patterns and formulas (Kindt, 2004)

This problem is so appealing because it offers room for seeing different patterns as
well as different solution strategies at different formalization levels. Such a diversity
of patterns and formulas is an opportunity for the teacher to challenge students to
compare their findings with each other and to defend their own work.

The algebra of patterns and structures, therefore, is about investigating, identifying and formulating similarities relating to general patterns and underlying algebraic
structures. During this process, generalization often plays a role: from specific cases
the students make a leap to the general level, to a class of cases. Consequently, the
variables often represent generalized numbers. Formulas are powerful means to capture and describe the patterns and structures. In Chapter 4, the algebra of patterns and
structures is explicitly addressed.

Restrictions

Algebra can be a powerful tool for problem solving activities, particularly if the
problem can be formulated in terms of equations or inequalities. The question in such

problem situations often is: what value(s) of the unknown variable satisfies the required conditions? Such problems not only originate from mathematics itself, such as geometry, analysis or probability, but also come from physics, economics, the life sciences and daily practice (professional or otherwise).

As an example, let us consider a linear programming problem taken from the Dutch journal *Pythagoras* (Vol. 5, issue 1, 1965) and presented in Figure 3.

A 'small businessman' has a company that can have no more than nine employees. The employees consist of trained employees and untrained ones (trainees). A trained employee can manufacture five units of the product the company makes per day, and a trainee can manufacture three units. If the businessman does not want to make his clients wait too long, then he must manufacture at least 30 units per day. His question is: *what are the ideal numbers of trained employees and trainees?* It goes without saying that this question concerns even more factors than those referred to above. For example, the trade union requires a minimum of two trained employees for each trainee, but the law does not allow more than five trained employees per trainee. Of course, the salary paid to both types of employees also plays a role. A trained employee earns € 40 per day and a trainee earns € 20 per day. Finally, the businessman must take into account the fact that he receives € 25 for each delivered unit.

Figure 3. Linear programming problem

A businessman, due to his algebraic training, reasons as follows. Assume that I have x trained employees and y trainees. There can be no more than nine employees, therefore $x + y \leq 9$. Altogether, they must manufacture at least 30 units, therefore $5x + 3y \geq 30$. The trade union stipulates that $x \geq 2y$. And the law requires that $x \leq 5y$. These four inequalities can be shown on a coordinate plane, and that leads to a quadrangular region (Figure 4). The four vertices of this area represent the possible distributions of personnel; after calculating the profit in each of the four cases, it turns out that the most advantageous composition is seven trained employees and two trainees.

A tempting misstep when establishing the restrictions is the reasoning: x trained, y untrained, two trained employees per trainee, which results in $2x = y$. This change of roles is known in the literature as the Student-Professor problem (Rosnick, 1981) and can best be refuted (or preferably prevented!) by first thinking about concrete numbers: if there are three trainees, then ...

Another difficulty for students is that a restriction on the total number of employees (here $x + y \leq 9$) is combined with a restriction on the total number of products (here $5x + 3y \geq 30$). This is like adding apples and oranges. Although the intersection of the lines $x + y = 9$ and $5x + 3y = 30$ happens not to play a role here, many similar problems can be thought of where such an intersection is essential. In that case, during the solution process, students should concentrate on the pure algebra and for the time being leave the context for what it is.

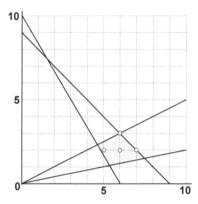

Figure 4. The allowable area

Generally speaking, the process of translating problems into algebra often consists of creating one or more equations and inequalities. One (or more) of the variables appearing in the problem is then the unknown, for which a numerical value is sought. Solving equations then becomes the key to solving the original problem. Chapter 2 goes more deeply into the historical background of the role of algebra as a servant for solving problems in geometry and other applications. In Chapter 5, the topic of restrictions is addressed in depth.

Functions

The functional approach sees algebra primarily as the study of relations and functions, which explains the term 'functional'. Algebra, then, is a means to formulate and investigate relations between variables. This involves covariance and dynamics: how does a change in one variable affect the other? The variables have the character of changing quantities. As a result, algebra offers the means to express and investigate relationships between quantities. An example of the 'algebrafication' of such a relationship is the well-known lens formula (Figure 5).

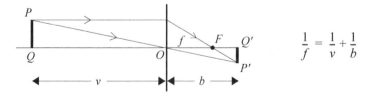

$$\frac{1}{f} = \frac{1}{v} + \frac{1}{b}$$

Figure 5. The lens formula sketched

The formula describes the relationship between three quantities: the focal distance, the distance from the object to the lens and the distance from the lens to the image. If the focal distance f and the distance from the object to the lens v are known, then the distance from the lens v to the image b can be calculated, and we find ourselves in a situation comparable to that in the previous section. However, an interesting question is the following: how does the distance from the lens to the image change with a given lens (where f is fixed) if the object moves away from the lens? The following geometric solution is based on the above construction. If the line segment PQ moves to the left, then the angle of the line PO makes with the horizontal axis becomes smaller, causing P' to 'crawl' towards F. The question can also be answered using the following algebraic reasoning. For a given lens, the sum $\frac{1}{b} + \frac{1}{v}$ is constant.

If v becomes larger, then $\frac{1}{v}$ becomes smaller. Because the sum does not change, $\frac{1}{b} + \frac{1}{v}$ must become larger, so b becomes smaller. Of course, the reverse is also true: if v becomes smaller, then b becomes larger. Consequently, we encounter a process of co-variation, in which the value of b depends on that of v, or vice versa, and where f is a parameter.

The functional connection between v and b can be represented most beautifully in algebra by an implicit formula, i.e. without expressing b explicitly in terms of v. However, the functions that frequently appear in our mathematics education are usually described with explicit formulas. If we consider the distance from the lens to the image to be a function of the distance from the object to the lens for various values of the parameter f, then an explicit algebraic function description, which effectively illustrates the input-output character of the function, is useful:

$$v \to \frac{1}{\frac{1}{f} - \frac{1}{v}} \text{ or } v \to \frac{f \cdot v}{v - f}$$

A second example has a geometry background. On the left of Figure 6, a geometry program has been used to construct a parabola. This parabola is cut by several parallel lines. We now pay attention to the midpoints of the intersections of the lines and the parabola. The geometrical locus of these midpoints appears to be a vertical ray. But is that really so? And how can we know the position of that line?

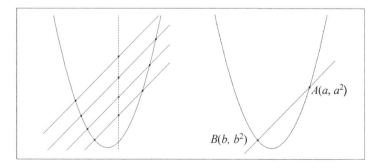

Figure 6. Cutting a parabola with a line with a fixed direction

This problem can be effectively tackled with algebra. Assume that a line with a fixed direction cuts the parabola at two points. We call the x-coordinates a and b, so the points are $A(a, a^2)$ and $B(b, b^2)$, as shown on the right side of Figure 6. The slope of AB is now

$$\frac{a^2 - b^2}{a - b}$$

Because in the geometric situation we have chosen the fixed direction of the lines, we know that this expression in a and b has a fixed value. The *algebra* tells us that

$$\frac{a^2 - b^2}{a - b} = a + b$$

We now know that $a + b$ is constant. So $(a + b)/2$ is also constant. The connection between algebra and geometry now becomes obvious: the x-coordinates of the mid-points of AB are $(a + b)/2$, so they are constant. From this follows the geometric fact that the midpoints lie on a single vertical line. If we look back at the solution, we see in the algebraic part that the simplification of the expression for the slope is an important link. Also important is the observation that the essential steps, the factor-ization of $a^2 - b^2$ and cancelling out a common factor $a - b$, are essentially algebra-ic and have no immediately visible referents in the geometric situation.

This example makes it clear how the translation of algebraic properties into alge-bra, followed by reverse translation back into geometry, plays a crucial role in solv-ing problems. In this way algebra can play a role in solving problems that at first glance do not call for this, which is one of the powerful characteristics of algebra. Translating and reverse translating between algebra and geometry are skills that are required to exploit this power.

The algebra of functions and graphs concerns the functional dependence relation-ships between quantities that are shown as a formula. Often, as in the example of the lens formula, we are interested in the effect of change. By emphasizing this dynamic, the algebra of relationships and functions comes closer to analysis. Variables have the character of changing quantities. Graphs provide generally useful visualizations for functions and relationships. In Chapter 6, functions and graphs are addressed in greater detail.

The language of algebra

A fourth and final approach to algebra stresses its language aspect and views algebra as a system of symbolic representations. Algebra uses its own standardized set of signs, symbols and rules about how you can write something; algebra seems to have its own grammar and syntax. This makes it possible to formulate algebraic ideas un-equivocally and compactly. This compact unequivocality is one of the reasons why algebra is also used in other subjects (see Chapter 9).

Chapter 2 describes how this compact and internally consistent algebraic notation developed. Historically, this development was shown primarily by algebra becoming increasingly independent from geometry, but also by the development of a system where it became possible to see – by grammar alone – if a formula could be viable. For instance, we immediately recognize '$a\ b\ +$' as nonsensical in the context of our notation system, while $(a+b)\cdot c$ is viable.

The language aspect of algebra involves more than compact notation; as rule, the use of algebraic grammar goes hand-in-hand with formalization and abstraction. Algebraic language is used to express algebraic ideas in a way that is detached from the initial, concrete problem. In this sense, abstraction takes place. It would be going too far to say that algebra is a language, but algebra does have a powerful language. In this symbolic language, variables are simply signs or symbols that can be manipulated with well-established rules, and that do not refer to a specific, context-bound meaning.

An important part of algebraic activity is what is often called the translation of a problem or situation into 'algebra'. In fact, this involves more than translation; it concerns building a structure that algebraically represents the problem variables and their mutual relationships in the situation; essentially, this is modelling. Of course, the reverse process – reformulating the algebra in words about the original problem – is also part of mastering the language of algebra. True algebraic translation involves the conversion of algebraic expressions into day-to-day words, and especially the reverse. It is advisable to focus attention on these aspects, for example by occasionally holding an 'algebra dictation' session in class. During the session students are asked to write down language expressions as algebraic expressions, for example 'the half of x, one half times x, the sum of the square of x and the square of y and the square of the sum of x and y. Note that the latter problem is ambiguous: depending on the position of the break in the sentence ('the square ... of x plus y' or 'the square of x ... plus y') the algebraic expression could be either $(x+y)^2$ or x^2+y. Parentheses play an important role in algebra 'sentences'. The reverse activity, converting algebraic expressions into sentences, is also a good exercise.

In this book, the language aspect of algebra does not have its own chapter, but is addressed throughout different chapters.

KEY DIFFICULTIES IN ALGEBRA: WHAT a IS, YOU CAN'T KNOW

Let us start with an observation made in a class of 13 year-old mid-achieving students, who were working with a 'number machine' (Goddijn, 1982). This machine works as follows: you put a number into the machine; it subtracts 8 from the number and the result comes out. The assignment for the students is to fill in the table of output values (see Figure 7).

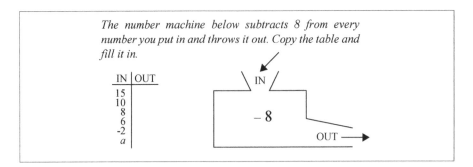

Figure 7. The number machine task

All students filled in the beginning of the 'out' column flawlessly, but a number of them stopped at *a*. The following discussion took place:

> Student: You cannot know what to fill in under *a*.
> Observer: How did you figure out the 7 under the 15?
> Student: I just subtracted, 15 – 8
> Observer: And how did you get that 0?
> Student: 8 – 8
> Observer: Try writing that underneath.
> The student writes: 15 – 8, 10 – 8, 8 – 8 underneath ... and even writes *a* – 8.
> Observer: So what comes 'out' at the right end of the row?
> Student: What *a* is, you can't know.

This observation, from which the title of this section is derived, shows one of the key difficulties in algebra. The student has understood the operation of the number machine: he can express the calculation process in words. But when the *a* appears, after some urging the student writes the requested *a* – 8 , but this does not satisfy him because 'what *a* is, you can't know'. For the student, the 'algebrafication' of the situation has no meaning, nor does it help him to understand the situation better.

Algebra is not easy; not easy to learn and not easy to teach. For many students it can be a stumbling block that creates obstacles for further education. What is so hard about learning algebra? Where is the difficulty? In the following section, we will attempt to understand this problem based on the following keywords and dualities: abstraction, generalization and overgeneralization, procedural fluency and symbol sense, and process and object.

Abstraction

One of the first difficulties in learning algebra is abstraction. In algebra education, tangible and meaningful situations are often used to introduce algebra. For example, situations with fixed and variable costs appear regularly in grades 7-9 of Dutch mathematics education. In the example shown in Figure 8, question a. is an item that would fit in the restrictions strand. Question b. has a somewhat more functional character, and with question c. a second formula must be created. When comparing the prices charged by various repair services, the recognition of the general structure and the linear relationships plays a role. Abbreviating the formulas is an obvious step, and in the first case leads to $30 + R \times 45 = K$. If we let go of the context and keep to the usual conventions for ordering the symbols (three order changes) we obtain the form $y = 45x + 30$ or, more generally: $y = a \cdot x + b$.

An appliance repair company has a call out charge of € 30 and an hourly rate of € 45. The following algebraic relationship applies to the cost of repair:

$$30 + \text{Repair time} \times 45 = \text{Total repair cost}$$

a. You only have € 100 in cash. How long can the repair take before you exceed this amount?
b. How much does the cost go up for each hour that the repair takes?
c. Another company has a call out charge of € 45 and an hourly rate of € 30. Which company is the cheapest for long repairs, and which is the cheapest for short repairs? How do you decide which company to call?

Figure 8. Contextual task

Most concrete questions concerning this context can be solved without algebra, for example by calculating in reverse. However, when students take a different point of view, algebra can become important. Consider the point of view of the repairman, who may be asked for a price in advance, or the point of view of the company manager, who wants to compare their rates with those of the competitor. Moreover, there are other tangible situations that are algebraically identical. Similar shifts in perspective can elicit the need for abstraction: letting go of the tangible concept and developing a transcendent world of algebraic objects and operations. This is difficult: letting go of a familiar frame of reference and building a new one. In this context, Van Hiele (1986) referred to the transition from the basic level to the first level, where a meaningful relationship network of mathematical objects is created. If abstraction indeed takes place, this abstract world of algebra can become increasingly tangible for the students. The core of the tangible-abstract problem is primarily that the originally abstract world of algebra must become a meaningful 'reality' for the students, which also helps them to solve tangible problems.

PAUL DRIJVERS, AAD GODDIJN, MARTIN KINDT

In some cases, the tangible problem situations are such that it is not necessary to enter the more abstract world of algebra; it is therefore better to omit this step. The subtle game of maintaining contact with the tangible context and temporarily letting go of this context to work with pure algebra is not easy, certainly not in cases where thinking about the tangible situation becomes a blockade for abstraction and vertical mathematization.

Generalization and overgeneralization

The description of the Patterns and formulas strand stated that generalization is an important aspect of algebraic thought and activity. Studying, describing and using generalizations is one of the core aspects of algebra. The algebraic permanence principle referred to above essentially means that we make algebra in such a way that generalization can be used as much as possible. Generalizing about situations is often linked with abstraction, because it frequently requires a more detached view of the topic of study. One of the difficulties here is the problem of overgeneralization. For example, consider the following simplification that students are sometimes tempted to apply:

$$x^2 + y^2 = 25 \text{ so } x + y = 5$$

This simplification indeed is visually very attractive (Kirschner & Awtry, 2004). The reasoning appears to be that you can take square roots 'piece-wise':

$$\sqrt{x^2 + y^2} = \sqrt{x^2} + \sqrt{y^2}$$

This idea isn't totally absurd because with x instead of $+$ it does work:

$$\sqrt{x^2 \times y^2} = \sqrt{x^2} \times \sqrt{y^2}$$

And with the operation 'multiply by 5' instead of 'take the square' it is also correct:

$$5(x^2 + y^2) = 5x^2 + 5y^2$$

But with the lens formula, it doesn't work:

$$\text{If } \frac{1}{f} = \frac{1}{v} + \frac{1}{b} \text{ then } f = v + b$$

Students who make such mistakes are guilty of overgeneralizing the distributivity of algebraic operations. One could call this an illusion of distributivity. Generally speaking, students have difficulty with identifying generalizations and the limits of generalization. It is possible to avoid errors such as that described above by referring to numerical or geometrical examples. However, it is striking that such errors continue to return in new, somewhat more complex situations, even though the students learned to avoid them in the simpler situation. In this respect, learning algebra is a growth process; this is why Chapter 7 is about teaching and maintaining skills. It argues clearly in favour of striking a balance between learning from meaningful activities and performing well conceived skill exercises. The chapter also argues for restoring practice for techniques at various levels.

A different way to focus attention on possible structural mistakes is to take advantage of the situation by addressing the mistakes explicitly and problematizing them, as shown in the example in Figure 9.

Simplify: $\dfrac{y^2 + 7y + 6}{y^2 + 8y + 12}$

One student tackles the problem as follows. The first step is to cancel out y^2 in the numerator and denominator:

$$\frac{7y + 6}{8y + 12}$$

After this you subtract $7y$ from the numerator and denominator:

$$\frac{6}{y + 12}$$

Then you subtract that 6 in the numerator from 12 in the denominator. Nothing remains in the numerator, so it disappears. So the answer is:

$$y + 6$$

The student made several mistakes. What are the mistakes and why are they wrong?

Figure 9. Problematizing algebraic mistakes

Procedural fluency and symbol sense

The above mistakes demonstrate the importance of procedural fluency. What does this fluency consist of? The mistakes that students make, like those shown above, are the ultimate manifestations of the algebraic difficulties they experience. Besides simple errors, which are caused by lack of concentration or time pressure, these mistakes also include structural errors related to the students' lack of algebraic experience; as a result, they lack insight during certain algebraic steps, such as reversing the order of operations or dividing or multiplying with an expression that is possibly equal to zero. Algebraic expertise involves an interplay of various types of skills. Initially, it is important that students develop procedural skills. These are skills such as solving simple equations or simplifying expressions. This concerns procedural algebraic calculations, which often have a local focus. It is important to be able to conduct such procedures fluently, routinely and without making errors. Besides requiring insight, this also requires students to practice skills and maintain them (see Chapter 7).

Algebra involves much more than mastering basic skills; it also involves choosing a sensible strategy to tackle problems, maintaining an overview of the solution process, creating a model, taking a global view of expressions, wisely choosing subsequent steps, distinguishing between relevant and less relevant characteristics and interpreting results in a meaningful fashion. In the professional literature, this type of meta-knowledge is called symbol sense (Arcavi, 1994, 2005; Fey, 1990; Zorn, 2002). Symbol sense is for algebra what number sense is for arithmetic: the flexible algebraic expertise or algebraic literacy that often operates in the background without our conscious awareness. Based on insight into the underlying concepts, it directs the implementation of the basic routines. Arcavi (1994, 2005) provided a number of examples of symbol sense. It plays a role in planning, coordinating and interpreting basic operations and consists of three interrelated skills:

- The strategic skills and heuristics to arrive at a problem approach; the capacity to maintain an overview of this process, to make effective choices within the approach, or if a strategy falls short, to seek another approach.
- The capacity to view expressions and formulas globally, in order to recognize the structure of expressions and sub-expressions, to understand the meaning of symbols in the context and to formulate expressions in another way. Process-object duality plays a role in that skill.
- The capacity for algebraic reasoning. This often involves qualitative reflections on terms and factors in expressions, symmetry considerations or reasoning with particular or extreme cases.

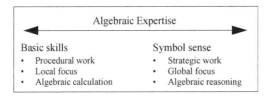

Figure 10. Algebraic expertise as a spectrum ranging from basic skills to symbol sense

The algebraic expertise spectrum has basic skills on one side and symbol sense on the other. Figure 10 illustrates this spectrum. One of the difficult facets of algebra is combining these two aspects: the interplay between the routine of basic operations and the implicit meta-skills that play a guiding role. For that matter, one element cannot exist without the other: algebraic reasoning is only possible once you have reasonably mastered the basic operations, and with algebraic computation you often need reasoning as well, certainly if the 'automatic pilot' is not functioning smoothly or the situation is unusual. A good balance between skill and insight, between acting and thinking, is therefore crucial. It is impossible to make a sharp distinction between basic skills and symbol sense. However, it is suspected that the development of the symbol sense side of the spectrum is given too little explicit attention in algebra education.

Process and object

A final difficulty of algebra is that students have to be able to view an algebraic expression as both a process and an object, and must acquire a sense of which view is most suitable at any one time. Initially for students, a formula often has the character of a *process description*, a calculation procedure or a step-by-step plan. To return to the example of repair costs from figure 8, 30 + Repair time × 45 = Cost may be understood as a recipe to calculate the repair cost from the repair time. Interpreted this way, the formula says 'if the repair time is 1.5 hours, then take that 1.5, multiply it by 45, add 30, and the result is the total cost'. The symbols +, × and = acquire an action character and appear to invite a calculation.

However, in algebra there often is nothing to be calculated at all. An identity such as $(a + b)^2 = a^2 + 2ab + b^2$ does not have a process character; it indicates that the expression on the left hand side is equivalent to the expression on the right hand side[i]. In this case, the equal sign does not stand for 'and the result is...', but stands for 'is equivalent to'. The plus symbol also has a different character: instead of 'take a and add b' the + in $(a + b)^2$ stands for 'the sum of a and b'. The expression $(a + b)^2$ is not a process description, but an *algebraic object* (Freudenthal, 1983).

Several authors have pointed out the students' difficulties with this dual nature of algebraic expressions, and with the object view in particular (Sfard, 1991; Tall & Thomas, 1991). For example, students find it difficult to accept an expression as a solution to an equation, because 'then you still don't know how much it is' (cf. the observation on the number machine task in Figure 7). As the object view is supposed to form a higher conceptual threshold than the process view, algebraic expressions are initially presented as processes. Nevertheless, the flexibility to switch between the two views is an important algebraic skill. In arithmetic, the process view is generally predominant. Consequently a didactic gap between arithmetic and algebra is a point of discussion (Van Amerom, 2002; Malle, 1993).

ALGEBRA IN SCHOOL: WHY AND HOW?

Now that we have more clearly delineated our definition of algebra and the possibilities that play a role in learning algebra, the question is why and how algebra can be taught in school.

Why teach algebra in school?

As clearly expressed in the quotation from Tall and Thomas at the beginning of this chapter, learning algebra requires a costly initial investment, but it ultimately returns a profit, especially in subsequent courses in subjects like physics. It is precisely due to algebra's detachment from the original meaning of a problem that it is an especially powerful tool:

> In fact, from one point of view, this is one of the strengths of symbols – they enable us to detach from, and even 'forget', their referents in order to produce results efficiently. (Arcavi, 1994, p. 26)

This is especially true for students who are headed for a subsequent programme in subjects like physics in higher education. For them, adequate preparation for higher education and the profession that follows is one of the most important aims of algebra education. However, even for students who will hardly come into contact with mathematics in their further education or profession, some degree of algebra education is still important. After all, algebra can be a means to organize and sort phenomena from their work and their environment, to discover patterns and regularities, and to reason logically with them. In this sense, algebra is a component of mathematical literacy, which is relevant for all citizens, helping them to find their way in a society full of numbers, procedures and patterns. Algebra education that focuses on this aspect is different than algebra education that prepares students for subsequent courses in physics: here, algebra is more a tool to solve practical problems than an objective in itself. It concerns an informal, application-oriented and close-to-reality approach to algebra. A third aim of algebra education is one of the motives of mathematics education in general; it concerns, as formulated by Polya (1945), learning to think. This general educational value of algebra is less tangible than the aims described above, but still deserves attention.

In summary, algebra education serves various aims: it helps to prepare students for their subsequent education, profession and their future roles in society, and it has a general educational value. The relationship between these aims and the way in which they are realized varies greatly and depends on the needs and capacities of the target group.

Our view on learning algebra

The point of departure of this book is our vision about learning algebra, which emerges from the more general perspective of realistic mathematics education (Freudenthal, 1991; Treffers, 1987). The core of this vision can be summarized as follows:
– Algebra as human activity.
   In the course of history, algebra has been constructed by people. From this cultural-historical perspective, it is important that students do not experience algebra as rigid and uncompromising, but as a human construction of tools and knowledge that can be used for solving recognizable problems.
– Algebra as brain activity.
   This not only means that people think about things, but also that students experience something of the detachment from tangible problems that often occurs when working with algebra. A context problem will initiate a process in which context-transcending reflections lead to the development of algebra at a more abstract level, i.e. algebra as an abstract world of mathematical objects. The brain activity

comprises a combination of skills and understanding, which are generally not separate from each other.

– Algebra as personal activity.

Based on their intuition and ideas, students can independently design representations and develop algebra along the route of progressive formalization. In this way, students can 'internalize algebra'.

– Algebra as meaningful activity.

Whether students use algebra at a tangible or an abstract level, it is crucial that the activity is experienced as meaningful. Sometimes this requires a tangible problem situation taken from the students' world of experience. In other cases, the meaning for the students is contained in a more abstract, theoretical context. But what is most important is that the problem situation is 'experientially real'; the students must experience it as meaningful and realize what they are doing.

CONCLUSION AND PREVIEW

The exploration of topics and themes in algebra education has resulted in a delineation of algebra and a division of the topic into three strands: patterns and formulas, restrictions, and functions and graphs. Various approaches to algebra have been distinguished, and a number of difficult aspects of learning algebra have been identified. Several themes have emerged in this process, including the historical development of algebra, algebra as a way of working with numbers and number structures, practicing and maintaining algebraic skills, and using technological aids with algebra. We have also addressed the fact that algebra can be used with problems from other subjects or sub-areas of mathematics. All of these aspects together have led to a vision of algebra education. The following is a brief outline of the remainder of this book. Chapter 2 describes the historical development of algebra in global terms. Chapter 3 addresses the relationship between arithmetic and algebra. This is followed by three chapters that discuss the three main strands: patterns and formulas in Chapter 4, restrictions in Chapter 5, and functions in Chapter 6. Chapter 7 addresses the question of productive practice of skills. The role of ICT in learning algebra is the topic of Chapter 8. Finally, Chapter 9 discusses how algebra is used in physics and other technical subjects.

NOTE

i   Some algebra textbooks use a special notation for equivalence $(a + b)^2 \equiv a^2 + 2ab + b^2$.

REFERENCES

Arcavi, A. (1994). Symbol sense: informal sense-making in formal mathematics. *For the learning of mathematics, 14*(3), 24-35.

Amerom, B. van (2002). *Reinvention of early algebra*. Utrecht: CD-beta press.

PAUL DRIJVERS, AAD GODDIJN, MARTIN KINDT

Arcavi, A. (2005). Developing and using symbol sense in mathematics. *For the learning of mathematics, 25*(2), 42-47.

Bednarz, N., Kieran, C., & Lee, L. (Eds.) (1996). *Approaches to algebra, perspectives for research and teaching.* Dordrecht: Kluwer Academic Publishers.

Fey, J. (1990). Quantity. In L.A. Steen (Ed.), *On the shoulders of giants: new approaches to numeracy* (pp. 61-94). Washington D.C.: National Academy Press.

Freudenthal, H. (1977). What is algebra and what has it been in history? *Archive for history of exact sciences, 16*(3), 189-200.

Freudenthal, H. (1983). *Didactical phenomenology of mathematical structures.* Dordrecht: Reidel.

Freudenthal, H. (1991). *Revisiting mathematics education, China lectures.* Dordrecht: Reidel.

Goddijn, A. (1982). Spijkers zoeken op laag water: algebra in het lbo. [Algebra at lower educational level]. *Nieuwe Wiskrant, tijdschrift voor Nederlands wiskundeonderwijs, 1*(4), 3-6.

Hiele, P.M. van (1986). *Structure and insight: a theory of mathematics education.* Orlando, Fl: Academic Press.

Kilpatrick, J.E., Swafford, J.E., & Findell, B.E. (2001). *Adding it up: helping children learn mathematics.* Washington: National Academy Press.

Kindt, M. (2000). De erfenis van al-Khwarizmi [The heritage of al-Khwarizmi]. In F. Goffree, M. van Hoorn, & B. Zwaneveld (Eds.) *Honderd jaar wiskundeonderwijs* (pp. 57-69). Leusden: Nederlandse Vereniging van Wiskundeleraren.

Kindt, M. (2004). *Algebra off course. Poster plus booklet with ideas for activities.* Utrecht: Freudenthal Institute.

Kirshner, D., & Awtry, T. (2004). Visual Salience of Algebraic Transformations. *Journal for Research in Mathematics Education, 35*(4), 224-257.

Klein, D. (2007). A quarter century of US 'math wars' and political partisanship. *Journal of the British society for the history of mathematics, 22*(1), 22 - 33.

Malle, G. (1993). *Didaktische Probleme der elementaren Algebra.* Braunschweig: Vieweg.

National Council of Teachers of Mathematics (2009). *Principles and standards for school mathematics.* Retrieved November, 12th, 2009, from http://standards.nctm.org/.

Polya, G. (1945). *How to solve it?* New Jersey: Princeton University Press.

Reeuwijk, M. van (2002). Students' construction of formulas in context. In Fou-Lai Lin (Ed.), *Common sense in mathematics education* (pp. 83-96). Taipei, Taiwan: National Taiwan Normal University.

Rosnick, P. (1981). Some misconceptions concerning the concept of a variable. *Mathematics teacher, 74*(6), 418-420.

Schoenfeld, A. (2004). The math wars. *Educational policy, 18*(1), 253-286.

Sfard, A. (1991). On the dual nature of mathematical conceptions: reflections on processes and objects as different sides of the same coin. *Educational studies in mathematics, 22*, 1-36.

Stacey, K., & Chick, H. (2000). Discussion document for the twelfth ICMI study: The future of the teaching and learning of algebra. *Educational studies in mathematics, 42*(2), 215-224.

Stacey, K., Chick, H., & Kendal, M. (2004). *The future of the teaching and learning of algebra: the twelfth ICMI study.* New York / Berlin: Springer.

Tall, D., & Thomas, M. (1991). Encouraging versatile thinking in algebra using the computer. *Educational Studies in Mathematics, 22*, 125-147.

Treffers, A. (1987). *Three dimensions, a model of goal and theory description in mathematics instruction - the Wiskobas project.* Dordrecht: Reidel.

US Department of Education (2007). *National mathematics advisory panel preliminary report.* Retrieved August 18th, 2009, from http://www.ed.gov/about/bdscomm/list/mathpanel/pre-report.pdf.

Wisconsin Center for Education Research & Freudenthal Institute (Eds.) (2006). *Mathematics in context.* Chicago: Encyclopaedia Britannica

Zorn, P. (2002). *Algebra, computer algebra and mathematical thinking.* Contribution to the 2nd international conference on the teaching of mathematics, 2002, Hersonissos, Crete. Retrieved 20 March 2003 from www.stolaf.edu/people/zorn.

AAD GODDIJN

2. ALGEBRA FROM AHMES TO APPLET

> Some things are so normal that it would seem that they have always existed. We are so accustomed to our method of writing equations that is difficult to conceive of anything else. Can you imagine that there was a time when people would not have recognized an expression such as $x^2 - 4x + 3 = 0$ as an equation? (Van Maanen, 1998, p. 12)

INTRODUCTION

There is no definitive history of algebra. Writing the history of a topic requires making choices, and this applies to the history of algebra in the same way it applies to the history of music or to the history of human capability to make the world liveable. These are choices such as: do we demonstrate the full power of algebra, such as how it evolved from cuneiform script to computer language, or do we emphasize the process of trial and error, searching for usable forms of notation and methods of solution? For an educational book such as this one, the latter appears to be the best choice; after all, we learn primarily from our mistakes in the hope of achieving success.

But what is 'searching'? Was Ahmes searching for $x \cdot \left(1 + \frac{1}{2} + \frac{1}{4}\right) = 10$ on the shores of the Nile when he wrote 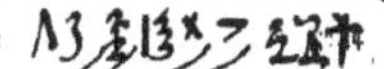, approximately 3700 years ago? No, probably not. Out of the sea of possibilities, it is most likely that specific notations and strategies floated to the top and ultimately made into the mathematics books of 2010. Whether or not Ahmes contributed to this process is not important to us at the moment. However it is important that we – in hindsight – can find something from the historical record which is inspiring for learning and teaching algebra today and which also enables us to improve our understanding of the essence of algebra, which is the aim of this chapter.

To this end, we will now include a series of algebra 'snapshots' to demonstrate the old and new faces of the phenomenon of algebra. These are ranked according to themes such as equations, notations, algebra and geometry, algebra and applications and several others. Such observations can inspire thoughts in the reader such as: my student actually took the same steps on his worksheet as Diophantus did. Or, after reading the history of the parentheses, I began to question how I approach things in class. Or, the geometric representation of products such as rectangles has advantages, but apparently also has disadvantages. Or, the historical development of the notation of variables inspires me to take a new didactical approach to the concept of the variable.

P. Drijvers (ed.), Secondary Algebra Education, 27–68.

However, you will not find a systematic chronological and exhaustive overview of the history of algebra here. If you are interested in this, there are many sources you can consult; the main sources on which this chapter is based are listed at the end.

In general terms, this chapter focuses on the theme of 'meaningful algebra'; consequently, there is more attention for the connections between notation, meaning and applications than on specific subjects such as negative numbers or square roots.

The following is a brief outline and description of the components of this chapter:

– Algebra is solving equations. This appears to be a central theme in the history of algebra. Three times some number is 15; which number is it? The question about the unknown value that ultimately leads to special theories.
– Algebra: a notation that clarifies and organizes. Algebra began with hardly any additional symbols besides those for numbers and normal words. The nature and importance of algebraic notation.
– Algebra and geometry: helpful neighbours or opposites? Algebra began in both the world of shapes and in the world of numbers. Geometric methods for solving equations, from Euclid to the present day.
– Analysis and synthesis, the lessons of Descartes. Algebra is not only a systematic use of mathematics with unknowns or variables, but it is also closely related in history to a specific mathematical method: analysis. This refers to analysis in the traditional sense, because modern analysis means something else. An extensive discussion about *La Géométrie* by Descartes, which is seen as the origin of analytical geometry; this book connected algebra and geometry in a new way.
– Has everything become computable with algebra? This was a dream that accompanied the application of algebra to geometry: to solve every problem (geometric and otherwise) by giving it to the 'automatic' calculation method known as 'algebra'.
– Towards the broad spectrum of modern algebras. In the 19th century, it was discovered that solutions of quintic and higher degree equations were subject to limitations. On Abel, Galois and the 20th century algebraic panorama.
– Back to algebra as taught in school. In school, algebra is overrun with graphs. Where do these graphs come from? Not from the history of algebra!

ALGEBRA IS SOLVING EQUATIONS

What we now refer to as solving equations is actually arithmetic, but in reverse. In the equation situation, 'someone or something' has begun with one or more numbers or quantities and has conducted some arithmetic operations with a numerical final result. The challenge is to retrieve the original number, numbers, or the lengths of segments. This is the perspective from school: that someone already knows the answer and asks you the 'trick question'. This school perspective is also present to some degree in history: there was much emphasis on polynomial equations, much time was spent linear and quadratic equations, and then within a much shorter time period mathematicians raced through the cubic and quartic equations as if it were a contest. But the history of algebra is richer than algebra as taught in school: number-theoretical problems together with geometric, indeterminate equations, precise case distinctions, a broad palette of solution methods for apparently simple – but fundamental – problems.

In this section, we will initially stay close to the appearance of mathematics as shown in the older sources; this will make it very clear that 'old' algebra did not use letters to stand for numbers, and that working with unknowns initially appeared in a totally different shape than that which we are used to today. However, it is interesting that the mathematics used by the Babylonians and other ancient peoples is still close to what is done in school today.

To make things not too difficult for the reader, we will often translate the sources into more modern forms of notation; although this type of translating always distorts the source, we also want to demonstrate the differences in notation and meaning with today's standards.

From Thebes in Egypt to Babylon, from arithmetic to algebra?

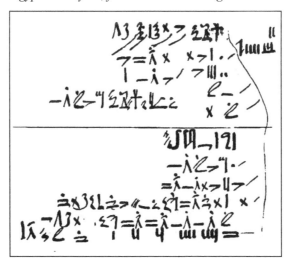

10 makes	whole it $\frac{1}{4}$ it $\frac{1}{2}$ it		heap		
	$\frac{1}{2}$	$\frac{1}{28}+\frac{1}{4}$	$\frac{1}{4}$ $\frac{1}{2}$ 1	1	←
	1	$\frac{1}{14}+\frac{1}{2}$	$\frac{1}{2}$ 3	2	
			7	4	←
$\frac{1}{14}$ $\frac{1}{7}$ $\frac{1}{2}$ 5 is heap together			$\frac{1}{4}$	$\frac{1}{7}$	←

Figure 1. Part of the Rhind papyrus (1650 BC) with transcription

We begin with two examples from the second millennium BC. First, the top part of Figure 1 shows a problem from the Egyptian Rhind papyrus, from around 1650 BC. It was copied by the scribe Ahmes, who stated that the original was about 200 years older. At the bottom is a partial transcription of the original hieratic. Like the original papyrus, read the transcription from right to left.

The first line states that we must take *it* one time whole, a $\frac{1}{2}$ time and a $\frac{1}{4}$ time to get 10 as the answer. The question (not explicitly stated) is: 'How big is *it*?'
In the column on the far right in the transcription, we see 1, 2, 4 and $\frac{1}{7}$ on top of each other under '*heap*', (*Hau* in the original). The solution is therefore built up under *Hau*.

First $(1 + \frac{1}{2} + \frac{1}{4})$ is written individually, directly to the left of the '1'. Then this is doubled (see to the left of the 2), and doubled again (left of the 4). $\frac{1}{7}$ of $(\frac{1}{4} + \frac{1}{2} + 1)$ is also determined, which is $\frac{1}{4}$; see the fourth line. The rows marked with arrows (compare the corresponding slashes in the original) give 9 for the '*heap*' together, and for the number of times that $(\frac{1}{4} + \frac{1}{2} + 1)$ is multiplied, $1 + 4 + \frac{7}{7}$ is used temporarily; in the heap, which is still 1 too little to make the required 10. This '1' will be built up from multiples of $\frac{1}{4}$ that correspond with the $\frac{1}{7}$ which belongs to the numbers that build up the final answer. Therefore, we must find the double of the double of $\frac{1}{7}$, because the double of the double of $\frac{1}{4}$ makes 1. For doubling unit fractions such as $\frac{1}{7}$ a table was available that also gives the result in unit fractions: in this case we encounter $\frac{1}{28} + \frac{1}{4}$.

This expression is located in the second row on the left, to the right of the $\frac{1}{2}$. Doubling this row easily yields the '1' next to the $\frac{1}{14} + \frac{1}{2}$ in row 3 on the left.

The overall solution $\frac{1}{14} + \frac{1}{7} + \frac{1}{2} + 5$ is shown at the left of row 4. The rows marked with arrows yield 9 corresponding to 5 and $\frac{1}{7}$; together with the $\frac{1}{14} + \frac{1}{2}$, this provides the final answer.

The lower half of the fragment also contains a calculation; this tells us something more about the method in general. The first row of text under Ahmes' line says: 'The start of the proof'. The second row under the line contains the same expression as the first row above the line, where the answer is at the far left; this is clearly visible in the original. This is what happens: with his calculations, Ahmes shows through direct calculation that the expression $\frac{1}{14} + \frac{1}{7} + \frac{1}{2} + 5$ is indeed the solution to the problem. The phase of *building* the solution is followed by *proving* that the solution answers the original question.

Could this be something like solving the equation $\frac{x}{4} + \frac{x}{2} + x = 10$? In this case, this is giving perhaps too much credit to Ahmes. In fact, this problem involves a division operation (reversing a multiplication operation), while most of the calculation takes place using the rather difficult system of unit fractions. In this system, the solution is achieved by doubling and then adding up the results. It is actually very similar to a long division problem. Giving the name of '*Hau*' to the right-hand column can also be interpreted as 'algebra', but the specific numerical computations are still the main part of the text.

The example of Ahmes places little or no emphasis on the general aspects of the method. It is certainly not yet algebra, in the modern sense of a systematic approach to a problem that is independent of the specific numbers. This is very different in another example from Mesopotamia, about 200 years later, where the specific numerical data do not completely control the solution process. Clay tablet AO 8862 – the original is in the Louvre, Figure 2 shows the transcription made by Neugebauer – is from the same period as the famous Code of Hammurabi, about 1700 BC.

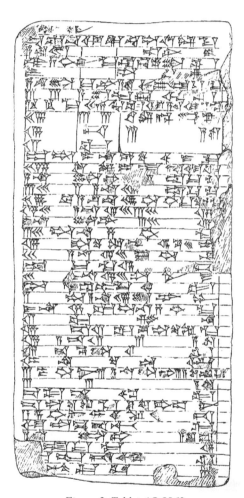

Figure 2. Tablet AO 8862

In cuneiform script on clay tablets, numbers up to 60 are written in a decimal tally system, which can be easily pressed into soft clay with a flattened piece of reed.

Based on the transcription of this fragment (Neugebauer, 1935-37), from line 8 the system becomes clear:

(27)   (183)

The 27 is evidently: $2 \times 10 + 7$. But where does the 183 come from? In the sexagesimal (base sixty) system[i], this number should be read as 3,3 where the first 3 stands for 3 times 60 and the second 3 stands for 3. The meaning of the uppermost rows on this tablet is the following:

> Length, width. I have multiplied the length and width and in this way formed the area. I have added the excess of the length above the width to the area: 3,3. I have added the length and the width: 27. Find the length, the width and the area.

We have already seen that 3,3 means 183, and the reader can get to work with the following system of equations:

$$xy + x - y = 183$$

$$x + y = 27$$

The approach used on the clay tablet is clever. It starts, translated to modern ideas, with substituting y' for $y + 2$. This is hidden in the mathematical operations; the step is taken without explanation. The system now becomes:

$$xy' = 210$$

$$x + y' = 29$$

and the solution is found by applying a famous Babylonian recipe. The arithmetic mean of x and y' is $14\frac{1}{2}$. $(14\frac{1}{2})^2 - 210$ is calculated, which is $\frac{1}{4}$. The square root of this number is $\frac{1}{2}$ and according to the recipe, the correct values for x and y' are then $14\frac{1}{2} + \frac{1}{2}$ and $14\frac{1}{2} - \frac{1}{2}$, respectively. The final solution is $x = 15$, $y = 12$; this can be seen on the pictured fragment under the line with 27 and 3,3, because the solution is shown first, and the method used is shown underneath. The area 3 (180!) is prominently visible.

The solution of the transformed system of equations concerns a standard solution process for a standard problem; this is shown by the fact that the x and y' are in turn called *length* and *width*. In this example, *length* and *width* indicate the factors of a product, which is consistently called the area. It is a subtle but relevant distinction: the *length*, *width*, and area in the Babylonian text refer to roles in the process, while our x, y and y' refer to specific numbers, which we still have to find. So we will resist the temptation of seeing the birth of the algebraic unknown in this example, also because another essential link is missing: the words *length* and *width* only appear in the surrounding text, but are *not* used in the calculations themselves, where we only find the numbers.

Of all calculation steps, only the result is consistently reported; the version with all the calculations is not shown on this tablet. This is also the case with calculating square roots. The emphasis is placed on the recipe-based structure of the solution process, and not on the dependency on the specific numbers. Consequently, we can see more algebra in these examples than in the work of Ahmes: the general solution process is made visible, even though it is only shown with explicit exemplary numbers.

Babylonian clay tablets contain many examples of this type. There are linear equations, quadratic equations, systems of two or sometimes three equations, of which one in the second degree. The tablets give exemplary calculations in the form of recipes to be implemented with the given numbers. We do not understand very well how the Babylonians arrived at the methods of solution. Based on various examples, extensive theories have been developed on this topic, which are still being discussed.

We may draw the conclusion that algebra at this high level requires a good calculation system for numbers which has been mastered impeccably, so that all attention can be focused on the method itself. Today, our students have such a perfect calculation system: their electronic calculator. The author of the clay tablet had multiplication and division tables at hand on other tablets!

Diophantus finds the unknown

There is a verse about Diophantus of Alexandria that was written around 500 AD. It is an epitaph in the form of a word problem. In a modern school book it was translated as follows:

> Here lies Diophantus, the wonder behold.
> Use x's and applets to tell us how old!
> 'God gave him his boyhood one-sixth of his life;
> One twelfth more as youth while whiskers grew rife.
> And then one-seventh more when his marriage had begun.
>
> In five years there came a bouncing new son;
> Alas, the dear child of master and sage
> after attaining half the measure of his father's age,
> died and was buried in a cold grave. With numbers Diophantus consoled his
> fate for four years more, living but then he also passed through life's final door.

Despite this verse, the dates of Diophantus' birth and death are unknown, but based on many links between his writings and those of others, the period 200–284 AD is a good guess.

Diophantus' *Arithmetica*, of which only six of the original thirteen volumes remain, is almost entirely about solving number problems told in words that lead to equations. Arithmetica: on positive integers and rational numbers. There are determinate and indeterminate equations, depending on whether there is a single solution or a number of solutions, although Diophantus consistently gives only one solution for equations in the latter category as well.

Here we focus on problem 39 from Book IV, because it provides a good example of Diophantus' skill. The details of the solution process provide insight into what an 'unknown' could have been in Diophantus' eye. For purposes of clarity, we will first show the solution in modern notation, and then go more deeply into Diophantus' famous notation for powers of the 'unknown'. This is the assignment:

> Find three numbers so that the difference between the largest and second largest number forms a given ratio with the difference between the second largest and the smallest number, in such a way that the sum of two of the three numbers is always a square.

The problem is stated in general terms; the given ratio is not even stated. But Diophantus' solution begins by specifying this ratio:

> Assume that the difference between the largest and second-largest numbers has a ratio of 3:1 with the difference between the second largest and smallest numbers.

If we know a single solution to the problem, we will know more solutions because you can multiply the three numbers of the solution with the square of any number to find a new solution. Diophantus does not explain this in the problem, but he does indicate the value of the smallest of the three squares[ii]:

> The sum of the second largest and smallest term must be a square; let it be 4. Then the second-largest term is larger than 2; let us assume it is $x + 2$, then the smallest term is $2 - x$.

Because the first two terms are $2 - x$ and $2 + x$, we know that the final term must be $2 + 7x$; the difference of $2x$ between the first two terms has a 1 : 3 ratio with the difference between the last two, so that must be $6x$. We therefore know that the other two sums of two of the three numbers are $8x + 4$ and $6x + 4$, which also must be squares. The original problem statement, which is fairly complex, has now been transformed into finding a single unknown, which we have named x.

The second square, the number $6x + 4$, lies between 4 and 16; Diophantus[iii] calls the side of the square 'unknown plus 2', which we have written as $z + 2$, where z is therefore smaller than 2.

Diophantus immediately gives $z^2 + 4z + 4$ for the square and calculates that the largest of the three squares must therefore be $1\frac{1}{3}z^2 + 5\frac{1}{3}z + 4$. Multiply this by the square $\frac{9}{4}$; result: $3z^2 + 12z + 9$ is a square.

Now the story takes an elegant algebraic turn. Diophantus expresses the side of the square as 'a number of times z minus 3'. From:

$$3z^2 + 12z + 9 = (mz - 3)^2$$

it is directly derived that:

$$z = \frac{6m + 12}{m^2 - 3}$$

The elimination of the 9 from both sides is prepared by stating that the unknown side of the square is 'a number of times z minus 3'. As a result, the equation can be reduced to a linear equation. An important observation: Diophantus chose 'a number of times z minus 3' with an eye to the further development of the problem, and with a great deal of insight into the strategy to be followed later on.

Diophantus concludes with deriving from $z < 2$ that $m = 5$ provides a good solution. During this process, a second-degree equation is solved in passing by completing the square. This is followed by $z = \frac{21}{11}$. The final solution for the problem itself is found by substituting this value in $z + 2$ and squaring: $\frac{1849}{121}$. This number is the second-largest square and must therefore be equal to $6x + 4$.

After finding the value of $x = \frac{1365}{762}$ this gives the following three numbers as a solution:

$$\frac{58}{484} \qquad \frac{1878}{484} \qquad \frac{7338}{484}$$

As shown by the final steps of his treatment, Diophantus no longer wants to use fractions in the numerator or denominator, but in this case he does use the common quadratic numerator, so that the fractions are not given in their simplest form. Diophantus closes with the statement: "And the proof is evident." It is certainly evident, and calculation shows that the solution is correct. Nevertheless, it is striking that Diophantus does not use the word 'proof' until this point in the text. We previously noted something similar, on the Rhind papyrus. In this papyrus, the solution was first constructed, and after this the result was explicitly checked in the original problem; Diophantus leaves the verification to the reader. Many other problems end with similar closing remarks. As a whole, the solution process has several striking characteristics:

– Unknowns are sometimes used consistently, but are not necessarily the solution to the problem; they appear to be more of conveniently chosen auxiliary variables.
– In the part where (in our notation) z is used, Diophantus presents an interim problem which must be solved first; he returns to the original problem when a number is found as a solution to that interim problem. By means of this meaningful structure, the processes do not become confused. This is important, because as we will see later, Diophantus did not have a way to distinguish different variables, like we use x and z.
– The coefficients of the problem (for example, the ratio given here) are written numerically. However, it is questionable whether the solution would proceed so smoothly if a ratio was chosen different from 3 : 1.
– Specific numbers are given as solutions. In the present case, the reader understands that values such as $m = 6$, 7, etc. also lead to solutions, but this 'parametrization' of the solution is not visibly present and is certainly not made explicit.

The practical algebraic manipulations that are required in order to verify all of this are not all included in *Arithmetica*, which is not a textbook for elementary algebra. Diophantus assumed that the algebraic rules for the addition, subtraction or multiplication of the various formula components were known to the reader. However, he initially provided rules for the transformation of the 'equations' that were created in this way; for example, he says the following about simplifying:

> If a problem leads to an equation in which specific terms are equal to terms of the same type, but with different coefficients, then it is necessary to subtract equivals from equivals until on both sides one single term is equal to one single term.

The introduction of the book states that 'a deficit times a deficit yields a surplus.' We should not read this as a rule that means a minus times a minus is a plus; negative numbers are not present in *Arithmetica*. The rule only indicates how to deal with 'difference times difference'. The avoidance of negative numbers is apparent in the solution to the above problem 39.

Finally, here is a quotation from the beginning of *Arithmetica*, which immediately follows the dedication to Dionysus:

> Perhaps the topic [of this book] will appear fairly difficult to you because it is not yet familiar knowledge and the understanding of beginners is easily confused by mistakes; but with your inspiration and my teaching it will be easy for you to master, because clear intelligence supported by good lessons is a fast route to knowledge.[iv]

Cubic and quartic equations

In the above examples, we have seen that before the year 1000, people were working on second-degree equations in various ways. We saw special examples with the Babylonians, and with Diophantus we found indeterminate equations, where whole or rational solutions were sought. Later on, we will address the geometric methods, which Euclid and the Arabic mathematicians used for quadratic equations in one unknown.

For many years, the geometric methods (where squares are actual geometric squares) and arithmetic approximations made that equations in the form (in modern notation) $x^2 + 10x = 39$ and $x^2 + 10 = 13x$ had to be treated differently. If we think about representations in the form of area or numbers, then it is clear why this was the case: all amounts on the left and right sides of the equation have to be positive. These equations showed to be of the same type only after it became possible to do algebra with a comprehensive system of negative and positive numbers from which we can take the difference and with which we can perform addition. Therefore, with the oldest solutions of equations, we still see extensive handling of cases.

For the most important step to the exact and general solution of the third and fourth-degree equation, we now go to the great Italian trading cities of the 15th and 16th centuries. It is known that Leonardo Pisano Fibonacci (1170–1250) provided an *approximate* solution to a third-degree equation, but for the story of the general exact solution of the third-degree equation, we have to wait three more centuries. It is a dramatic story of broken promises and has been described in many histories of mathematics. A brief version of the story belongs here as well; due to the easily accessible sources on the internet, this is an outstanding research assignment for students, even if they cannot entirely understand the third-degree equation and its solution. The leading roles are played by:

– Scipione del Ferro, 1465–1526, mathematician at the University of Bologna
– Antonio Fiore, 1506 –?, from Venice, and a student of Del Ferro
– Nicolo Tartaglia, 1499–1557, mathematics teacher in Brescia
– Girolamo Cardano, 1501–1576, physician in Milan
– Ludovico Ferrari, 1522– 1565, student of Cardano

Equations of the type $x^3 + px = q$ were solved by Del Ferro around 1515, but he did not publish the method. Del Ferro died in 1526. Fiore, who probably became acquainted with the solution while studying in Bologna with Del Ferro, challenged Tartaglia in 1535 to solve a series of thirty problems of the type $x^3 + px = q$. Of course, the challenger must have been familiar with the solutions. Tartaglia replied with his own list of problems, which was more varied. Just before the expiration of the deadline, Tartaglia discovered the correct method, solved all the equations within two hours and beat Fiore, who had solved almost none of the problems on Tartaglia's list. Tartaglia was satisfied with the honour and waved off the thirty banquets that had been planned for the winner.

In 1539, Girolamo Cardano, who was busy writing his own *Practica Arithmeticae,* heard about Tartaglia's accomplishments and tried in vain to find the solution of $x^3 + px = q$ himself. After this, he tried to get Tartaglia to reveal his solution. Tartaglia did so, but only after Cardano offered to use his influence on Tartaglia's behalf with the military commander of Milan. According to Tartaglia, Cardano swore an oath not to publish the solution before Tartaglia.

Later on – in cooperation with Ludovico Ferrari – Cardano was also able to adapt the solution method for equations of the types $x^3 = px + q$ and $x^3 + q = px$. Moreover, Ferrari succeeded in solving a fourth-degree equation by reducing the problem to solving a third-degree equation. But what could he do with all these wonderful discoveries? Cardano and Ferrari felt that they were bound by the oath. In one version of the drama, they heard rumours that Scipione del Ferro knew the solution even before Tartaglia. It required little difficulty to find this information in Del Ferro's legacy; indeed, it was clearly stated.

In 1545 Cardano published the complete solution for all three types of equations in his *Ars Magna*; he reported both Del Ferro and Tartaglia as being the discoverers of the solution for equations of the type $x^3 + px = q$, claimed the other two types for himself, and gave Ferrari the honour for the fourth-degree equation. He was honest, that is certain. However, the publication elicited the boundless fury of Tartaglia, who claimed that he had solved the three types himself.

Let us now look at the solution method, which was a long-held secret, with the following example:

AAD GODDIJN

(a cube and six times its side is 20)

Because this is how the equations were written. In our notation: $x^3 + 6x = 20$. Cardano (Del Ferro, Tartaglia?) replaced the side (x) by a difference between two other lengths. In other words, he substituted $x = u - v$.

Reducing $(u - v)^3$ to $(u^3 - v^3) - 3uv(u - v)$ is now crucial.

$x^3 + 6x = (u - v)^3 + 6(u - v) = (u^3 - v^3) - 3uv(u - v) + 6(u - v) = 20$.

If it is possible to choose u and v so that $u^3 - v^3 = 20$ and $3uv = 6$, then $x = u - v$ is a solution for $x^3 + 6x = 20$. Because these conditions for u and v are equivalent (everything is positive!) to $u^3 - v^3 = 20$ and $u^3 v^3 = 8$, there is no longer a problem because every mathematician in this era could deal with this system of simultaneous equations: given the difference between and product of two numbers, find the numbers themselves. But the present-day reader finds $\sqrt{108} + 10$ and $\sqrt{108} - 10$. So here is the solution of $x^3 + 6x = 20$, as shown in *Cardano's formula*:

$$x = \sqrt[3]{\sqrt{108} + 10} - \sqrt[3]{\sqrt{108} - 10}.$$

In this case it all appears fairly simple and very elegant, but in those days there were many cases where impassable obstacles still appeared during the solution process, even if it could be easily seen that a real solution must be possible. Rafael Bombelli (1526–1572) succeeded in interpreting cubic roots so that he always found a solution, even if there were negative numbers inside the root sign. During this process he used what were later called complex numbers.

General solutions: François Viète

François Viète (1540–1630) took two important steps to clarify the relationship between roots and equations. First of all, he used a notation of equations in which the specific value of the coefficient was no longer given, but both the coefficient and the unknown were represented by a letter. For the unknown (known as the cosa), Viète used a vowel; for the coefficients, he used consonants. He wrote a second-degree equation as follows:

B in A quadratum, plùs D plano in A, aequari Z solido.

Translated:

B times the square of A plus area D times A will be equal to the volume Z.

Our equation

$$BA^2 + DA = Z$$

is an efficient but meagre shadow of the original. Viète clearly believed it was important for the equation to be formulated homogeneously, that all components had to be either linear, plane or solid. Apparently he assumed that B is a line segment. B in

38

A quadratum is therefore a 'solido'. If *D* plano is an area, *D* plano in *A* is also a so-lido. *A* itself is clearly linear. In our present-day notation, these aspects are no longer visible.

Viète, in his *De equationem emendatione*, took a route that appears very similar to that of Cardano, and found a solution to the equation

$$A^3 + 3BA = 2Z$$

namely:

$$A = \sqrt[3]{\sqrt{B^3 + Z^2} + Z} - \sqrt[3]{\sqrt{B^3 + Z^2} - Z}$$

In this equation, *Z* therefore represents a volume and *B* an area; to make sure that all the operations in the radical expression make sense, it is useful to briefly check this. The conclusion must be that 2 and 3 in the original equation are dimensionless.

Here the advances made on Diophantus' work are clear: you only have to fill in a newly chosen *B* and *Z* in the pattern, and the new solution rolls right out. With Di-ophantus' approach, at the beginning of the solution process for a problem another constant value could be chosen, but after this the entire solution process had to be gone through again; we noted a similar difference with Ahmes and his Babylonian colleague.

Regarding the concept of generalization, which is in Chapter 1 mentioned as an essential characteristic of algebra, something special is also taking place here. For Viète, the generalization aspect was not in the unknown, *A*, of the equation, but in the coefficients, here *B* and *Z*. In the final section of this Chapter, which deals with school algebra, we will return to this aspect in connection with the current insights.

Further developments

It is remarkable that Viète also knew that the solution of an equation determines the coefficients in a certain sense. Viète:

> *Si A cubus $\overline{-B-D-G}$ in A quad. $+ \overline{B\ in\ D + B\ in\ G + D\ in\ G}$ in A, aequatur B in D in G:*
> *A explicabilis est de quadlibet illarum trium, B, D, vel G.*

In today's language:

> *If $A^3 + (-B-D-G)A^2 + (BD+BG+DG)A = BDG$*
> *then A is equal to one of these three: B, D or G.*

However, here we are given the strong impression that *A*, *B*, *D*, and *G* have equiv-alent roles in the equation. After all, *A* is equal to one of the three. Thomas Harriot (1560 – 1621) made this much more explicit by ascertaining that if *a*, *b* and *c* are the solutions of a third-degree equation, then the equation must be:

$$(x-a) \cdot (x-b) \cdot (x-c) = 0$$

Later on (in 1673), in a letter to Huygens, Leibniz used pure algebra to shown that if *a*, *b* and *c* are given by the solution formulas of Cardano/Bombelli, then the third-degree equation can indeed be found. This is a completely algebraic verification of the formulas, which had not been done until then.

Ferrari, Viète, Harriot, Tschirnhaus (1651–1708) and others found solutions for the general fourth-degree equation; once again this was done by inserting an extra variable that led to a solvable third-degree equation. The calculation work that was required for this discovery does not provide us with much more insight into the historical development of algebra.

Almost two centuries later, it turned out that there can be no solution formula (in a strictly defined algebraic sense) for the general fifth and higher-degree equations. But in this *proof* of inexistence, the understanding that the coefficients of the equation can be expressed in the roots plays an important role. There will be more about this in the section on the question whether everything has become computable with algebra.

ALGEBRA: NOTATION THAT CLARIFIES AND ORGANIZES

The nature of algebraic text

From the above it can be seen that during the search for the solution of equations, new forms of notation appeared. This is an important phenomenon which we will now explore more deeply; it is also a good time to reflect briefly on the role of various notations in algebra. There are two extreme standpoints regarding the relationship of algebra to its notation:
1. Without notation using letters, there would be no algebra.
2. Algebra concerns relationships and structures; notation is only a memory aid.

The first standpoint is a superficial definition of algebra; the second standpoint appears to go far beyond the superficial appearance, but does disregard the fact that we require such a memory aid in complex situations. And isn't it obvious that algebra could not have developed without notation?

The title of this section indicates that the situation is not that simple. In a certain sense, the notation of algebra has evolved from being a memory aid to an active mechanism, which has its own part in solving complex problems. In this section, we will map out this idea in greater detail based on the historical development of two components of 'our' notation: the notation of powers and the representation of structure in algebraic expressions.

Notation is a means of communication: a notation must clearly indicate what is meant. All of this leads perhaps to the following question: is mathematics (or algebra) a language? The answer can be yes or no, it does not make much difference, because the statement that mathematics is a language (or not) says little about what doing mathematics actually is. Nevertheless, 'the language of mathematics' is a very popular expression, and has a history that seems to begin in the 17th century. Probably Galileo's most widely quoted statement is:

> This [the book of nature] is written in the language of mathematics and the main characters are triangles, circles and other geometric figures, without which it would be impossible for people to understand a single word. Without this language, people would get lost in a maze.[v]

Galileo claimed especially that geometric objects are necessary for us in order to find our way in the universe. This is a philosophical point of view that outstandingly exemplifies the 17th century; Galileo's *scritto in lingua matematica* is a gripping way to express this view, but the one-sided emphasis on the aspect of language in the quotation disregards the importance of the geometric objects that Galileo also refers to: triangles and circles.

How does this apply to algebra? What are mathematical objects in algebra and what is their relationship in and with language? These days, an algebraic formula or equation in a running text usually takes the grammatical role comparable to a name; the name has its own inner mathematical structure, not influenced by the structure of the sentence. For example:

The equation $x^2 = 10 \cdot \sin(x)$ has 10 solutions

This is syntactically similar to:

"The Londoner Jack the Ripper committed 5 murders."

The fairly literal translation that we made of a proposition of Viète

*If $A^3 + (-B - D - G)A^2 + (BD + BG + DG)A = BDG$,
then A is equal to one of these three: B, D or G.*

is a mixed form in which the sign of equality between two algebraic formulas acts as a verb in the conditional subordinate clause. This clearly shows that the algebraic notation can function as an abbreviation system within regular language. The reader is advised to check the Viète original above.

Not everyone will have objected to this example of Viète, but mixing a mathematical notation with everyday language may have a strange effect in other situations:

> The length of a football field = 90 meters and the width = 60. What is its area?

The separation of normal written language and the formalism of the mathematical objects is the product of a long development. In a later example, we will clearly see that the conjugations of Latin words still held a grip on the names for unknowns in algebraic expressions until well into the 17th century.

The mathematical text also places special restrictions on the meaning of normal words. In the mathematical context, words such as line, variable, point and function have their own, limited meaning. This is not so remarkable; the words used in other disciplines also have restricted meanings. *Jargon*: the half-formalized language elements of a specific discipline.

Unknowns and their powers: from abbreviation to complete arithmetization

On the Rhind papyrus, we previously saw that no sign was used for finding an unknown or variable in a problem. We also saw that the Babylonian mathematician consistently referred to the unknowns-to-be-found, of which he knows the sum and product (the 'area'), as the 'length' and 'width'. He gave functional names to a quantity in a specific situation, but did not use the terms in the calculations themselves. This was different with Diophantus.

Diophantus

The assignment in Figure 3 appears in problem 39 from Book IV. In the Greek sentence it is easy to see where the mathematical components are located; with the modern transcription underneath, we quickly understand the notation method. We will examine several components.

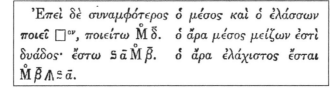

Because the sum of the middle term and the smallest term is a square, let it be 4. Then the middle term is larger than 2. Let it be $x + 2$. Then the smallest term is $2 - x$.

Figure 3. Problem 39 from Book IV by Diophantus

$\square^{ov}$. First of all, we are struck by the use of the small square, which is used like a word, in the second row of the text. The square is an abbreviation for the Greek word τετραγωνον: the square of a number. There appears to be an exponent (on) after this element, but it is actually an inflection; for us, this emphasizes how the formal element of the square in the text is still an actual part of the running language.

M̊ δ̄ The Greeks wrote numbers with letters, from 1 through 9 simply in the sequence of the alphabet, often written with a line above the letter for clarity. α, β, γ, δ, ε, ϛ, ζ, η, θ. This represents 4, because the *M* with a circle above means (according to Diophantus) that it concerns units, *Monaden*; so here the 4 is just a number. The letter ι next to θ represents 10, the following letters stand for 20, 30, etc. This is followed by the nine hundreds. There were separate words for 1000 and 10,000.

ϛ ā M̄ β̄ We can now read the '1' and the '2' units (monads). The sign ϛ in the front is new; this is the building block of Diophantus' fame. Diophantus said that this was the *unknown* quantity of units to be found, the *arithmos*. Note that the letter alpha (α)explicitly indicates that the arithmos is taken only once. Here is something that we would like to read as $1x + 2$.

M̊ $\bar{\beta}$ ⋀ ⊆ $\bar{a}$ Diophantus did not use a real minus sign, but he did have a difference sign, ⋀. We can see this from the fact that this sign is never placed at the front. 'Two take away one times x' is a good translation, or $2 - 1x$.

Equality is simply expressed in words, but with an abbreviation.

In ϛ$\bar{\eta}$ M̊ δ ῐσ. □ᵖ, καὶ ϛϜ M̊ δ ῐσ. □ᵖ. we read: $8x + 4$ is a square and $6x + 4$ is a square. But in this case we can also read 'the number $8x + 4$ has the square-property'. Like 'this rose is red', which doesn't imply equality of a rose and a colour. Diophantus gave each power of the unknown its own sign.

The transcription of $\Delta^{Y} \bar{\gamma}$ ϛ $\bar{\iota\beta}$ M̊ $\bar{\theta}$ is our trinomial $3x^2 + 12x + 9$.

Diophantus used the Δ (dynamis) for the square of the unknown and K (kubos) for the cube, both with an index ^{Y}, that undoubtedly descended from the second letter, the Greek upsilon. The fourth and fifth and six powers were created by making combinations. The symbol combinations:

$$\Delta^Y, K^Y, \Delta^Y\Delta, \Delta K^Y, K^Y K$$

now 'mean' x^2, x^3, x^4, x^5, x^6 respectively.

But the conversion to a letter such as x and an exponent obscures the original notation. For various powers of the same unknown quantity, Diophantus used various signs, but in the structure of the sequence of powers, it can be seen which power a product of two powers leads to.

Diophantus was unable to make a difference in notation between two unknowns, but in modern interpretations of Diophantus this cannot be seen; for example, the modern interpretations refer to x and z and act as if Diophantus was able to do something similar. This is very misleading!

The transcription of problem 39 shows how Diophantus dealt with the situation. For example, while solving the main problem, a step is made to solving a 'sub-problem'. In this sub-problem, the arithmos temporarily functions in a different role. When the sub-problem was solved, Diophantus returned to the original story line with the original arithmos. This was a story within a story, a well known narrative device in classical literature. For example, in Homer's *Odyssey*, a singer at the court of Alkinoös tells a story about the Trojan war, while Ulysses himself is present, who then tells the story of his own travels. Both stories are stories within the *Odyssey* itself.

It is very clear that Diophantus' algebraic notation has the character of handy abbreviations. Due to these abbreviations, Nesselman (1842) refers to syncopic notation, as opposed to rhetorical notation in which everything is written out in text form. In syncopic notation, the symbols do not yet have their independent symbolic meaning and algebra-only mutual relations; Nesselman refers to symbolic notation only after Viète. It is very clear that there are three types of notation, but linking them to historical periods, as is frequently done, is not very sensible. They also appear at the same time, often in the same text.

Notations for the unknown and powers of the unknown, 1450–1637

During the European Renaissance, many words (and their abbreviations) for the unknown were in circulation. One of the most well known was cos (the thing) with its variants cosa and coss. But other words were also used such as res (the matter), latus (the side, note the link with square) and thynge (Robert Recorde, Engeland, 1556). Every writer could use different terms for the powers of the unknown, often according to the Diophantic pattern, but sometimes based on a different structure. For example, Pacioli (1494) wrote cosa-censo-cubo, where we would write x, x^2, x^3. He abbreviated to co, ce and cu and then continued with ce.ce for x^4, ce.cu for x^6 and p.r. (primo relato) for x^5. So we must see the ce.cu as the second power of the third power of the unknown, and not as the second power times the third power.

Still similar to Diophantus, William Oughtred wrote in 1647 in his *Clavis mathematicae* $1qc - 15qq + 160c - 1250q + 6480l = 170304782$,
which is our $x^5 - 15x^4 + 160x^3 - 1250x^2 + 6480x = 170304782$, because the q, c and l stand for quadratus, cubus and latus. With this construction, Oughtred kept to the conservative side; at that time, other methods were already becoming popular[vi].

The arithmetical structure of our notation with powers of variables, where multiplication of two powers leads to the addition of the exponents, was preceded by notations that only wrote down the so-called index, instead of writing the unknown and its powers with abbreviations. If there was only a single unknown (as we have seen with Diophantus), this approach was sufficient. For example, in the notation used by Chuquet (1445–1488), 10^2 stood for 10 times the square (of the unknown).

Although there were predecessors, we have chosen the Dutchman Gielis van der Hoecke as an example with his *In arithmetica een sonderling excellēt boek* (Antwerpen 1537). Van der Hoecke provides a list of symbols for the notation of powers of the unknown, but also provides a rule for the multiplication of powers. See Figure 4.

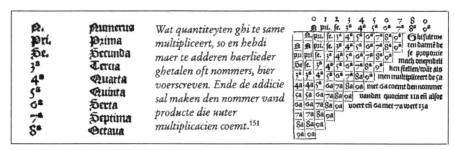

Figure 4. The rule for adding exponents, here called 'nommers'

The symbols are actually the Latin ordinals, where the first two words are written out and the rest after Terza are shown as numerals. We encounter Diophantus' Monade in the first line: Numerus, number. A number without the unknown, therefore the absolute numbers.

Van der Hoecke not only provides an explanation, but also uses a table to show how powers can be combined during multiplication. 'So en hebdi maer te addiren haerlieder ghetalen oft nommers' (You only have to add their numbers). In the table we see a 0 (zero) above the *N* of Numerus to show the number that people have to add in this case.

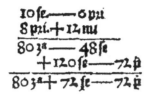

Figure 5. Multiplications of two binomials

Finally, Figure 5 shows an example of the multiplication of two binomials, which shows *10se – 6 pri times 8 pri + 12 ni*. The notation is still not entirely symbolic; in this example it is especially the *n* of numerus that reveals its role as an abbreviated text element concerning the declension to the plural (ni, for numeri), including the notation of the small letter *i* above the *n*. But the result is correct, and the multiplication scheme is clear.

From Descartes to the present

In 1637, Descartes used almost the same notation as we still use today. Descartes still deviated from present-day notation for the second powers, which were frequently, but not always, represented by doubled letters. Figure 6, taken from his Géométrie, shows some of the variation.

> tiplier l'vne par l'autre; Et $\frac{a}{b}$, pour diuiser *a* par *b*; Et *a a*, ou $\overset{2}{a}$, pour multiplier *a* par foy mefme; Et $\overset{3}{a}$, pour le multiplier encore vne fois par *a*, & ainfi a l'infini; Et $\sqrt{\overset{2}{a} + \overset{2}{b}}$, pour tirer la racine quarrée d' $\overset{2}{a} + \overset{2}{b}$; Et $\sqrt{C. \overset{3}{a} - \overset{3}{b} + a b b}$, pour tirer la racine cubique d' $\overset{3}{a} - \overset{3}{b} + a b b$, & ainfi des autres.

Figure 6. Fragment of La Géométrie (Descartes, 1637)

Descartes provided guidelines for the use of the letters in the same way as Viète. We consistently find the final letters of the alphabet (*x, y* and *z*) being used for the unknowns, and the first letters (*a, b*, and *c*) being used as coefficients in the equations

45

or problem situations. This division of the alphabet into its first and final letters replaced the division into vowels and consonant used by Viète. Later on, the convention was established to indicate typical counting variables, such as indexes for rows, by the letters *n, m, i, j* and *k*.

Standardization of the notation took place very gradually. It was only after the infinitesimal calculus in the style of Newton or Leibniz became widely known (which was many years later) that some uniformity was established. These two mathematicians established the ultimate norms for mathematical notation in principle, in the same way that the great Bible translations (Luther, King James) established the norms for grammar and spelling in various countries.

Fractional, negative and literal exponents

Nicole Oresme (1323–1382) used what we could call fractional exponents in his *Algorismus proportionum*, but these did not become commonplace. In his *Van de Spiegheling der Singh-konst* (Theory of the art of singing) Simon Stevin (1548–1620) was already using fractional exponents; in this book, Stevin addresses the mathematics of equal temperament, i.e. the division of the musical octave into twelve equal parts (semitones). In mathematical terms, this amounts to determining the twelfth root of two and its powers. Stevin used a notation with fractions, but only in this book, which was not published in his lifetime; he did not use fractions in his algebraic books.

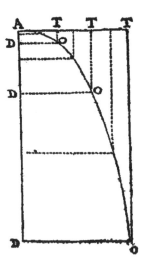

Figure 7. Wallis' investigation of the sum of powers

In the work of John Wallis, we encounter the active use of fractional exponents and negative exponents; in his *Arithmetica Infinitorum* from 1656, he investigated sums of powers of this type $0 + 1 + 4 + 9 + 16 + 25 + 36$ in proportion to sums of the value of the largest term, in this case $36 + 36 + 36 + 36 + 36 + 36 + 36$. Wallis used what he called induction[vii] to show that such a proportion approaches $1 : 3$. The illustration next to proposition 23 (Figure 7) clearly shows the essence of the problem: the area of *ATTTOOOA* above the parabola with respect to the area of the entire rectangle. For the cube, Wallis discovered the proportion $1 : 4$, and so forth.

Later on in the book, Wallis investigated other number sequences (and therefore other types of parabolic curves), for example a series of various types of roots and sequences that are created by multiplying or dividing the terms from two sequences. During this process he explicitly referred to what he calls the index of the sequences. In this way, for example, the sequences of square roots

$$\sqrt[2]{0a} \qquad \sqrt[2]{1a} \qquad \sqrt[2]{2a} \qquad \sqrt[2]{3a}$$

is multiplied by a series of fifth roots

$$\sqrt[5]{0b} \qquad \sqrt[5]{1b} \qquad \sqrt[5]{2b} \qquad \sqrt[5]{3b}$$

via the interim steps

$$\sqrt[10]{0a^5} \qquad \sqrt[10]{1a^5} \qquad \sqrt[10]{32a^5} \qquad \sqrt[10]{243a^5}$$

and

$$\sqrt[10]{0b^2} \qquad \sqrt[10]{1b^2} \qquad \sqrt[10]{4b^2} \qquad \sqrt[10]{9b^2}$$

to

$$\sqrt[10]{0a^5b^2} \qquad \sqrt[10]{1a^5b^2} \qquad \sqrt[10]{128a^5b^2} \qquad \sqrt[10]{2187a^5b^2}$$

where a series is created that Wallis described with index $\frac{7}{10} = \frac{1}{2} + \frac{1}{5}$.
In the book, Wallis used sums and difference of indices in expressions such as:

$$2 + \tfrac{1}{2} = \tfrac{5}{2} \text{ and } 2 - \tfrac{1}{2} = \tfrac{3}{2}.$$

But Wallis did not use the index as an exponent; he still wrote the denominators of the index with radicals, and still classified the negative indices of differences of indices as division.

Finally Newton had the honour of being the first to use letters in the exponent; he immediately used also fractions such as *m/n* in the exponent.

Review and conclusion

The history of the notation of powers shows how algebraic formalism began by describing problems in words, then used abbreviations and symbols, and finally developed into a mechanism where the notation of a problem took over the role of the 'brainwork'. In that regard, the table of Van der Hoecke (Figure 4) illuminates an essential aspect: in algebra, simple calculation rules can be provided, and correctly following the rules leads to the correct result, in this case the rule for multiplying exponents (product rule) by adding them. This is an important aspect when doing mathematics with algebra (in the sense of mathematics using letters and symbols): the shift from reflection to algorithmic action based on rules that describe the form of the written algebra, but no longer explain it. Whether we as teachers like it or not, this loss of meaning is essentially built into this process.

The loss of visible meaning could also be seen in the gradual transition from the old, geometry-based notation of A-squared and A-cubed to A^2 and A^3. The notation with numerals puts the old geometric meaning out of the picture, and almost automatically places the two powers of A in a sequence, which begins with A, moves onto A^2, then A^3 and A^4 and never stops. The new, less geometrically oriented notation of powers made it possible to consider the power A^n, the general model for the elements in the series A^1, A^2, A^3, ...

Aggregation, grouping
In the following four expressions

$$(x^2 + 4) \cdot (3 - 2x) \quad \sqrt{x^2 + 4} + \sqrt{3 - 2x}, \quad \frac{3 - 2x}{x^2 + 4}, \quad a^{x^2 + 4} + b^{3 - 2x}$$

$x^2 + 4$ and $3 - 2x$ are sub-expressions. Parentheses, root signs, the horizontal line and exponentiation are forms of notation that group related symbols together. This is known as aggregation. Today, aggregation determines the order of the operations, but in history it was limited primarily to grouping with respect to adding and subtracting a series of terms.

Here is a small selection of historical uses that deviate from present-day custom. The selection is large enough to ascertain that the meaning in specific situations interferes with discovering general forms, and that ultimately a systematic grouping method developed: the paired parentheses. However, until about 1825, forms of notation were used that seem bizarre from a modern perspective.

Parentheses are one of the oldest grouping methods. In this example from Bombelli (1550), square brackets are used in combination with underlining:

$$R^3[2\tilde{m}R[0\tilde{m}.121]] \text{ for } \sqrt[3]{2 - \sqrt{-121}}$$

Regarding the use of parentheses (or brackets), this is an early and isolated example. In the printed versions of his book, Bombelli also used the letter L (Legata) and its mirror image to show what was covered by the R.q (square root). Note the minuscule signs for the variable above the 20 and the 2 on the right-hand side of the equation.

$$4 \cdot p \cdot R.q \cdot L \; \imath 4 \cdot m \cdot \imath o. J \quad \text{Egualei } \imath.$$

That is $4 + \sqrt{24 - 20x} = 2x$. For many years, the preference was given to grouping items with a single, additional graphic element, and not with two pair-forming signs, as is the case with parentheses.

Lines above the letters, Newton (1669):

$$\overline{\overline{y - 4 \times y + 5 \times y - 12 \times y + 17}} = 0.$$

for

$$(((y - 4) \times y + 5) \times y - 12) \times y + 17 = 0.$$

This was very common in the 17th and 18th centuries. The lines were also used in combination with roots; the long tail of the root sign that we use today has its origin in this line.

In *La Géométrie* (1636), Descartes used no parentheses at all, but we do find forms such as the following, often with even more layers of terms next to the braces:

Points were also frequently used to mark the aggregation, especially in combination with roots. For example, with Descartes $\sqrt{.2 - \sqrt{2}}.$ plays the role of our $\sqrt{2 - \sqrt{2}}$ and the points could therefore be read as a pair of parentheses. But the point behind the root could also indicate that the root must be taken over the remaining part of the formula. We therefore also encounter:

$$\sqrt{.2 - \sqrt{.2 + \sqrt{.2 + \sqrt{.2 + \sqrt{.2 + \sqrt{2}}}}}}$$

for the side of a regular 128-sided polygon with outer radius 1, i.e.

$$\sqrt{2 - \sqrt{2 + \sqrt{2 + \sqrt{2 + \overline{\sqrt{2 + 2}}}}}}$$

This example is from a text by Dibaudius (1605) on book X of Euclid's *Elements*, which contains root expressions of the type $\sqrt{A + \sqrt{B}}$. In this situation, this notation is ideal.

With *binomial* coefficients, from the 17th century until far into the 19th century factors such as $n, n-1, n-2$ were often separated only by points, so that the following notation regularly appeared: $n \cdot n - 1 \cdot n - 2$. Or were n and 1 held together by the points, as with the root notation? This example is from the *Exercises de Calcul Intégral* van Legendre, from 1811! These forms of notation were very common for mathematicians such as Wallis, Leibniz, Bernoulli, Euler and Gauss.

We find a special notation for writing polynomials in an ordered form for the first time with Descartes, but it also appears later. With the expression $x^6 - bx = 0$, the missing powers of x and the constant term are now visibly absent.

$$x^{.6} * \quad * \quad * \quad * .. bx * \infty 0$$

AAD GODDIJN

Universal substitution

The examples of the points used with roots and binomial coefficients demonstrate that notations were often linked to the specific algebraic context and were not generally applicable. Lines (with roots and in division) and parentheses (as a universal grouping indicator) did not have that drawback, and these two types of notation therefore continued until the 21st century.

This is a good time to reflect on an important characteristic of modern notation: the possibility for universal substitution. As a starting point, take an expression such as

$$\frac{2}{1+x}$$

Without destroying the syntactic structure of the formula, the elements 2, 1 and x of this expression can be replaced not only by other numbers and letters, but also by entire formulas. To ensure that the new component does not interfere with the rest, we place it inside a pair of parentheses if necessary; this makes the formula into a block which cannot be influenced from the outside. In this example, if you replace 1 with $x^2 + y^2$, replace 2 with some integral formula and replace x with the original formula, the overall formula retains a correct grammatical-syntactical structure:

$$\frac{\int_{-x}^{y}\frac{dt}{2+\sin t+\cos t}}{(x^2+y^2)+(\frac{2}{1+x})}$$

Comparing the two expressions (the old one and the new one) shows that our modern notation unites both the global structure and the detailed structure. Every detail can become a new whole, in the same way that a word in a sentence can be replaced by a long description. Modern notation primarily shows the syntactical structure, and to a much lesser extent an operation to be executed (cf. Chapter 1 on the operational-structural dimension). If values for x and y for the large formula above are given, then it is not at all obvious what must be 'done' first or calculated first. Our modern algebraic notation is initially a syntactical notation, and only secondarily a calculation notation.

New notations for human and computer calculation Algebra as taught in school has retained at least one notation element from the New Math era: the so-called arrow language. In this language, the arrows represent operations. The upper part of Figure 8 provides an example. The lower part of Figure 8 shows an arrow chain created in the educational applet Algebra Arrows[viii].

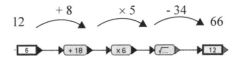

Figure 8. Two types of arrow chains

Arrow language emphasizes the sequence in which operations are conducted. The sequence is written out completely, and the notation does not provide any visible grouping into sub-formulas, as is the case with traditional notation. Notations are focused on a specific type of reader. For example, if the reader is a machine performing calculations, then such an arrow-based notation is extremely functional. The most prevalent form of this notation in the computer world is the so-called postfix system, which we will illustrate with the following example.

This is a calculation written in postfix notation (also called Reverse Polish Notation or RPN):

$$4 \ 5 + 25 \ \sqrt{\ } \ 2 - \times$$

The operations take place by reading from left to right, while taking the following steps:
– putting numbers on a stack
– performing operations on the topmost elements of the stack
– if necessary, the result goes back onto the stack
– if the entire sequence has been executed, the result remains on the stack.

The status of the stack after every step is shown in Figure 9 from left to right; below the stacks are the objects read from the input line.

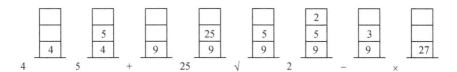

Figure 9. Visualization of the calculation process

An essential aspect of RPN is that there are no parentheses. This is because grouping is unnecessary. However, we can leave the operation steps in standard notation, and then the machine provides an algebraic expression as the result: the grey fields below are therefore pieces of the formula built up in standard notation. In Figure 10 we see an automatic translation process from RPN to standard notation.

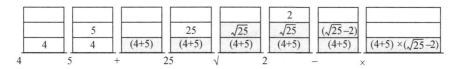

Figure 10. From postfix to standard notation

In this way, the formula can be built up in steps in a given arrow chain; an activity that would appear to be educational; nonetheless, it is rarely used in school.

We find another new notation method in spreadsheets generated by software such as Excel. A spreadsheet is a grid in which every cell represents a value, which is calculated by a formula linked to the cell, which can also refer to other cells.

C7	▼	f_x = B7+C6				
	A	B	C	D	E	F	G
1	1	1	1	1	1	1	1
2	1	2	3	4	5	6	7
3	1	3	6	10	15	21	28
4	1	4	10	20	35	56	84
5	1	5	15	35	70	126	210
6	1	6	21	56	126	252	462
7	1	7	28	84	210	462	924
8	1	8	36	120	330	792	1716

Figure 11. Spreadsheet with Pascal's triangle

In this way we have a two-dimensional scheme of variables, each of which is given the name of its coordinate pair on the grid. In Excel, for example, the formula $B7 + C6$ can be placed in cell $C7$. The values of the cells left of and above $C7$ are then added. If we place the value of 1 in the cells in column A and in the cells in row 1, and if we copy cell $C7$ to the remainder of the cells, then we have a slanted version of Pascal's triangle.

The power of spreadsheets is, among other things, that a formula from a cell can be copied to a group of other cells, where references will be copied relatively or absolutely as desired. Entirely new possibilities and methods have been created in this process, not only for bookkeeping and calculating weighted averages with tests, but also for mathematics itself!

ALGEBRA AND GEOMETRY: HELPFUL NEIGHBOURS OR OPPOSITES?

Euclid and Applet Area Algebra

Around 300 BC, 1200 years before the word 'algebra' began to take its place in mathematics, Euclid formulated proposition II, 4:

> If a straight line is cut at random, the square on the whole equals the squares on the segments plus twice the rectangle contained by the segments (Heath, 1910).

Even the oldest known manuscripts of Euclid's elements contain figures. In proposition 4 of Book II, we find the drawing shown in Figure 12 on the left. For a reader from the 21st century, it is tempting to read the following into this figure:

$$(x+y)^2 = x^2 + y^2 + 2xy$$

referring to an applet from the Wisweb[viii] , as shown on the right. They do appear very similar. But why does Euclid use the diagonal line *BD*? It doesn't have anything to do with the problem, or does it?

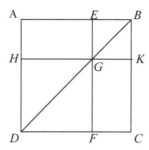 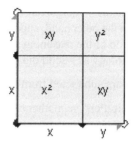

Figure 12. Euclid and Geometric Algebra applet, both geometry and algebra

The answer becomes clear when we examine Euclid's proof. This proof consists of constructing a square on *AB*, which is based on proposition 46 from Book I; this proposition is included in the Elements just before the Pythagorean theorem. After this, the diagonal line *BD* is drawn, and finally *HK* is drawn parallel to *AB* through the intersection of *CF* and *BD*. The proof consists of a long argument to show that *DFGH* and *GKBE* are equal to the squares on the segments *AE* and *EB* and that *HGEA* and *FCKG* are each equal to the rectangle built by *AE* and *EB*.

The diagonal *BD* plays a dominant and essential role in this reasoning. It creates all kinds of equal angles and a game with isosceles triangles is the backbone of the substantiated construction of the figure, which – for Euclid – is the actual proof of the proposition.

At first glance, it would thus appear that Euclid does not have much to do with $(x+y)^2 = x^2+y^2+2xy$. The formula looks like a calculation with objects that appear to represent something numerical; the geometric proof refers to shapes of figures, taking together what the lines 'contain'.

The present-day student and the creator of the applet no longer see the possibility of positioning the squares and rectangles in the figure as a problem. The emphasis in the applet Geometric Algebra is on other aspects:
– identifying a product of two factors as an area;
– investigating the geometric-combinatorial structure that corresponds with the addition of line segments *x* and *y* to become *x* + *y*, and multiplying this term by itself to become $(x+y)^2 = x^2+y^2+2xy$.
– interpreting $(x+y)^2 = x^2+y^2+2xy$ as a summary of the result.

Viewed in this way, the applet becomes more of an algebraic continuation of Euclid's proposition problem in a somewhat different direction and using other means, rather than a contrasting approach to that of Euclid.

Classical Greek mathematics is itself dualistic. There is the Pythagorean movement, which is based on numbers, and there is the geometric movement, where figures made of points and lines set the tone. The geometry books of Euclid's *Elements* are vital to the latter movement. In these books, Euclid did what no modern teacher would dare: present the Pythagorean theorem without mentioning the 3-4-5 triangle. Diophantus, on the other hand, appears to represent the numerical tradition. However, in his description of the reasoning steps in the calculation process, Diophantus uses the same terminology as Euclid did in his *General Rules*, which states, for example:

If equals are subtracted from equals, then the remainders are equal.

In the Arabic-Persian mathematics that took place during our Middle Ages, the Greek geometric style was continued. Equations were solved by means of geometric figures, and the link with the geometric algebra of Euclid is obvious. However, an example from the *Hisab al-jabr w'al-muqabala* by Al'kwarizmi (780–850) of Baghdad leads one to suspect that there is something more going on than was the case with Euclid. In this tradition, Jabr has the meaning of adding the same to both sides of an equation in order to eliminate terms from both sides that could be removed (the frequently used formulation 'to eliminate negative terms' is somewhat anti-historical; moreover, jabr has other meanings such as regrouping and setting broken bones).

In the following example, something is added to both sides of the equation. The question is:

A square added by 10 of its roots is equal to 39, how big is the square?

First there is a solution presented as a mathematical recipe: take half of 10, which is 5. Add the square of this number to 39, the result is 64. Take the square root, which is 8. Subtract 5. The answer is 3. It is once again immediately clear how the recipe can be generally applied to similar equations. As proof for the method, we draw a square that represents (or is) the square to be found. On the four sides, rectangles are placed with a width of $2\frac{1}{2}$. Added together, these four rectangles are 10 times the square root. The four squares that are attached to the four corners, taken together, form the square of 5. We now know the length of the side of the large square: 8; after all, the total area is 64. So the square root is 3, because this is 8 minus two times $2\frac{1}{2}$.

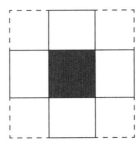

Figure 13. Visualization of the proof

The proof of the method is purely geometric, in the style of Euclid. But nevertheless, it has a different flavour! Euclid drew a general position of squares, and a relationship between areas follows from the mutual position; in the Arabic-Persian style, the figure is in a certain sense already based on the square to be found. After all, the problem is determined by the given values of 10 and 39. That's why the drawing in Figure 13 is on scale!

Arabic mathematics continued the tradition of allowing other means of construction besides straight lines and circles when building a solution; Omar Khayam was especially famous for his solution of a cubic equation using a circle and hyperbola. Omar was actually even more geometric than Al'kwarizmi. He made sure that the various quantities in the equation are all linear, plane or solid, for example by constructing a rectangle with a given length and a unit length.

Viète made a very explicit distinction between numbers and quantities. In his *In artem analytice isagogen* (1591), he built a system of quantities in which only the same species can be taken together/added. In concrete form, we saw this previously in the way in which Viète wrote his equations: homogeneously.

However, quantities can always be multiplied. This process results in new types of quantities such as area and volume. But Viète used quantities to build a general, abstract system, in which a cube can also be multiplied by a cube, to form a new quantity, which cannot be interpreted so concretely!

The true unification of the diversity of geometry and algebra came about in the 17th century. During this process, algebra matured, developing from a child who plays with somewhat non-worldly problems involving equations into a craftsman who is extremely skilled in helping to solve mathematical and even non-mathematical problems.

ANALYSIS AND SYTHESIS, THE LESSONS OF DESCARTES

In 1637, René Descartes (1596–1650) published his *Discours de la méthode pour bien conduire sa raison et chercher la vérité dans les sciences*. The Discours itself was followed by three essays, *La Dioptrique, Les Météores* and *La Géométrie*, which demonstrated the method in various areas. *La Géométrie* is therefore part of his general method for scientific problems. His point of departure is that only the mathematical method can lead to true certainty in science. This resulted in a method which, in simplified form, amounts to the following:
a. every question about quantities can be reduced to a geometric problem;
b. every geometric problem can be reduced to an algebraic problem;
c. every algebraic problem can be reduced to solving one or more equations with one or more unknowns.

Regardless of the value of the philosophical-methodological point a, points b and c provide a methodology that can be evaluated and discussed from a mathematical standpoint. Descartes comes straight to the point in the first sentence of Book I of *La*

AAD GODDIJN

Géométrie (Figure 14): "Any problem in geometry can easily be reduced to such terms that a knowledge of the lengths of certain straight lines is sufficient for its construction". The final word states the mathematical method that is used for this process: 'construire'. The importance of this word cannot be underestimated: it means determining the solutions of problems by explicitly constructing the solutions; in this framework, a proof by argumentation is not a complete solution for a problem. Explicit constructions are required, and Descartes also provides geometric constructions for solving equations.

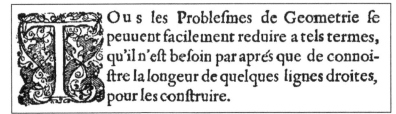

Figure 14. The opening phrase of La Géométrie

For transforming a geometric problem into algebra, Descartes then provides a concrete operational plan. The first step of the plan is important and requires additional explanation, because the step is the core of the method:

1. pretend that the problem has already been solved;
2. give names (letters) to all line segments, both known and unknown;
3. try to express a single quantity in two different ways in the above-named line segments; these expressions are equal, which results in an equation;
4. solve for the unknown of the equation.

The analytical method
Pretend that the problem has already been solved: with this statement, Descartes refers to Pappus (4th century A.D.). According to Pappus, to find the solution to a problem (i.e. the construction of the proof that is sought), you can begin from the situation where the construction has already been completed. You then study the figure in order to find the essential characteristics and the relations with simpler propositions. This is the phase of *analysis*, during which the situation is essentially untangled. This phase is followed by *synthesis*, during which the construction, or the proof, is built up from the analysis.

In Greek geometry, the synthesis phase is the actual solution, because the proof – or the construction that is to be found – is 'the solution' to the problem. In this approach, the analysis phase is actually a preliminary research phase, a technique to find a proof.

The analytical method in geometry owes its name to this distinction of Pappus. The new aspect of Descartes' method is that during the analysis phase, he uses algebra in a special fashion, in the global manner described above. Later – and certainly today as taught in school – the algebraic process is viewed as the only solution phase, culminating in finding values for unknowns or for equations that establish the solution set. The calculation of 'the solution' in the initial situation and the possible geometric tests are then used to check the solution, and do not form the solution themselves. For people who feel certain about their algebraic technique, these checks are not even essential. This is an important shift in the core of the mathematical activity: from construction to analysis. However, in many places in *La Géométrie*, it is very clear that the synthesis phase has not yet been forgotten, on the contrary.

Multiplication, unit, abandoning homogeneity

At the beginning of Book I, Descartes shows the basic operations of algebra, applied to line segments. Taking together or removing compare to addition and subtraction, the traditional relationship. The first real construction in the book, shown in Figure 15, concerns multiplying line segments, and it is striking.

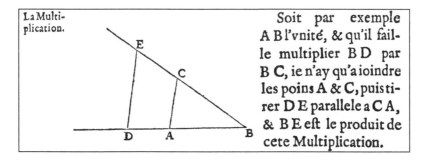

Figure 15. First construction in La Géométrie

Previously, Descartes indicated that he assumed a unit segment, which can be chosen randomly. In the figure, that is line segment *AB*. *DB* and *CB* are given line segments. *ED* is made parallel to *AC*, and then *AB* is to *DB* as *BC* is to *EB*. *EB* is the fourth proportional of *AB*, *DB* and *BC*. The text next to the illustration reads: "*EB* is the product of *DB* and *CB*". In this example, the product of two line segments is another line segment, and not an area, as with Euclid, Viète and in the Wisweb-applet!

Thus, a^2 is defined as the fourth proportional of 1, *a* and *a*, in other words by $1:a = a:a^2$. To make it very clear, Descartes frankly states that he is using the terms square and cube with their customary meanings, but that a^2 and b^3 really are line segments. As a result, expressions such as $ab - c$ become meaningful; the requirement that algebraic forms and expressions must be homogeneous has been abandoned. However, Descartes does explain that by adding or removing units in the terms of $aabb - b$, a quantity of dimension three can be created, from which the cube root can be taken. Descartes determines the cube root of a quantity, a line segment *a*, by means of continued proportion, therefore through the x in $1 : x = x : y = y : a$, and not by finding a side x of a given cubic quantity a.

True to the title of *La Géométrie*, Descartes' algebra is an algebra of line segments, created to solve geometric problems and to deal with algebraic problems geometrically.

Making algebra from geometry, algebraic modelling

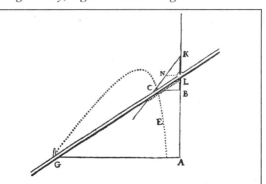

A prés cela prenant vn point a diſcretion dans la courbe, comme C, ſur lequel ie ſuppoſe que l'inſtrument qui ſert a la deſcrire eſt appliqué, ie tire de ce point C·la ligne C B parallele a G A, & pourceque C B & B A ſont deux quantités indeterminées & inconnuës , ie les nomme l'vne y & l'autre x. mais affin de trouuer le rapport de l'vne à l'autre; ie conſidere auſſy les quantités connuës qui determinent la deſcription de cete ligne courbe, comme G A que ie nomme a, K L que ie nomme b, & N L parallele à G A que ie nomme c. puis ie dis, comme N L eſt à L K, ou c à b, ainſi C B, ou y, eſt à B K, qui eſt par conſequent $\frac{b}{c} y$: & B L eſt $\frac{b}{c} y - b$, & A·L'eſt $x +$ $\frac{b}{c} y - b$. de plus comme C B eſt à L B, ou y à $\frac{b}{c} y - b$, ainſi a, ou G A, eſt á L A, ou $x + \frac{b}{c} y - b$. de façon que mulpliant la premiere par la derniere. & ainſi l'equation qu'il falloit trouuer eſt .

$$yy \infty cy - \frac{cx}{b} y + ay - ac.$$

de laquelle on connoiſt que la ligne E C eſt dn premier genre , comme én effect elle n'eſt autre qu'vne Hyperbole.

Figure 16. x and y as distances to two given lines

Give names to all line segments in the figure, both known and unknown.
In combination with 'Pretend that it is solved', this is a powerful description of what we would currently call the modelling phase of a problem. In his solution strategy, Descartes also provides a wonderful tip: choose the letters *a*, *b*, *c*, *d* for the known line segments and *x*, *y*, *z* for the unknown line segments. It goes without saying that this tip has been generally followed ever since.

La Géométrie is about geometry, the algebra used in the book is an aid. Descartes primarily aimed to classify which means of construction were required for specific problems. A special and widely applicable tool that he developed in this process is his method of determining points by using the distance to two given lines. Because the point to be found is unknown, these distances are indicated with *x* and *y*, in accordance with the tip given above.

The problem shown in Figure 16 is the first one in the book where this happens. The problem concerns the dotted curve, which was made with a simple mechanism. Mechanically generated curves were an important theme in the geometry of the 17th century; for example, consider the cycloid, the curve defined by the path of a point on the edge of a circular wheel as the wheel rolls along a straight line.

GA is a fixed line segment. Point *L* moves on the vertical line through *A*. The fixed triangle *KLN* slides as *L* moves over the vertical line. Point *C*, the intersection of line *GL* with the line passing though *K* and *N*, describes the dashed curve. Here, line segment *CB* is named *y* and *BA* is named *x*. In addition: *GA* = *a*, *KL* = *b*, *NL* = *c*, the known (fixed) quantities in the problem.

In the figure, direct proportionalities can be found due to two pairs of similar triangles: *KNL~KCB* and *GAL~CBL*. The line segment *BL* can therefore be calculated in two ways; Descartes thus arrives at an equation which shows the relationship between *x* and *y*. It is a problem with an indeterminate solution: there are many possible points – or pairs of line segments *x* and *y*, if one prefers. In this case, the solution is a locus, a set of points, satisfying the conditions of the problem. This is a second-degree equation; Descartes refers to a *curve du premier genre*. He concludes that the curve is a hyperbola.[ix]

Equations of the third and higher degree

Solve for the unknown in the equation. Descartes provides explicit instructions for solving equations from the third through sixth degree. In the constructions for third and fourth-degree equations, a circle is cut by a parabola; the position and measurements of these figures are expressed in the coefficients of the equation. For the fifth and sixth-degree equation, Descartes intersects an extra curve, which is generated by a mechanism of a rotating line and a sliding parabola. In the above example in Figure 16, *GL* is a rotating line and *KN* is a sliding line; in the new construction the sliding line is replaced by a sliding parabola. An important theme in *La Géométrie* is indicating which curves – which are produced in similar ways – are geometrically acceptable in constructions. For the third and fourth-degree equations these are the conic sections, for the fifth and sixth-degree equations it is the above-named Cartesian parabola. The degree (in an algebraic sense) of the Cartesian parabola is higher than that of the normal parabola; Descartes' suggestion at the end of the book that all constructions (of roots of equations) can be solved with his general method is perhaps too abrupt, because he does not work it out any further. However, it does appear that Descartes saw his approach as essential for his plan to be able to solve all geometric problems.

Throughout *La Géométrie*, the reader encounters many other practical algebraic tips. For example, in many situations we know a point to be found or a curve to be investigated, and we search for the second intersection with the curve of a line passing through that first point. In algebraic terms, this amounts to finding a second solution for an equation when a first solution is known. In this case, it is clumsy to solve generally; it is easier to divide out the factor corresponding to the known solution. Descartes demonstrates this process extensively, including the long division for dividing a polynomial by a linear factor.

Final remark

It is widely assumed that René Descartes was the first to use analytical geometry (in the sense of using coordinates in geometry), and that this was his greatest contribution to mathematics. However, this assumption is incorrect. Fermat and Mersenne used related methods, and English mathematicians also claimed priority. But even worse, this assumption does not take into consideration Descartes' main goals. His primary accomplishment in *La Géométrie* was to expand the construction repertoire of geometry from the circle and line to the higher-degree curves, which he systematically generated. Descartes also indicated which curves he believed were acceptable for this purpose. The title of the book in which Bos (2001) provides detailed support of this vision of *La Géométrie* is significant: Redefining geometrical exactness: Descartes' transformation of the early modern concept of construction.

HAS EVERYTHING BECOME COMPUTABLE WITH ALGEBRA?

Descartes' statement about being able to solve all problems via the geometric-algebraic route sounds overconfident. Nevertheless, it is a good idea to explore the relationship between geometry and algebra in what is historically perhaps the most important area of application for mathematics: astronomy. This tells us something about the limited computability of 'the world'. The five greatest books in Western European astronomy from before 1700 are without a doubt:
– *Almagest* (Ptolemy, 85–165 AD);
– *Revolutionibus orbium coelestium* (Copernicus, 1543);
– *Harmonices mundi* (Kepler, 1619);
– *Dialogo dei massimi sistemi* (Galileo Galilei, 1624);
– *Philosophiae Naturalis Principia Mathematica* (Newton, 1687).

Ptolemy described the cosmos, with the earth as the central point of a complex system of moving spheres and circles. In other words, he used geometry. The presentation of the material also followed the lessons of geometry. In his approach, Copernicus linked up closely with Ptolemy; he used the same geometric methods, but he opened the point of view that the earth does not have to be the fixed central point of the universe. Galileo supported him especially in this point of view, and also kept to the geometric style. In *Astronomia Novae* Kepler also provided a geometric model that determines the mutual distances between the planetary orbits: the nested spheres with the five regular polygons in between. Later he introduced the elliptical orbit of the planets around the sun.

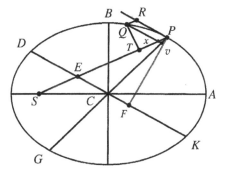

Figure 17. Newton's proof for the elliptical orbits of the planets

Of Newton it is sometimes said that he used analysis (calculus) to prove that the elliptical orbits of the planets are a result of the universal law of gravitation, which states that this force is inversely proportional to the distance between the attracting masses. Figure 17 is Newton's sketch for accompanying central proposition 10, which addresses the elliptical orbit.

Here, Newton shows that if planet P is held by a centripetal force to S in an elliptical orbit[x], that force must be inversely proportional to the square of SP. In other words, he used geometry. The small components of the figure, near planet P, essentially represent the motion directions, and these can certainly be analysed in the modern sense of the word. Regarding the concepts of motion and limit (Newton used other terminology), this is correct. But it is not algebra like we saw in Descartes' geometry. The proof takes place entirely in Euclidian style by means of composed ratios while using the properties of the ellipse. But here as well, a limit has been reached. In *Principia*, the elliptical shape of the planetary orbit is proved geometrically. However, predicting the moment when a planet will be at a specific position of its orbit is another story. During the calculation process, given the average anomaly M and eccentricity e, the true anomaly E (in radials) is found from

$$M = E - e\sin E$$

AAD GODDIJN

Solving for E in this transcendent equation is impossible with the tools of classic geometry (and algebra). Moreover, the ellipse represents the two-body problem. In this problem, one planet moves around one sun, without being disturbed by other planets. It is precisely these visible disturbances of orbits that led later on to the discovery of previously unobserved planets such as Uranus and Neptune. The calculation of these disturbances, and the reverse process of determining the positions of unknown planets based on these disturbances, are great achievements. These calculations are truly algebraic/analytical.

TOWARDS THE BROAD SPECTRUM OF MODERN ALGEBRAS

The algebraic solution of polynomial equations, which in this chapter we left with the work of Ferrari, remained an important focus of mathematical interest. The attempts to find an explicit solution for fifth-degree and higher equations using algebraic means also led to a great deal of research.

As early as 1798, Carl Friedrich Gauss (1777–1855) showed that the regular 17-sided polygon could be constructed with compass and straightedge. Algebraically, this meant that the complex solution of the equation $x^{17} = 1$ could actually be calculated by solving a series of second-degree equations, where the coefficients of the following equation are rational expressions in the roots of the previous ones.

Gauss also found which regular p-gons (p prime) could be constructed in this way: p must be a Fermat prime number, therefore a prime number of the form $2^{2n} + 1$. The only known prime numbers of this form are 3, 5, 17, 257 and 65,537. In 1799, Gauss also showed that every polynomial equation with real or complex coefficients has a solution in the complex plane; this is the so-called fundamental theorem of algebra. However, theorizing about the existence of solutions does not say much about finding the solutions, let alone about expressing them in the coefficients. Of course, the search for explicit algebraic expressions in the coefficients of the equation for the roots was continued. But without success! 'Algebraic' means with expressions built up from the coefficients, with the usual basic operations and extracting roots, where the index of the root is a natural number, therefore with so-called radicals.

Paolo Ruffini (in 1799) and Niels Abel (in 1824) showed that such expressions cannot exist for the general 'quintic' (the fifth-degree equation). Ruffini's proof made use of modern tools such as the permutation properties of the roots of an equation. His proof is complete, except for a small defect. Abel was given the honour of providing the complete proof. The relationship between the solutions of the equations and the number structures in which they exist (the so-called fields) was investigated later by Galois, who was able to define which equations could be solved with radicals. Galois' work also relied strongly on the permutation properties of the roots of equations, especially on subsets of permutations that do not move some of the roots. His most important results are known under his name: Galois Theory.

During the 1920s and 1930s, Emmy Noether and Bartel van der Waerden brought 19th-century algebra to a higher level of abstraction. Structures such as groups, rings, modules, fields and vector spaces now define the image of algebra; equations and their solutions became an illustration in the margin of a theory that they originated initially.

Following this step to higher levels of abstraction, progress continued with transcendental extensions, an 'algebrafication' of what a derivative of a function is, ideal theory, curves and manifolds, which on the one hand appear to be special ideals in a polynomial domain, and on the other hand solution sets of a set of equations. Topology also acquired its algebraic characterization methods. In knot and graph theory, the classification of the elementary particles in quantum mechanics and so forth, everything appears to be characterized by groups. The general cataloguing of finite and infinite group structures was therefore an important theme of research during the past 200 years!

BACK TO ALGEBRA IN SCHOOL

The perhaps somewhat overly modernized students of today find the solution of an equation such as $x^2 - 4x = 77$ in a totally different fashion than Ahmes, Diophantus and Galois did. They enter the left and right parts of the equation into their graphing calculator, have the graphs for both parts drawn on a broadly chosen domain, and use the Intersect option (see Chapter 8). After several moments of approximation, some correct decimals are shown. This method differs from traditional algebra in various ways:

- *Variable and unknown*

   Traditional algebra sees 'x' as indicating a solution for which the existence is assumed, and after transforming the equation to a different form, for example by reducing to zero and factorization, the unknown is essentially revealed. It turns out to be simply 11 (or -7). The graphing calculator approach shows that both $x^2 - 4x$ and 77 are descriptions of lines in the plane. The solutions ($x = 11$ and $x = -7$) are now associated with the intersection points of these geometric curves. In these descriptions, x must be seen as a changing quantity, which can take on all possible values in a domain in order to provide the graph. In traditional algebra, there is no such interpretation of the letter x in the equation.

- *Analysis versus algebra*

   The graph concept is closely linked with the concept of change, which has a rather limited place in algebra, but is of great conceptual importance for analysis. The intersect button of the graphing calculator is also part of analysis; with the numerical graphing calculators this is based on a step-by-step approximation process, and not on an algebraic strategy constructing the roots with some general solution formula (although some students expect this).

- *Function versus equation*

   When solving equations, with Descartes we also encountered geometric figures – still in a coordinate-like system – but these were of an entirely different nature: the solutions for an equation were constructed geometrically and the drawn figures (lines, circles, parabolas) had nothing to do with the equation to be solved in the sense of a figure that represents the equation. An essential aspect of analytical geometry with a Cartesian coordinate system is the equivalence of the x and y directions. This concerns the plane, and the coordinates describe the points. With a graph, also in the graphing calculator example just mentioned, one variable – here the x – has the independent role, and the other variable is dependent, in this case via a formula.

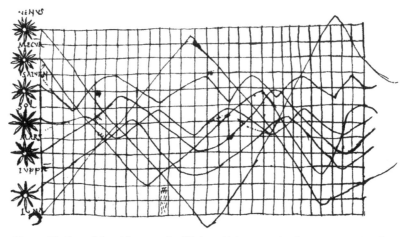

Figure 18. One of the oldest graphs (10th or 11th century): planetary positions?

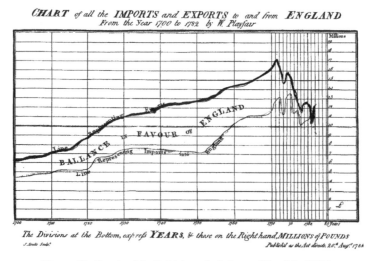

Figure 19. Graph of the British trade balance (Playfair, 1782)

The graph, as a representation of change processes in time, also has its historic roots, but these do not lie in the history of algebra. In Figure 18, we see one of the oldest known graphs, a 10th or 11th century figure which possibly[xi] represents the positions of planets (in any case: these are the symbols on the left) in the course of time. Time charts, now with typical economic variables such as import and export, are subsequent examples in history; the example in Figure 19 is from Playfair, 1782. High school mathematics pays a great deal of attention to these types of graphs. However, little historical support is available to link these graphs with algebra.

The true graphs, as shown in these two historic examples, are highly suited for visual representation of data, and especially for comparing different time series in a single figure. Historically, graphic representations of formulas originated from analytical geometry; the approach used for problems involving tangent lines and areas also has its historical roots in analytical geometry. However, since the 1960s the school curricula have linked the analytical geometry approach and the graphical approach directly to each other, the latter as visual representation of change in analytical geometry, possibly with occasional confusion between the two.

School algebra took its own track in history even in more ways. In arithmetic books from the 16th century, we often find a chapter that includes algebra, sometimes referred to as 'the Rule of Cos'. An interesting author is Robert Recorde, who wrote a book about arithmetic with the title *The Whettstone of Witte* (1557). In this book, Recorde makes a distinction between 'abstract nombers' and 'nombers denominate'. Abstract nombers are the pure numbers themselves, and nombers denominate are, among other things, expressions such as 10 shillings or 13 miles. Surprisingly, the denominate nombers also include the Cossike nombers 3 times cos, 4 times the square, with a Diophantus-like notation. Today (2010), if teachers were to explain expressions such as $3a + 5b$ with images of 3 apples and 5 bananas, they would no longer be taken very seriously by mathematics educators, but they would have an important English schoolbook writer from the 16th century behind them!

Recorde discusses exercises and operations with these nombers for many pages, and only then arrives at the actual Algebers Rules for solving equations. Such an equation always arises in a specific situation. The first example is of a type that is still loved (and perhaps maligned):

Alexander, when asked his age, said that he was two years older than Ciphesto. Yes, said Ciphesto, and our father is 4 more than our ages together.

Taken together, the years of ourselves and our father are 96. How old are we?

The student is then given an important tip (the book is written in dialogue form): indicate the unknown.

.... I will begin with the youngeste mannes age, and that will I call $\textbf{1} \, \textit{ze}$ which is the common supposition in all such questions.

The sign $\mathbf{1}\,\overset{\star}{\rho}$ stands for one times the number to be found. There is also a sign ρ. for abstract numbers, once again the same as with Diophantus and others. The amount taken together is quickly set equal to 96: $4.\,\nu\rho\,.-\!+\!-8.\rho\!=\!=\!=\!96.\,\rho\,.$. Eight units are removed from the left and right; and then it turns out that Alexander is 22.

In contrast with the *Whettstone*, Descartes' *La Géométrie* does not emphasize the student who drills and learns; the accent is primarily on building up new theory. These are therefore two distinct types of literature, one for students and one for scientists; this distinction appears to typify the early and modern history of algebra. For example, until 1900, geometry education appeared to be largely dominated by Euclid's *Elements*, in which the axiomatic system was clearly visible[xii]. Schoolbooks followed, although with more and more deviations from the original system and insertions from translators and adaptors to the work as it was handed down. However, teaching algebra appeared to go its own way and quickly tended to disseminate techniques and rules, supported at most by imitation applications in questions about fathers that are three times older than their four daughters together will be in five years from now. This resembles some aspects of modern mathematics education, such as competitive taxi rates from which the client can choose, even though the client is more concerned about whether there will be even a single a taxi waiting at the station. None of these were realistic applications.

Looking back on history, we see that the systematic formation of theory in algebra took place later than that in geometry, and that the theory immediately reached such a high level at the beginning of the 19th century that it was almost completely outside the reach of general preparatory education, which we now know as secondary education. Beautiful elements from the theory of equations were the recognition of the sum, product and other symmetrical functions of the solutions of an equation in the coefficients. We saw this with Viète, it was one of the pillars of Galois theory. Before the Dutch secondary education mathematics curriculum reform in 1968, such an element was still a backwater of the formula for second-degree equations.

With traditional Euclidian geometry, the relationship between school and theory was different still in the 19th century. Amateurs such as Napoleon (emperor), Brocard (lieutenant), Lemoine (musician) and Emmerich (teacher) contributed substantial new discoveries. And – clearly with the latter – also kept in the link between research and education alive.

The emphasis on precise algebraic calculation at the cost of reasoning in education possibly has its fundamental origin in the 17th and 18th centuries, especially due to the belief that all problems could be solved by means of industrious calculation.

In the novel *War and Peace* by Leo Tolstoy, the somewhat old-fashioned and strict Prince Nicholas Bolkonski gives lessons in geometry and algebra to his daughter Mary. In pedagogical terms, he characterizes the two disciplines as follows:

> He used to say that there are only two sources of human vice: idleness and superstition. He acknowledged only two virtues: activity and intelligence. He

himself undertook his daughter's education, and to develop these two cardinal virtues in her gave her lessons in algebra and geometry. He arranged her life so that her whole time was occupied by lessons and other useful activities.

Activity as opposed to intelligence, algebra as opposed to geometry; the 'meaningless' algebra as taught in school has its roots in times that go further back than the educational reform following World War II, they go back at least to Napoleon's Russian campaign in 1813.

In the 21st century, school algebra still seems to be growing completely away from its own mathematical challenge (or perhaps it has grown away yet again). Is there a way to go back to meaningful algebra? Of course there is a way back, and innumerable moments from the history of algebra offer many starting points for restoring meaning to algebra.

NOTES

i   This sexadecimal number notation, in which the 'digits', ranging from 1 to 59, are notated in a decimal sub-system, existed in Mesopotamia since about 3000 BC. Extensive tables were available for division, multiplication, inverse and square roots. The system is not as much a position system as we are used to; the arithmetical context informs the interpretation. Sexadecimal fraction calculation is also possible, similar to our decimal fractions. This sexadecimal fraction calculus in particular survived until the Italian Renaissance.
From the sexadecimal system we inherited our sexadecimal angle measuring system in degrees, minutes and seconds, as well as our time measurement. These two are closely related. Time and angle meet in the cosmic clock within astronomy.

ii   Diophantus' notation will be addressed in more detail below.

iii   In the original text Diophantus uses the same sign for the new unknown.

iv   According to Paul Tannery, who edited a text edition of Diophantus' *Arithmetica* in 1895, this Dionisius was bishop of Alexandria from 248-265. Diophantus may have been Christian and a disciple of Dionisius. This quote is also included at the start of this book.

v   Egli è scritto in lingua matematica, e i caratteri son triangoli, cerchi, ed altre figure geometriche, senza i quali mezi è impossibile a intenderne umanamente parola; senza questi è un aggirarsi vanamente per un oscuro laberinto.[Galileo Galilei, Il Saggiatore, in Opere di Galileo Galilei (a cura di Franz Brunetti), UTET, Torino, 1980, vol. I, pp. 631-632]

vi   Ougthred's equation has as solution the two final digits of the year of publication.

vii   Wallis does not provide Induction in the moderns sense. He is satisfied with showing a pattern of fractions with differences increasingly smaller than 1/3 for the cases with top term 1, 2, 3, 4, 5 and 6.

viii   See http://www.wisweb.nl for many more applets on algebra.

ix   Frans van Schooten (1615 – 1660) translated *La Géométrie* in Latin, to improve the book's dissemination. He added in his book a (synthetical) proof that it concerns the hyperbola.

x   He finishes the proof later, in proposition 17, by showing that a given starting point and initial velocity determine one unique orbit of planet P.

xi   The exact meaning of the graph is unknown. It seems to suggest a back-and-forth movement of planets, but these cannot be linked to the real movements of the planets. As there are no related graphical representations available from this period, every interpretation – even the one that this is a graph indeed – remain speculative.

xii There are some exceptions, such as *Éléments de géometrie* by Alexis Clairaut (1741) and *Grondbeginsels der Meetkunst* (Principles of Geometry) by Pibo Steenstra (1763). More applied geometry books are available in the 17th century, mainly for architects, land surveyors, and fortress builders.

REFERENCES

The most important sources used for this chapter are shown below.

Adams, J. (2005). Cardano and the Case of the Cubic, The fictional account of a mathematical detective. *Math Horizons, 12*.

Ahmes (copyist)(1550 BC). Papyrus Rhind.

Baumgart, J.K. (1969). The history of algebra. In *Historical topics for the classroom, the thirty-first year-book* (pp. 232-332). Washington DC: National Council of Teachers of Mathematics.

Bos, H.J.M. (2001). *Redefining geometrical exactness: Descartes' transformation of the early modern concept of construction*. Berlin/New York: Springer.

Boyer, C.B. (1991). *A history of mathematics*. John Wiley & Sons, Inc.

Buffum Chace, A. (1979). *The Rhind mathematical papyrus. Free translation and commentary with selected photographs, transcriptions, transliterations, and literal translations*. Washington DC: National Council of Teachers of Mathematics.

Cajori, F. (1929). *A History of mathematical notations*. Chicago: Open Court.

Descartes, R. (1637). La Géometrie. In The geometry of René Descartes / transl. from the French and Latin by David Eugene Smith and Marcia L. Latham with a facsimile of the first edition. La Salle, 1952.

Fauvel, J., & Gray, J. (1987). *The history of mathematics, a reader*. Basingstoke, UK: The Open University.

Heath, T.L. (1910). *Diophantus of Alexandria*. Cambridge: Cambridge University Press.

Maanen, J. van (1998). Descartes en zijn Nederlandse profeten. [Descartes and his Dutch prophets.] *Pythagoras, 37*(3), 12-20.

Nesselman, Q.H.F. (1842). *Die Algebra der Griechen*. Berlin.

Neugebauer, O. (1935-1937). *Mathematische Keilschrifttexte*. New York/Berlin: Springer.

Pesic, P. (2003). *Abel's proof, An essay on the sources and meaning of mathematical unsolvability*. Boston: MIT.

Struik, D.J. (1959). *A concise history of mathemathics*. London: Bell.

Waerden, B.L. van der (1983). *Geometry and algebra in ancient civilisations*. Berlin/New York: Springer.

Waerden, B.L. van der (1980). *A history of algebra. From al-Khwârizmî to Emmy Noether*. Berlin/New York: Springer.

Websites:

The MacTutor History of Mathematics archive: http://www-groups.dcs.st-and.ac.uk/~history/
http://www-groups.dcs.st-and.ac.uk/~history/HistTopics/Quadratic_etc_equations.html

TRUUS DEKKER, MAARTEN DOLK

3. FROM ARITHMETIC TO ALGEBRA

"You can't know that (...), do you? You don't know how many there are."
(Student during classroom observation, this chapter)

INTRODUCTION

Algebra, isn't that just advanced arithmetic? It's not quite as simple as that. In practice, the relationship between arithmetic and algebra is not an easy one, and the transition between various types of education creates an additional complication. Students in secondary education continue to work with arithmetic, but differently than in primary school. Education for young children pays little attention to algebraic thinking, even though there are certainly opportunities to do so. Important aspects of algebraic thinking include implicit reasoning and generalization. If young students are encouraged to develop algebraic thinking, and this thinking is maintained and expanded in the subsequent years, a longitudinal learning trajectory for algebra is created. This can not only narrow the gap between arithmetic and algebra, but also between the various types of education. This chapter shows how such a longitudinal learning trajectory could be given shape.

Teachers in primary education have long thought differently about arithmetic lessons than teachers in secondary education. Many high school mathematics teachers appear to think that their students have not learned arithmetic properly before they came into their class, while teachers in primary education tend to say that arithmetic skills are not properly maintained in secondary schools, and that students start using the calculator too early. It is unclear whether there is a transition problem here that can be solved by making better agreements about the content of education, or whether the education in one or both types of schools is below par. This discussion has been going on for many years, as shown by the following examples from the Netherlands.

In the first volume of the journal *Euclides*[i], Beth (1925) wrote that the level of both primary and secondary education, generally speaking, had declined. In that era, the discussion focused partly on the question of what aspects of arithmetic should be addressed in secondary education. Beth lamented that reducing composite fractions and taking square roots and cube roots contributed little to the formation of concepts. A short time later, Wijdenes (1927) described his mathematics lessons during the first year of the HBS (grade 7 in the former Dutch high school). He clearly focused on doing arithmetic with letters, which he distinguished from algebra. According to Wijdenes, doing arithmetic with letters concerns the first manipulations with sym-

P. Drijvers (ed.), Secondary Algebra Education, 69–87.

bols, for example simplifying expressions such as $2a + 3c + 9a + 2b$ to become $11a + 2b + 3c$.

'Arithmetic with letters' also included reversing the order of addends ($a + b = b + a$) and reading formulas. Today, we would refer to these activities as algebra, not arithmetic. Much later, this delineation was again addressed when people began discussing algebra in primary education. At that time Wijdenes (1953) supported the idea that primary education should provide an introduction to algebra by doing arithmetic with letters. Negative numbers, and certainly rules such as 'minus times minus is plus', appeared to belong to the domain of algebra, and therefore to secondary education.

In 1989, a group of instructors from various teacher education programmes in the Netherlands again addressed the developments during the transition from primary to secondary education (Goffree & Buys, 1989). Based on the theme of negative numbers, this group explored the twilight area between primary and secondary education; this chapter also explores this area. We will focus primarily on the relationship between arithmetic and algebra, in particular on promoting algebraic thinking, which could start early in primary school. We will also pay attention to building upon arithmetical strategies and developing arithmetical skills in secondary education. The examples we have chosen are all from the algebra strand Patterns and Regularities. For that matter, they can be supplemented with many other examples from the other learning-teaching trajectories.

ALGEBRA AND ALGEBRAIC THINKING

In the first chapter of this book various facets of algebra (as taught in school) are described. For example, it is noted that the use of the verb form is important. In this respect, the authors of that chapter are walking in the footsteps of Freudenthal (1968), who proposed that we should not speak of mathematics, but of mathematization. By extension, we prefer the term 'algebraic thinking' to 'algebra'. Algebraic thinking consists of aspects such as generalized arithmetic (using literal symbols), the development of mathematical models and the development of the language of algebra. Usiskin (1997) distinguished five aspects of this algebraic language: unknowns, formulas, generalized patterns, place value and relationships. These aspects of algebra as a language are also important to algebraic thinking, but they are not didactic goals in themselves.

We believe that the following mathematical activities are important for developing algebraic thinking:
– implicit and explicit reasoning and generalization;
– developing mental models;
– constructing fundamental algebraic ideas;
– observing, formulating, researching and visualizing patterns and relationships;
– solving problems.

Very young children sometimes develop their own methods of what we could call algebraic thinking. For example, Susan (3 years old) is playing Mankala with her grandmother; this is a game with beautifully coloured pebbles that you can play even if you cannot yet count (Figure 1). The player with the most pebbles at the end of the game is the winner.

Figure 1. The game of Mankala

Grandma: I think you won, Susan. Your pile is bigger than mine.

Susan hesitates, she is obviously not convinced.

Susan: You can count, grandma, so you should count them.
Grandma: One, two, three, four,..... I have 20 and you have 24. So you have more. You win!

Susan is still not convinced. Of course, numbers don't yet have any meaning for her.

Susan: I can also do it this way. I'll keep taking one from your pile and then one from my pile.

The double row of pebbles becomes longer and longer; and yes, Susan's row is longer. So... but you don't know Susan. She pushes the two rows back into two piles:

Susan: My pile is bigger, so I win.

As far as Susan is concerned, it is now clear how you can tell if you won the game. She has devised a method herself, which agrees with what her grandma already said. But she did not take it on her grandma's authority who won. Susan can compare the size of two quantities, although she cannot count. She also uses this method later on when playing a game with her sister to determine who has more marbles. Reasoning, generalizing, and developing a mental model are all part of this process, although implicitly.

Actually, it would be preferable for all children to acquire comparable experiences at school, which the teacher would also notice at the right time. This is not possible, of course, but arithmetic education for young children offers plenty of opportunities for addressing algebraic thinking. However, the teacher must direct this process; it does not happen by itself.

The following is an example to clarify this situation. You can explain to the students that in our system for writing numbers, the 2 in the number 23 actually means 20, and that the 3 means three ones. The students will probably accept this explanation on the authority of the teacher. But there is another way to go about this, where the teacher thinks up meaningful activities, guides the students in the right direction, helps organize things and asks questions. The children discover new patterns and structures and try to persuade each other and themselves. During a class discussion and/or discussions with individual students, the teacher tries to focus on the development that the students are going through, and makes use of their struggle to acquire control over a new concept. When you have discovered the structure of the number system for yourself, you will not forget this as quickly as when you are simply told how the number system is structured. This will be helpful when you have to deal with the structure of various number systems in secondary education, and it helps you to independently continue developing fundamental algebraic ideas starting from an informal level. Appropriate questions are asked such as: Do you see a certain pattern? Is this always the case? Can you know that for sure?

In the video of the Taking Inventory activity (Dolk & Fosnot, 2004), we can see how something like this can happen in daily practice at school. This video shows how the children can independently develop strategies, and can reason and generalize as a group.

Students between 5 and 6 years old are taking an inventory of school supplies in the classroom. Because, says Jodi, the teacher, then we will know how much of everything we have, and if someone has borrowed something, then we will know for certain if we have gotten it back. Do you remember when were missing some scissors? This is a meaningful assignment and sufficiently open to enable the children to work at various levels. Some children count everything one-by-one, which sometimes makes for a lot of counting, while others make packets of five – and then ten – to simplify the counting. One group of students is counting envelopes by making packets of ten held together with rubber bands, while in another group blocks are being counted by colour. There is a discussion about how you should write one hundred twenty, is that 10020 or 120?

At a certain point, after a discussion about flexible counting by making packets of items, Jodi draws a table on the blackboard with the following headings: type – number of packets of 10 – number of loose objects – total number of objects, and asks the students to write down their results. Jodi repeatedly asks the following questions, but alternates the sequence of the questions: "How many packets (of blocks, books, envelopes, etc.) have you counted? How many loose objects do you have? How many is that all together?", until Cosmo, who first thought that two packets of 10 and three loose objects together are 13, suddenly sees a pattern being formed, and calls out: "The board! It's right there on the board!"

Two packets of 10 and three loose objects are the same as the total of 23.

type	packets of 10	Loose	total
books	4	7	47
envelopes	8	2	82
blocks	2	3	23
	1	2	14?

Instead of being confused, the children are now thinking about a pattern that is being created. However, the 'why' question must still be answered. During the class discussion, Jodi asks: "Does it always works this way with groups of 10 and loose objects?" When a child remarks "I'm not sure", Jodi asks him what he needs to be convinced. Certainty, persuading each other, realizing this pattern always holds true, this is where algebraic thinking begins. This is not just knowledge about the decimal number system, but independently developed knowledge about the number system. Finally, when Jodi points out the findings of one group – 14 in total, one packet of 10 and 2 loose items – some of the children think at first that the general pattern has been broken. And then a girl says: "I think it might be a mistake, and maybe 14 should be 12." The children are relieved because the pattern still holds true.

Some children reach a certain level sooner than others. They use this knowledge to help others in their group, and to go further together.

Thinking about the structure of numbers can begin at a very young age, and can be considered as an example of algebraic thinking. The teacher provides direction to the process and asks questions that help the children organize their thoughts and reason mathematically. By integrating activities focusing on developing algebraic thinking into the standard curriculum of primary education, not only the transition from basic arithmetic to advanced arithmetic becomes easier, but it also eases the transition to algebra in secondary education.

A LONGITUDINAL LEARNING TRAJECTORY IN ARITHMETIC

There is a lot of arithmetic in primary school; most schools have arithmetic on the programme every day. We estimate that in the Netherlands between ten and twenty percent of school time is spent on arithmetic. During the arithmetic lessons, there is only a limited differentiation in subject matter and student levels; usually the children are first given class instruction, and then they work on the practice material, which is differentiated according to level and pace (Janssen et al., 1999; Kraemer et al., 2005).

If you scan a randomly chosen schoolbook for Dutch primary education, you see immediately that most of the material concerns working with numbers (approximately 80%) and measuring/geometry (about 20%). You will also notice that all kinds of activities are combined during the arithmetic lesson. The following example is from a randomly chosen page from an arithmetic book for students aged 10 (Figure 2).

TRUUS DEKKER, MAARTEN DOLK

- One sequence of big numbers, for example 52,100; with tasks to take away 10, add 10, take away 100, add 100;
- One sequence of 'easy' numbers above 1000, with tasks to take away a small number, for example 2300 – 7;
- How long does it take? Calculations with time, for example from 08:30 hours to 10:00 hours;
- Adding and subtracting two or three numbers above 100;
- Complete a number to make 10,000, for example 7,250;
- A cheese is cut into pieces; how much do the pieces in the picture cost? In the example where $\frac{2}{3}$ of the cheese is shown, the whole cheese costs € 60.

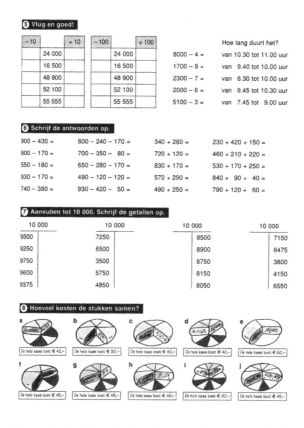

Figure 2. Page from a Dutch fourth grade arithmetic textbook

This arrangement of assignments is very suitable for practicing and maintaining arithmetic algorithms. Undoubtedly, there will be a certain structure underlying the various types of assignments throughout the book and through the years. To know this for sure, however, a more in-depth study of the various textbooks for Dutch primary education is required than would be suitable for this chapter. We should also emphasize that not all students in primary school achieve the same final level of arithmetic skills. For some students, their arithmetic skills will remain at the fourth-grade level, while others will not only reach the sixth-grade level (students aged 12), but they will also complete extra assignments. Teachers in secondary education must be aware of this. The differences between students can be large, even in the fairly homogeneous groups that are customary in Dutch secondary education.

In secondary education (starting around age 12-13), advanced arithmetic is on the programme, and the students indeed work on lots of arithmetic assignments. Skills with fractions and percentages are brushed up and maintained, although many students continue to have difficulty with these topics. The students are now required to have more insight than simply being able to find the answer quickly using arithmetic algorithms. This is especially true for students who are already skilled at using the algorithms. For teachers in primary and secondary education, it is not always clear that arithmetic at this stage has a somewhat different character, and this also applies to the students. When they begin secondary school, the students sometimes say: "I used to be good in arithmetic, but now I just don't get it."

Consider the previous example about the place value of numerals. In secondary education, students are not only expected to understand our common number system, but also other systems such as the binary numeral system. What does place value mean in these other systems? Working with fractions not only means that the students can use arithmetic rules properly, but they also have to know that there is an infinite number of fractions, they must be able to place fractions on a number line, use fractions in all kinds of situations, understand the relationship of fractions with decimal numbers and so forth.

The calculator is a standard part of secondary education, but there is also a great deal of emphasis on estimating, smart calculations and especially on interpreting an answer. Can this answer be correct in the given situation? How many decimals are reasonable in this context? Should you round off or round up? There is less emphasis on procedures, and more insight is required into the structure of numbers and using flexible calculation. Students decide for themselves if the calculator is useful in certain situations. For that matter, it seems that many students decide to use the calculator in all situations, even if they have to calculate 3×3!

In secondary education, much less time in total is spent on doing arithmetic than in primary school; in the first grades of secondary school, two or three lesson hours (of 50 minutes per week) are available for mathematics, of which arithmetic is only a small part. Especially in vocational education, advanced arithmetic takes a bigger role in providing 'numeracy', focusing on enabling the students to get by in society. Of course, there is disagreement about the right amount of arithmetic in the mathematics textbooks, but in any case a longitudinal trajectory is visible, from arithmetic to advanced arithmetic, and from primary education to secondary education. However, the demands that are placed on the arithmetic skills of the students change in secondary school, which perhaps explains the gap between primary and secondary education that is experienced by the students. In that respect, primary and secondary school teachers can certainly learn something from each other. The encouragement of algebraic thinking referred to above – encouraging students to think about number systems and not just follow procedures using numbers – can help in this process.

A LONGITUDINAL LEARNING TRAJECTORY FOR ALGEBRA?

In Dutch education, we have seen that there is a longitudinal learning trajectory from arithmetic in primary school to arithmetic in secondary school. But is there also a longitudinal trajectory from algebraic thinking and informal algebra in primary school to more formal algebra in secondary education? In the textbooks used in primary education that we have seen, this is limited to incidental topics without mutual coherence, in the same way that various components of arithmetic are offered. For example, an introduction to negative numbers is very suitable for primary education. In one of the Dutch primary school textbooks, these are introduced in the context of temperature and reading thermometers in degrees Celsius. This book also asks a question that precedes calculating with negative numbers:

– What is the difference between 4° and –1°?

(A better question would be: the temperature early in the morning was still –1°, but later in the day the temperature rose to 4°. How many degrees did it warm up during the day?)

There is only a single, isolated problem on negative numbers, arbitrarily placed between other assignments. In the following section, negative numbers are applied to a coordinate system. Of course, it is possible to link the isolated assignments in the book by using guided questioning during a classroom discussion, by discussing more examples in class and by providing more problems. This is up to the teacher. Some teachers will tend to skip such a mathematical component because they think it is unimportant. The teachers' own mathematical knowledge is often inadequate to enable them understand the usefulness of the topic. The fact that such assignments seem to appear arbitrarily in the book then invites these teachers to skip them. The processes of generalization (is it always true, and how do you know that?), abstraction (separating an idea from the context) and formalization (using symbols and formal mathematical language) are currently not visible in textbooks for primary education. However, when using the existing textbooks there are still good possibilities to address these processes. As a teacher, you must use these possibilities to make the longitudinal learning trajectory visible, also for the students. For example, how can you introduce negative numbers in a way that encourages algebraic thinking and improves the preparation for what is expected later in secondary education?

The introduction should preferably take place using various contexts. The contexts can also be found outside the arithmetic lesson, for example if there is an article in the newspaper about an imminent breach in a dike or when the geography lesson is on polders (low-lying tracts of land enclosed by dikes): how high is the dike above sea level, how many centimeters below sea level is the water in the sluice? When it freezes in the winter, reading the thermometer (in degrees Celsius) is bound to come up for discussion. Negative numbers can also come up when working with money and shortages of money. Another possibility, which is somewhat more formal, is to have the children play an arithmetic game where they count backwards from 100 with jumps of 7. Does anyone in the class go beyond 2 on their own initiative? What does it actually mean that you cannot calculate the difference $26 - 34 = ...$?

This is followed by the expansion of the number line with negative numbers, which the students have previously seen and used only with positive numbers. Students often independently come up with the idea of expanding the number line below zero. Are there also negative fractions and negative decimals? Do negative numbers also continue forever, like the numbers on the positive side of zero? In this way, insight into the expansion of the number system is created in a way that is feasible for most students in primary education.

Simple operations such as addition and multiplication with a whole (positive) number are also possible, especially if the students have the support of the number line. In the example 'Taking Inventory', we saw that young children can develop knowledge about the number system. After the negative numbers are introduced, it becomes clear that the number system has been expanded: we suddenly have many more numbers at our disposal. This observation leads to a whole series of questions. Can you make general rules for adding two positive numbers, two negative numbers or a positive and a negative number? How can you show that your general rule always applies (for example by using the number line)? In secondary education, this knowledge is reviewed and expanded with multiplication and division of a positive and a negative number, and with the very abstract multiplication and division of two negative numbers, for example by using the concept of slope. And mathematical operations are practiced; this takes place in a way that challenges the students, as shown by an example of Martin Kindt[ii] in Figure 3.

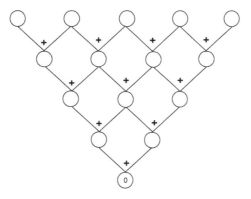

Figure 3. Filling in a number tree (Kindt, 2010)

TRUUS DEKKER, MAARTEN DOLK

No, there are no missing numbers in this example. Students are challenged to independently fill in numbers on this tree so that the final answer is zero. Some students even use decimals or fractions in their own productions. Or they make the problem more difficult for themselves, for example by not beginning at the bottom, but by filling in a large number somewhere about halfway. In this way, each student can work at his or her own level while practicing the mathematical operations.

At the present time in the Netherlands, there is no clear long-term learning trajectory in algebra from primary school to secondary education. Some cautious steps have been taken, but these have become stalled in isolated assignments without much coherence. This makes it difficult for teachers to encourage algebraic thinking in primary education and to develop algebra at an informal level, which can then be built upon in secondary education. This situation should be addressed in teacher training programmes, so the teachers can fully utilize the possibilities that are available. Moreover, it is questionable whether mathematics teachers in secondary education have sufficient knowledge about the preparations in their subject area that have been made in primary school.

ALGEBRAIC THINKING IN PRIMARY SCHOOL: A COMPREHENSIVE EXAMPLE

How can you prepare students in primary school for the algebra that will be taught in secondary education? A few examples are shown above. In this section, we will outline a comprehensive algebra programme from practice.

How do you ensure that students do not memorize rules, but learn to think mathematically/algebraically? In any case, the problems must give students the opportunity to build, expand and generalize their own mathematical concepts based on known mathematical operations. This cannot happen if there are only incidental mathematical problems among the regular arithmetic problems. Instead, a series of assignments with a clear structure must be provided. In addition, these assignments must be provided in such a way that the students can work at different levels, because the differences between the students often become quite large around the end of primary education.

The extensive example below is from the *Mathematics in Context* (MiC) textbook series, which was developed for middle school students (ages 10-14 years) in the USA by the Freudenthal Institute in cooperation with colleagues from the University of Wisconsin at Madison (e.g., see Roodhardt et al., 1997). This textbook series provides a longitudinal learning trajectory for algebra. Every year, the students work through a number of units, where each unit focuses on a specific mathematical domain: algebra, number, geometry and measurement, and statistics. But even when the main topic of the unit is algebra, the students still do a lot of arithmetic; after all, arithmetic skills must be exercised and maintained. But you will not find rows of more or less the same arithmetic problems, as in the Dutch schoolbooks. Similar to the Dutch curriculum, however, a great deal of attention is paid to the students' own solution strategies; many problems can be solved at various levels. The students first use informal algebraic models and strategies, followed by pre-formal and then formal ones. When a new concept is addressed, you often see students returning to previously used informal strategies. This helps them to understand the new concept and build their own mathematical expertise, instead of accepting a concept on the authority of the teacher without understanding it. The experiences with MiC have shown that students can start thinking algebraically at a young age. For this reason, we will go more deeply into the algebra strand of MiC. The algebra in MiC has three longitudinal learning trajectories: Patterns & Regularities, Restrictions and Change & Growth. The underlying idea is always that of progressive formalization.

Patterns and Regularities

When describing patterns and regularities, codes and symbols are used along with both formal and pre-formal algebraic language; expressions and formulas – closely related to the situation – play a role. A typical example is shown in Figure 4.

Figure 4. V-patterns

The above pattern can be endlessly continued. What does pattern number 5 look like? Number 10? Number 100? An arbitrarily chosen pattern from the row?
In informal algebra language, the pattern can be described as:
Twice the pattern number, and one more.
In pre-formal language, this can be something like
$$2 \times \text{pattern number} + 1$$
Expressed in formal language, this is:
$$2n + 1 \text{, where } n \text{ starts at } 1$$
When two expressions are added, this is first done informally by determining the expressions that correspond to number strips. Figure 5 shows an example of addition using number strips, at a pre-formal level. You can perform the operations for each step and for each number strip, and then look for the corresponding expressions. Some students, who can already work at a pre-formal level, immediately determine the expressions next to the number strips and then find the missing expression, where they use the numbers on the strips to check their answer. In any case, the numbers on the strips can be used by all students as a support[iii].

TRUUS DEKKER, MAARTEN DOLK

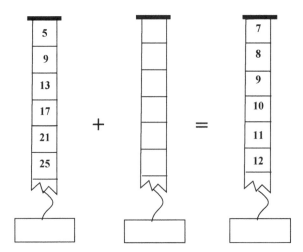

Figure 5. Addition using number strips

At a formal level, the following question is asked:
Fill in the empty place: $(5 + 4n) + \ldots = 7 + n$.

Students can always go back to the source and to the meaning of the problem. Some students will make a number strip to solve the latter problem, but it is not required.

Restrictions

Equations and inequalities are the formal algebraic tools that are used for describing and solving problems that are addressed in this learning trajectory. As with the other MiC materials, problems are usually placed in a context.

It is important to note that the three learning-teaching trajectories are not independent, but are interwoven. The number strips from the next example have a somewhat different form than those used before that (Figure 6). The question posed here is: does the same number ever appear in the two strips? This question leads to the observation that the difference between the numbers on the two strips must then be equal to zero, which in turn leads to the realization that this amounts to solving the equation: $34 + 5n = 9 + 6n$.

80

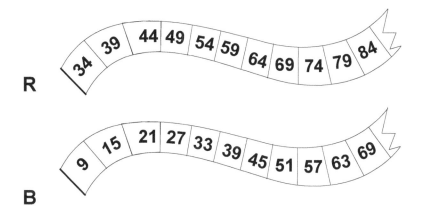

Figure 6. Other types of strips

It is more useful to calculate and examine the difference between the expressions if this difference is equal to zero:

$$34 + 5n$$
$$\underline{9 + 6n}\ -$$
$$25 - n$$

Now it becomes simple: $25 - n = 0$ if $n = 25$. So the answer is yes, the same number does appear on both strips, in the 25th box on the strip.

Change and Growth

The topics of the Change and Growth strands are closely related to calculus and concern situations in which continuous processes are described. Graphical representations play an important role; in this chapter, we will not provide any additional examples of this learning trajectory.

The V-pattern problem

The example on the following page is intended for students 10 years of age and is part of the Patterns and Regularities strand. This subject matter rarely appears in Dutch textbooks for primary education, but would actually be very suitable for them.

In the algebra unit Patterns and Symbols (Roodhardt et al., 1997), the children are given these assignments after the concept of even and odd numbers has been brushed up with a series of introductory questions. The students have already used symbols and codes as a shortcut to describe patterns. In this example, symbols are used to represent the actual objects: birds. The students are being prepared for a generalization of the pattern (Question 1c). The data are organized in a table, and the students make a formula in words (Question 4). The final question, Question 5, reviews a property of odd numbers:

$$\text{odd} + \text{odd} = \text{even}.$$

Of course, a class discussion accompanies this series of questions. When students work in groups, they can first consult with each other and try to persuade each other, before they do this in front of the entire class in a general discussion.

The material was tested at a Dutch primary school with students between 10 and 11 years of age. The students at the school where this material was tested had never done similar problems. The school is located near a lake, the IJsselmeer, so most of the children had seen a group of water birds flying in a V shape; we discussed this extensively. The context is therefore very familiar. In the real world, you seldom see such perfect V shapes. "But", said one of the students, "We can pretend!"

Sometimes you see birds flying in a V-formation:

Figure 7. Birds in a V-formation

1. It is easier to draw such a pattern with dots. Here are the three smallest V-patterns:

Figure 8. Dots in a V-pattern

  a. Draw the fourth V-pattern in the series next to the first three.
  b. Can a V-pattern have 84 dots? Why or why not?
  c. How many dots are there in V-pattern number 6?
     And how many in number 10?

---

2. Draw a V-pattern with 19 dots.
3. Sometimes it is useful to show your results in a table. The first part of such a table is shown below:

V-number	number of dots
1	3
2	5
3	7
4	
5	
6	

a. Fill in the rest of the table.
b. From the V-number, you can tell how many pairs of birds there are in each V-pattern. Do you see any other patterns in the table?

4. You can make the row with V-patterns as long as you want. How many dots are there in the pattern with V-number 100? How do you know that?

Two groups of wild geese are flying above the IJsselmeer, both in a beautiful V formation. Before they fly south, the two groups join together.

5. Can the new group form a perfect V? Why or why not?

In the trial class, a series of questions about odd and even numbers from the same unit were first discussed. One student wrote a number with 10 numerals on the board, ending with 1, and said: "I can't pronounce this number, because it is too big. But I know for sure that it is an odd number." Of course, then he had to explain to the class why he was so sure. The class was very impressed.

It was very striking that many children saw every question as being completely separate, even though the questions were related to each other. This was later confirmed by the teacher. When a series of questions appeared in the arithmetic book (question a, b, c, ...), the teacher said he had the same experience. Because the questions in the arithmetic book usually do not have any connection with each other, it was difficult for the students to realize that a new question could have something to do with the previous one.

Most students answered Question 1b correctly. There were answers such as:
– No, that's impossible because it is an even number.
– No, if you split it up, you have 42 on each side, and one of the birds still has to be in front.
– No, because there is still one extra at the back of the formation.
– No, because a V-pattern is an odd number.

Clearly, some of the students are still reasoning at an informal level. With Question 4, some of the students even used the image of the birds instead of the more abstract pattern of dots:
– 201, because one bird is the leader
– 2×100 and then the leader, so 201
– 201, it is doubled with one extra

And one student, who didn't understand the problem at all, wrote:
– On one side 51 and on the other side 49.

In this context problem, the pattern is generalized; how can you describe the pattern in general terms? This is an important step in the development of algebraic thinking. A (word) formula is not yet expected; instead the students make an informal description in words: "It is doubled with one extra", "Two times the V-number plus 1". Of course, a class discussion should also address the fact that you must be able to verify the formula: is this true for the V-numbers that I already knew? And how do I know that the result is always an odd number, as we found with 1b?

With Question 5, the children usually did not refer back to the properties of odd and even numbers that they previously discovered. The students sometimes approached the teacher to ask how they should solve this problem, because:

You can't know that because you don't know how they're going to be flying, do you? You don't know how many there are.

This reminds us of one of the observations in Chapter 1! One group found the right answer:

No, because then you no longer have a leader.

And there was also a student who wrote:

No, because together it makes an even number.

For the students in the school, this lesson was the only one of this type. But the MiC textbook series returns to the V-patterns later on, and extensively addresses similar but more abstract patterns, such as W-patterns (Figure 9). These patterns are also introduced in a realistic context, this time concerning aeroplanes flying in formation.

Figure 9. W-patterns

Then the formulas become more complicated as well. Some students are already writing formulas by using shortcuts, using letters instead of words, so they are working at a pre-formal level.

In primary school, students become acquainted very early with odd and even numbers. In the upper grades of primary school, with older students, you could continue with this topic by asking the students to make rules for calculations with odd and even numbers How can you know for certain that a number is odd or even? Do you always get an even number when you add two even numbers? How can you know that for sure? Can you convince everyone by just giving examples? What happens if there are two odd numbers or one odd and one even number? You can optionally expand this theme to include characteristics of divisibility.

This example has been chosen because it demonstrates a clear, continuous trajectory from informal to pre-formal solution strategies. This trajectory should be continued in secondary education, so that students are well prepared for creating formulas from regularities in a table or a series of figures. Unfortunately, this rarely happens. Is it therefore so surprising that students in the upper grades of secondary education often have serious difficulty with creating formulas? What percentage of Dutch students aged 15 do you think gave the wrong answer to the problem in Figure 10 (from the PISA study, see PISA, 2004) or skipped the problem entirely? For this problem, 25% of the Dutch students scored 0 points! Would students at the end of primary school be able to solve such a problem if they had worked with assignments such as the V-patterns? And would it be sensible to ask them such a question?

In the lower grades of secondary education, students are sometimes asked to construct an equation in order to solve a problem. However, this makes finding a solution often more difficult. Consider the following problem:

Three consecutive numbers added together are 54. What are the numbers?

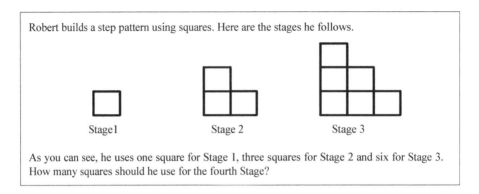

Robert builds a step pattern using squares. Here are the stages he follows.

Stage 1   Stage 2   Stage 3

As you can see, he uses one square for Stage 1, three squares for Stage 2 and six for Stage 3. How many squares should he use for the fourth Stage?

Figure 10. Stair patterns

In this case it is not very obvious that you should first construct the equation $n + (n + 1) + (n + 2) = 54$, like the book asks you to do. After all, if all three numbers were the same, the answer would be 54 : 3 = 18. So 18 is the middle number, and the three consecutive numbers are 17, 18 and 19. The one time that the students are asked to create expressions, they are not even useful or necessary!

In the lower grades of secondary education, a learning trajectory for Patterns and Regularities should perhaps be given more attention. What do the variables in a formula mean, what happens in the situation to which the formula applies if something is changed in the formula, or what happens to the formula if something changes in the situation? Students in the upper grades of secondary education would then have a good foundation for expanding their knowledge about creating and using formulas.

CONCLUSION

Are the teachers from primary school and secondary education correct when they complain about the poor linkage between primary and secondary education? We have shown that there is indeed a longitudinal learning line from arithmetic to advanced arithmetic, but there is a discontinuity regarding what is expected from the students. The skills that were learned in primary education must be practiced and maintained, but the students should also be expected to develop more insight. This process can begin in primary school. Teachers in the first years of secondary education sometimes make inadequate use of their students' mathematical knowledge.

In addition, it turns out that there is virtually no continuous line of algebraic thinking from arithmetic to algebra, even though there are good opportunities for this. Primary school teachers must take advantage of these opportunities, but to do this they must also have an adequate mathematical background, which they should have received through education or professional development.

In this chapter, we have provided only a few examples of possible activities in primary and secondary education to benefit the development of algebraic thinking. Such a longitudinal learning trajectory is possible and desirable; the textbook series developed by the Freudenthal Institute for the American market for students from 10 to 14 years old makes this clear.

The examples in this chapter are not worked out in sufficient detail to use them directly in education. But this was not the purpose of this chapter. We wanted to show that a longitudinal learning trajectory in algebraic thinking is valuable for nearly all students as they continue in secondary education, and that there are good examples of text books in which this actually happens.

NOTES

i   Journal of the Dutch Association of Mathematics Teachers.
ii This example as well as many others used here are taken from *Positive Algebra* by Martin Kindt (2010).
iii More practice with number strips can be found at www.wisweb.nl.

REFERENCES

Beth, H. (1925). Het 'meer en meer wiskundig' karakter der H. B. School met 5-jarigen cursus [The increasing mathematical character of the 5-year secondary school]. *Euclides, 1*, 90-100.

Dolk, M., & Fosnot, C.T. (2004). *Taking inventory, kindergarten-grade 1: The role of context* (cd-rom). Portsmouth NH: Heinemann.

Freudenthal, H. (1968). Why to teach mathematics as to be useful? *Educational studies in mathematics, 1*, 3-8.

Goffree, F., & Buys, K. (Eds.) (1989). *Tegengesteld.* [Opposite] Baarn: Bekadidact.

Janssen, J., Schoot, F. van der, Hemker, B., & Verhelst, N. (1999). *Balans van het reken-wiskundeonderwijs aan het einde van de basisschool 3: uitkomsten van de derde peiling in 1997.* [Balance of mathematics education at the end of primary education: results from the third survey in 1997.] Arnhem: Cito.

Kindt, M. (2010). *Positive algebra.* Utrecht: Freudenthal Instituut.

Kraemer, J.M., Janssen, J., Schoot, F. van der, & Hemker, B. (2005). *Balans van het reken-wiskundeonderwijs halverwege de basisschool 4.* [Balance of mathematics education in the middle of primary education.] Arnhem: Cito.

Programme for International Student Assessment & Organisation for Economic Co-operation and Development (2004). *Learning for tomorrow's world: first results from PISA 2003.* Paris: Organisation for Economic Co-operation and Development.

Roodhardt, A., Kindt, M., Burrill, G., & Spence, M. (1997). Patterns and symbols. In National Center for Research in Mathematical Sciences Education & Freudenthal Institute (Eds.), *Mathematics in context.* Chicago: Encyclopaedia Britannica Inc.

Usiskin, Z. (1997). Doing algebra in grades K-4. *Teaching children mathematics, 3*, 346-356.

Wijdenes, P. (1927). Over het onderwijs in rekenen in de eerste klas van de H.B.S. [On arithmetic education in grade 7.] *Euclides, 3*, 121-142.

Wijdenes, P. (1953). Algebra op de lagere school. [Algebra in primary education.] *Euclides, 28*, 188-195.

PAUL DRIJVERS, TRUUS DEKKER AND MONICA WIJERS

4. PATTERNS AND FORMULAS

Horizontal mathematization leads from the world of life to the world of symbols. In the world of life, people live, act – and suffer; in the other world, symbols are shaped, reshaped, and manipulated – not only mechanically, but also
with understanding and reflection. This is known as vertical mathematization.
(Freudenthal, 1991, p. 41-42)

INTRODUCTION

The previous chapter sketched out the subtle relationship between numerical calculations and algebraic thinking, and suggested ways of introducing young students to
algebraic thinking through the 'world' of arithmetic. The present chapter elaborates
on this topic and specifically addresses the topic of patterns and formulas. In
Chapter 1, the domain of patterns and formulas has been identified as an important
strand in algebra education. At the heart of this strand is the ability to recognize patterns and structures in problem situations, to capture and generalize this regularity by
using the mathematical language of formulas. The work with these formulas takes
place within the abstract world of algebra rather than in the tangible world of the
problem situation. In terms of Freudenthal's proposition quoted above, this strand
therefore involves both horizontal and vertical mathematization.

Patterns and formulas are fundamental to algebra. Formulas are powerful means
that can be used to describe patterns and express generalities. As such, they reflect
both the meaning and the power of algebra. Due to its abstract and general character,
however, this strand is difficult for many students to grasp. This chapter therefore is
written with middle to high achieving students (10 – 15 years old) in mind. For low
achieving students, the functional use of algebra in concrete and applied problem situations is more meaningful than the abstract algebra of patterns and formulas. For
the latter group, horizontal mathematization, i.e. in learning to recognize how a problem situation can be transposed into mathematical action, is more relevant than algebra as a mathematical domain in itself.

As an introductory example, Figure 1 shows a series of figures that consist of
black and grey dots. The task is provide an expression that describes the relationship between the number of the figure (n) and the number of black dots in that figure,
and similarly for the number of grey dots.

P. Drijvers (ed.), Secondary Algebra Education, 89–100.

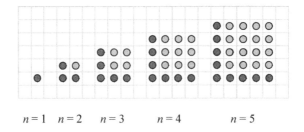

$n = 1$ $n = 2$ $n = 3$ $n = 4$ $n = 5$

Figure 1. Dot pattern problem

The problem is about describing the regularity in a pattern (Palha & Van Reeuwijk, 2002). Such a problem can be approached in various ways. For example, a 12-year-old student wrote the following:

> For the black dots it adds 2 every time, and for the grey it is
> the number $-1 \times$ itself.
> Black: $n - 1 + n$ Grey: $n - 1 \times$ itself

This student describes the number of black dots recursively, i.e., expressed in the previous number. For the number of grey dots he provides a direct description. After this, he writes down two direct formulas. The use of the variable n indicates that this approach has transcended the informal level. However, the current notation is still in a mixed form of natural and mathematical language. In addition, the mathematical language is still not entirely formal: although this probably will not lead to errors, the parentheses surrounding 'number $-$ 1' are missing in the student's formula. We therefore consider this solution to be an approach at what we would call the preformal level.

For a teacher, such diversity in solutions can be exploited to compare strategies and to discuss their advantages and disadvantages with the students. Questions such as 'which figure in the series contains more than 1 million grey dots?' lead to equations, which can also be formulated and solved at various levels of formalization. The teacher can also ask the students for an expression to indicate the total number of dots. This is not only equal to the square of the number of dots n in a row, but also to the number of grey and black dots together. In this way, the algebraic identity $n^2 = (2n - 1) + (n - 1)^2$ emerges, which is a reason for the students to think about algebraic equivalence, a concept which is not self-evident for them.

The dot pattern in this problem is not a realistic context problem in the sense that it is something you encounter in daily life. However, it is realistic in the sense that it is imaginable and meaningful. Isn't it fascinating to know for certain how many grey and black dots there are for $n = 12345$, without having to draw the enormous dot pattern or having to calculate all preceding cases? The satisfaction of being able to solve such a problem is unique to mathematics.

The process of discovering and representing patterns and structures can be a playful, challenging and productive algebraic activity, one which can lead in a natural way to generalization and building formulas. For example, Figure 2 shows part of a problem from the textbook series that the Freudenthal Institute developed, in collaboration with the University of Wisconsin, for middle school students in de United States (Wijers et al., 2006). The problem describes how the metal beams for a roof structure are constructed welding rods into a triangular pattern. In the larger context of investigating what such a roof structure looks like, one task for the students is to fill in a table which indicates the relationship between the number of rods and the length of the beam. The following task is to describe the pattern that they see in this relationship.

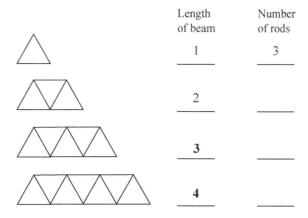

Figure 2. Building beams with triangles of rods

An interesting aspect of this problem is that it offers possibilities for seeing different patterns. Figure 3 shows several formulas that were created by students. In these formulas, N represents the number of rods and L represents the length of the beam, expressed in rods. Each of the (equivalent!) formulas reflects the student's specific way of looking at the pattern and its structure. Besides making such direct formulas, students also wrote down recursive formulas such as *'Next = Current + 4'*.

This diversity of formulas provides an opportunity for the teacher to challenge students to compare formulas with each other and to defend their own formula: "Are they all correct? How can you determine that they all amount to the same thing? How are the direct formulas and recurrent formulas related?" The power of this context is its strong link between the structure of the formula and the geometric interpretation of the pattern. At various levels – by sliding matchsticks around, by drawing or by conducting algebraic operations – it becomes clear that the various patterns that the students have written down reflect the same underlying algebraic structure.

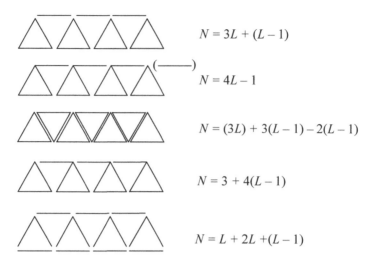

Figure 3. Pattern descriptions made by students

A more complex problem is shown in Figure 4 (Algebragroep W12-16, 1991). First, the students are asked to find algebraic expressions for the numbers of grey and white blocks as a function of the block structure's number in the row. The second question is whether the number of white blocks will ever catch up with the number of grey blocks – and if so, when? "How can you see which of the two formulas will ultimately 'win', based on the structure of the formulas?" The latter question invites a dynamic view of the situation because the students determine how both formulas behave when the independent variable increases. The block's number acquires the character of a dynamically changing quantity that runs through the natural numbers. This situation can also lead to thinking about proportionality and the order of growth.

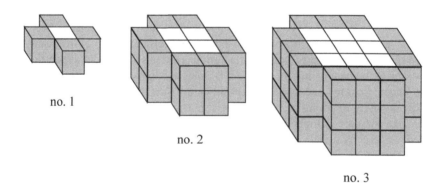

Figure 4. Block structures

The key to the above examples on pattern recognition is that students can describe a pattern by using an informal representation or a more formal formula. Expressed in terms of the quotation from Freudenthal at the beginning of this chapter, this is the phase of horizontal mathematization. Discussing and exploring the various formulas and representations invite simplification and shortening, which leads to thinking about equivalence. As a result, vertical mathematization comes into the picture, because the students reason about the algebraic relationships themselves, which may become detached from the original problem context. The 'world of algebra' becomes a domain in itself; it is a world in which mathematical objects exist and where you can think about their properties and relations.

The examples in this section show that the patterns do not have to originate from daily life to be suitable for introducing students to this form of algebraic modelling. Problems with a puzzle-like character in the world of mathematics are very suitable for this purpose. Examples can be found in the booklet *Positive algebra* by Kindt (2010). Problems such as the ones shown above can lead to different answers from the students. To ensure that the students will not feel uncertain about their answers, a class discussion during which the various approaches are compared can be very helpful.

FORMULAS AND VARIABLES

The algebra of patterns and structures concerns the investigation, identification and representation of patterns and underlying algebraic structures. Generally speaking, an algebraic model for a pattern is set up by *building a formula*. This type of algebraic modelling is not a simple task; variables are chosen, and sometimes assumptions and simplifications are made. Pattern recognition situations, as discussed in the previous section, are a suitable starting point for building formulas.

When they begin modelling, students often use action language that is close related to the description of the problem situation. In the example of Figure 4, one pattern description could be: "You can determine the number of white blocks by taking the cube of the sequence number". If these actions are expressed as an algebraic formula, this often has the character of a 'recipe' for the students: a step-by-step plan to describe the calculations. As such. the formula has the character of a compact *process description*. At this stage, word formulas are useful, with variable names that refer to the context:

NumberWhite = Object number cubed

Once a formula is constructed, often something has to be done with it. For example, the formula must be rewritten to allow comparison with another formula. An equation must be solved, or an inverse formula must be determined in order to carry out reverse calculation. In such situations, word formulas are no longer very useful; abbreviating the formula by using simple symbols turns out to be easier and more efficient. For example, the above formula becomes $w = n^3$. In this way the character of the formula changes; it is no longer a condensed calculation process, but it becomes 'a thing' that you can use and on which you can conduct mathematical operations. For example, you may want to expand parentheses in order to write the formula in a different way, or factorize. As a result, the formula gradually acquires an *object character*. This development can be encouraged in various ways, for example by comparing different formulas for the same phenomenon (see the example in Figure 3), or substituting formulas in other formulas. Chapter 7 contains several examples of such tasks. Switching between the process perspective and the object perspective was identified in Chapter 1 as one of the difficulties in algebra education, and therefore deserves attention (Sfard, 1991). When the link with the problem situation disappears entirely in the notation, as in the example $y = x^3$, this is referred to as an abstract formula.

A formula can describe a pattern or structure, but it also has a structure itself. It is important that students are aware of the structure of a formula, because this is often a prerequisite for being able to appropriately select an operation or a solution strategy. To develop insight into the structure of formulas, students can set up formulas themselves in problem situations. Or they can discuss a variety of formulas that other students have made. The reconstruction of the meaning in the work of the co-students is one way to promote insight into the structure of formulas.

Sub-expressions have their own specific meanings in the formulas students create. In the example of the dot patterns shown in Figure 1, the sub-expressions on the right-hand side of the equation $N^2 = (2N-1) + (N-1)^2$ are recognizable as the number of black and grey dots, respectively. In the example of the beams in Figure 2, the sub-expression $(L-1)$ in the equation $N = 3L + (L-1)$ stands for the number of connectors that join the individual triangles together. In this way, the sub-expressions have a specific meaning as part of the roof construction, and they also display different growth behaviours: $3L$ grows three times as fast as $(L-1)$. The capacity to understand the structure of a formula, and to identify the relevant sub-expressions in it, is an important element of algebraic expertise.

This capacity to take a global view of formulas and expressions, and to see the underlying structure, is part of what we referred to as symbol sense in Chapter 1 (Arcavi, 1994). However, if students do not have this global view on expressions and equations, they may be tempted to immediately carry out operations that the visual appearance of the formula invites (Kirshner & Awtry, 2004). In the case of $N = 3L + (L-1)$, this might be to simplify by removing the brackets, which does lead to a simplified form, but obstructs the relation with the problem situation.

Paying attention to insight into formulas deepens the student's understanding of variables. For students, variables initially function as placeholders for numerical values, or as unknowns, the value of which can be determined by solving an equation. But in formulas, other aspects of the variable must be understood. The example of the winning formulas refers to the dynamic aspect of the variable: the variable has the character of a changing quantity, which represents not just a single value – known or unknown – from the domain, but a quantity that runs through the domain set.

When working with formulas, the variable as a generalized number also emerges: the variable represents the entire set of numbers. This is visualized in Figure 5 with number strips (Kindt, 2000). Working with such number strips[i] visualizes the fact that these relationships apply to all numbers. Therefore they provide a natural transition from systematic calculation with numbers to calculation with formulas (see also Chapter 3). By labelling the strips, the step to symbolic algebra is taken in a natural way. For example, it becomes clear that the formula

$$(2 + 3N) + (5 + 2N) = 7 + 5N$$

does not apply to a single specific value of N, but to all values of N from the domain of natural numbers. N therefore does not represent just one of these numbers, but the entire set $\{0, 1, 2, \ldots\}$

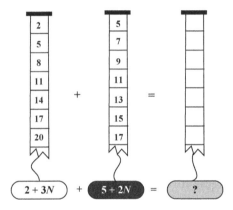

Figure 5. Number strips as an introduction to a different perspective on variables

Chapter 8 addresses the variable concept in greater depth and will discuss how ICT can play a role in its development.

GENERALIZATION AND PROOF

The two previous sections showed how building formulas for patterns and structures can provide an introduction to generalization and interpretation. Generalization is an important aspect of algebra; based on specific cases, a conceptual leap is made to the general case, or preferably to the class of all cases. In the example of the roof beams, a rule such as $N = 4L - 1$ shows the relationship between the length of the beam and the number of rods for all values of N and L. The process of generalization requires attention for the difference between 'there is a value of x where ...' and 'for all values of x ...', a distinction that is important in mathematical reasoning. Examples where the domain consists of natural numbers are perhaps more accessible for generalization than examples where the domain consists of the set of real numbers.

PAUL DRIJVERS, TRUUS DEKKER AND MONICA WIJERS

When performing algebraic modelling and generalization, it is important that students work on meaningful problems, where they are given the opportunity to develop their own strategies, mental models and forms of notation and representation. Initially, this has priority above general, formal proofs. Nevertheless, we believe there should also be attention for reasoning and proving. After all, one strength of algebra is that it can be used to compactly formulate coherent reasoning, which provides certainty about specific phenomena. Although this is an ambitious goal, one of the aims of algebra education is to make students experience something of this themselves. We will provide two examples of reasoning and proof that emerge from pattern recognition.

Earlier in this chapter we have shown how the world of numbers may provide access to the world of algebra in a natural way. Surprising calculation patterns may invite algebraic reasoning and proof. For example, consider the following method of squaring. To obtain the square of 65, we multiply the first digit, 6, by 7, which is 42. Then we add the square of 5, the second digit, to the back. This gives 4225, which is correct. With 15 this is even easier to check: 1 times 2 is 2, and then 25 attached to the back is 225. It also works with 95! Students who are 13 or 14 years old are often astonished that this works, and this astonishment can be exploited by the teacher. A sensible place to start is to estimate 65 times 65 by calculating 60 times 70. But why do we end up with 25 less? Does this technique always work out correctly? And how can we know for sure? With algebra, of course! The key is to expand $(10a + 5)^2$.

The second example concerns the sequence below, in which the difference of two products is always equal to 1:

$$9 \times 9 - 10 \times 8 = 1$$
$$10 \times 10 - 11 \times 9 = 1$$
$$11 \times 11 - 12 \times 10 = 1$$

Here as well, there are obvious challenges. How can the series be continued? How big is 999×1001 approximately? Is the difference always equal to one? How can you know that for sure? What would a line look like if it starts with $9\frac{1}{2}$ instead of 9? How can you formulate and write down a general rule? By asking such questions in class, the teacher can invite the students to reason and to find more or less formal proofs. The formal proof requires much: formalizing in order to write down the reasoning, generalizing about all numbers (whole, rational?) and abstracting from the calculation context. In this case, the students can prove their findings by expanding the product at the end of $a^2 - (a + 1) \cdot (a - 1)$. The geometrical proof in Figure 6 may complement the algebraic one.

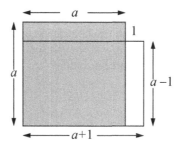

Figure 6. An illustration with $a^2 - (a+1) \cdot (a-1) = 1$

Teachers who want to go further can invite students to find similar surprising sequences of arithmetic tasks, or show their students variant such as

$$9 \times 9 - 11 \times 7 = 4$$
$$10 \times 10 - 12 \times 8 = 4$$
$$11 \times 11 - 13 \times 9 = 4$$

Finally, the generalization of generalizations can be made:

$$a^2 - (a+b) \cdot (a-b) = b^2$$

This may lead to the familiar formula for the difference of squares $(a+b) \cdot (a-b) = a^2 - b^2$. Of course, this result must also be proven, which can be done both algebraically and geometrically (Kindt, 1999). This formula for the difference of squares is useful to know by heart, as this will ease recognizing its potential application while working on algebraic tasks.

Although generalizations and proofs can be difficult, the examples in this section show that there are indeed opportunities for giving algebraic proofs a place in the curriculum for mid- and high-achieving students of 10 – 15 years old. The power of algebra as a method to express compact and coherent reasoning must not remain obscure for this target group.

CONCLUSION AND RECOMMENDATIONS

The main conclusion from this chapter is that the theme of Patterns and Formulas is important in algebra education and that it deserves attention in the mathematics curricula for mid- and high-achieving students of 10 – 15 years old. It is a topic that lends itself to inner-mathematical activity and both horizontal and vertical mathematization. Moreover, it is a fascinating topic that enables students to experience essential facets of algebraic thinking. If the degree and pace of formalization are adapted to the target group, we expect that students will experience this topic as meaningful and will understand the power of algebraic methods and representations. Sub-topics within this theme include patterns and structures, formulas and variables, and generalization and proof.

The question is then, how can teachers shape the teaching of this rather difficult topic? Without being exhaustive, we now present some pedagogical recommendations that are organized along three questions.

Do teachers need concrete problem situations to make the algebra of patterns and formulas recognizable and meaningful for students?

Concrete problem situations from daily life or from professional practice (current or future) can motivate students, but do not always trigger abstraction or lead to the development of algebraic thinking. It is not a good idea to artificially involve algebra with problems that can be approached with common sense reasoning and informal strategies. For example, consider the following problem: the sum of three consecutive numbers is 66. What are the numbers? From an algebraic perspective, the teachers expect their students to construct and solve the equation

$$a + (a + 1) + (a + 2) \ = \ 66$$

However, a more common sense approach comes down to noticing that the middle number must be one-third of the total, which in this case is equal to 22. Such a clever solution strategy deserves to be rewarded, and not rejected because no algebra has been used.

The algebra of patterns and formulas can also be recognizable and meaningful for students in a challenging, puzzle-like context, such as numbers, number patterns and numerical calculation, for example. This chapter provides some examples of this approach. We also recommend using such problem situations when the actual objective is to reach for vertical mathematization and abstraction. This involves situations that are realistic, not in the sense of being taken from everyday reality, but in the sense that the students can imagine the problem, can feel ownership, can understand what they can do to solve it and why their methods always work.

How can we encourage students to take the step to abstraction?

A problem situation involving a pattern or structure initially requires students to transform the situation into mathematical symbols and operations. This transformation process between the world of the problem and the world of mathematics, which can be conducted at various levels, is called horizontal mathematization. By having students construct formulas themselves in many situations, they acquire a perspective on the meaning of algebraic (sub-)expressions and they become experienced in this transformation process.

The stage at which thinking, representation and manipulation take place within the world of mathematics, where new mathematical objects and structures are formed, is vertical mathematization. Abstraction can be seen as the result of vertical mathematization; from this perspective – paradoxically – it amounts to the mathematical world being increasingly experienced as concrete and meaningful. To encourage students to take such steps towards abstraction, it is important that the problem situation itself is not just a common sense problem from daily life, as noted in the previous recommendation, but invites for gradual formalization and progressive abstraction.

As a pedagogical strategy, we recommend asking 'silly' questions, which serve no practical purpose, but are intriguing. In the example of the dot patterns (Figure 1), the question "Which number of figure contains more than 12345 grey dots?" is obviously not relevant for daily life, but at the same time it is fascinating and invites abstraction.

Finally, we recommend to encourage students to make their 'own productions'. For example, after the sequence of sums from the previous section, the students can be asked to make their own sequence which will always have the same answer, but which is now not equal to 1. Such productions contribute to the students' understanding of the issue at stake, and are challenging. Chapter 7 addresses such tasks in more detail.

How important are algebraic language and formalization?
The students' work on the dot pattern task (Figure 1) shows that they are capable of describing the algebraic essence of a problem by using informal mathematical language or sometimes even natural language. However, for students aiming at higher educational levels, it is important to become acquainted with formal algebraic language and notation. Algebraic language and notation are essential and powerful tools to support reasoning and proof. Algebraic thinking without algebraic language is not impossible, but difficult indeed. We therefore recommend paying attention to formal algebraic language by carefully and gradually increasing the abstract character of tasks or solution methods, and by directing the teaching more to the properties of the algebraic objects in the mathematical world than to the applications from which they emerge.

NOTES

i   An applet for operating with number strips is available at http://www.fi.uu.nl/wisweb/en/

REFERENCES

Algebragroep W12-16 (1991). En de variabelen, hoe staat het daarmee? [And how about variables?] *Nieuwe Wiskrant, tijdschrift voor Nederlands wiskundeonderwijs, 10*(1), 12-19.

Arcavi, A. (1994). Symbol sense: informal sense-making in formal mathematics. *For the learning of mathematics, 14*(3), 24-35. Retrieved April, 8th, 2010, from http://flm.educ.ualberta.ca/index.php?do=extras&lang=en.

Freudenthal, H. (1991). *Revisiting mathematics education, China lectures.* Dordrecht: Kluwer Academic Publishers.

Kindt, M. (1999). Legpuzzel-algebra. [Jigsaw-algebra.] *Nieuwe Wiskrant, tijdschrift voor Nederlands wiskundeonderwijs, 19*(2), 17-22.

Kindt, M. (2000). Discrete algebra. [Discrete algebra.] *Nieuwe Wiskrant, tijdschrift voor Nederlands wiskundeonderwijs, 19*(4), 31-36.

Kindt, M. (2010). *Positive algebra.* Utrecht: Freudenthal Instituut.

Kirshner, D., & Awtry, T. (2004). Visual Salience of Algebraic Transformations. *Journal for Research in Mathematics Education, 35*(4), 224-257.

Palha, S., & Van Reeuwijk, M. (2002). Zie je het verband? [Do you see the relation?] *Nieuwe Wiskrant, tijdschrift voor Nederlands wiskundeonderwijs, 22*(1), 12-15.
Sfard, A. (1991). On the dual nature of mathematical conceptions: reflections on processes and objects as different sides of the same coin. *Educational studies in mathematics, 22*, 1-36.
Wijers, M., Roodhardt, A., Reeuwijk, M. van, Dekker, T., Burrill, G., Cole, B.R., & Pligge, M.A. (2006). Building formulas. In Wisconsin Centre for Education Research & Freudenthal Institute (Eds.), *Mathematics in Context*. Chicago, USA: Encyclopedia Britannica Inc.

DAVID WEBB, MIEKE ABELS

5. RESTRICTIONS IN ALGEBRA

If we want students to truly understand the power of equality, they need to have experiences seeing the mathematical symbols of equality used in varied ways, not always as the symbol that comes before the answer to an arithmetic problem. (This Chapter)

INTRODUCTION

This chapter focuses on describing the restrictions sub-strand within algebra and how concepts and relationships are developed across grade levels. Many examples are also included to support meaningful connections to other mathematics, and hopefully provide additional motivation for discussing such relationships with students.

As discussed in Chapter 1, school algebra is generally understood to include patterns, generalization, solving equations, and graphing functions. Yet, one of the most powerful set of tools and techniques in algebra for representing realistic phenomena and analyzing mathematical behaviours is found in the domain of Restrictions, generally defined here as mathematical tasks involving the intersection and union of multiple solution sets and problems involving multiple variables. These types of tasks often call for the consideration of one or more equations and how they, together, represent the situation. By representing different aspects of the same problem, they support the modelling and solving of problems that would otherwise be unwieldy and complex if attempted holistically. When thinking of algebra through the lens of Restrictions, equality is a necessary concept that is used to identify and interpret solutions. And so it is with the concept of equality that we begin.

EQUALITY

Children recognize equality of groups and quantity at a very young age, with some research suggesting its origins in infancy (Gallistel & Gelman, 2000). In studies of children only six months old, Starkey, Spelke and Gelman (1990) found that children could quantify small sets of objects and would react when a screen was placed in front and later removed with one of the objects missing. The idea that one group 'is the same as' or 'is not the same as' another group seems so basic, so intuitive. However, by the time students study algebra the equal sign has lost its meaning as identifying a relationship between two expressions.

The often used equation in algebra is certainly more than something that needs to be solved. A well-trained student, when seeing the equation $2x + 1 = -x + 7$, will

P. Drijvers (ed.), Secondary Algebra Education, 101–118.

likely, without prompting, solve for x and find that the solution is $x = 2$. Lost in this reflex to solve for x is the recognition that these two linear expressions are equal to each other, and that the one solution found for x is true only because one expression, $2x + 1$, is restricted by another expression, $-x + 7$, or vice versa. Both of these expressions on their own could have infinite values depending on the value of x. By setting the expressions equal to each other, infinite possibilities for one expression are restricted to just one value. Of course, cases of no solution and infinite solutions can also occur depending on the expressions that are compared.

Equality is a relationship. As far as student understanding of algebra is concerned it may be an essential concept. Unfortunately, as we attempt to familiarize young students with the equal sign, they often do not see it as a mark of a relationship but as something that needs to be done. This object duality, as discussed by Drijvers, Goddijn and Kindt in Chapter 1, can serve as a source of confusion for students. Worksheets and workbooks with lists of arithmetic problems often overuse the equal sign. By the time students have completed hundreds of these practice sheets, students understand the equal sign as 'find the answer'. As Faulkner, Levi and Carpenter (1999) found, when given problems of the type $8 + 4 = \ldots + 5$, the most common but incorrect response for sixth grade students was 12 (84% of 145 students). And yet, the percentage of third grade students who responded with 12 was 49%, much less than sixth grade students! As these results suggest, as students progress in school the equal sign as a relational symbol takes on a different meaning, such as 'compute' or 'find the answer.' When teachers used problems that emphasized the relational aspects of equality, they began to see the equal sign in $8 + 4 = + 5$ as separating values that needed to be the same (Carpenter, Franke & Levi, 2003). Students would often describe their reasoning as follows: "Since five is one more than four, the other number has to be one less than eight – or seven. If one number goes up the other has to go down, to make it equal."

If we want students to truly understand the power of equality, they need to have experiences seeing the mathematical symbols of equality used in varied ways, not always as the symbol that comes before the answer to an arithmetic problem. When students communicate the relationships equations describe rather than seeing equations only as something to solve, a deeper understanding of algebraic relationships is developed. Likewise, when students are given an opportunity to reason about arithmetic problems that promote the meaning of equality, they are more apt to develop number sense along with an understanding of the restrictive properties that will come into play later as they study algebra.

THREE METAPHORS FOR EQUALITY

Even though young students can reason about equality using tasks involving numbers and symbols, problem contexts can motivate mathematical reasoning in ways that are more meaningful and interesting for some students. Some problem contexts are so closely related to mathematical processes, they serve as metaphors in which students associate a context with specific mathematics.

A first metaphor considers *bartering*. The process of exchanging one set of objects for an equally valued set, offers an opportunity to reason about substitution and equality for many variables (Van Amerom, 2002). In this way bartering serves as a familiar context to support student discussion as well as serving as a mathematical metaphor for equality (see Figure 1).

Figure 1. The bartering metaphor illustrated

For example, consider a problem context in which one goat can be traded for six chickens, and two chickens can be traded for one bag of salt (Figure 2). How many bags of salt can be bartered for three goats? These sets of equivalent statements, with some deductive reasoning, can be used to create chains of associated sets such as the one suggested in the following figure (Webb, Hedges & Abels, 2006).

Figure 2. The goat-chicken-salt task

Within the context, students often associate these trades with 'the same as' or equality, and write statements such as:
– 'one goat for six chickens'
– G = CCCCCC, or
– 1G = 6C

Students use combinations of these statements to substitute equivalent values and, eventually, find the solution to the problem – i.e., nine bags of salt. These multiple representations of equality that describe this context can also be thought of as sets of equations, or a system of equations.

A second common metaphor that is often used to convey equality and equal sets is comparing the weights of objects on a *balance*. Notice how the problem shown in Figure 3 (from Kindt, Abels, et al., 2006) represents notions of algebraic reasoning without explicitly using equations. It is important to note that the letters students might use here to abbreviate bananas and pineapples (e.g., 10B = 2P) are not variables, since the context focuses on counts of fruit, not weights or prices. But the transition to the use of variables is not too far removed from this type of problem or representation of the situation.

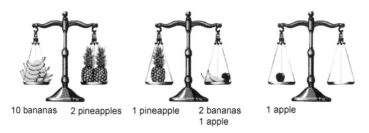

10 bananas   2 pineapples   1 pineapple   2 bananas   1 apple
                                             1 apple

Figure 3. The balance metaphor

A third metaphor (from Kindt, Abels, et al., 2006) that can be used to represent equality is a situation similar to the game 'tug of war'. Two or more groups of animals are pulling the same rope in opposite directions (see Figure 4).

Four oxen are as strong as five horses

An elephant is as strong as one ox and two horses

Figure 4. The tug of war metaphor

The problem posed in the above diagrams models two equations:
− 4 Oxen = 5 Horses
− 1 Elephant = 1 Ox + 2 Horses

These equations for tug of war suggest that four oxen are *as strong* as five horses; in the second equation, one elephant is *as strong as* one ox and two horses. Using this information, which group of animals will win the tug-of-war in the diagram below?

Figure 5. Tug of war task

So for this problem, the goal is not to find the "work" or "pull" of each animal, but to instead find which group is greater, or a solution to an inequality. Also notice that with all metaphors, the value of one variable is in relation to another variable. That is, none of the objects have been assigned a specific value or weight. This approach emphasizes algebraic reasoning over computation and guess-and-check. The focus is on relational thinking.

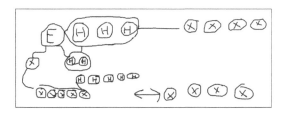

Figure 6. Student work on tug of war task

Figure 6 contains a typical example shared by a 15-year-old girl in a high school algebra class showing how students use this tug of war representation in their own solution strategy. Notice how in her representation of the problem she replaced the pictures of animals with letters. As she described her strategy, she explained that the elephant (E) is the same as an ox (X) and two horses (HH). Replacing the elephant leaves one ox and five horses on the left side and four oxen (XXXX) on the right side. From the first diagram, four oxen have the same strength as five horses. Replacing the horses with the oxen leaves five oxen on the left versus four oxen on the right. The left side must be stronger.

To solve this problem students primarily use a substitution method, and need to identify strategic uses of equivalent sets and represent the final statement in way that clearly shows which team wins or if both teams are the same.

REPRESENTING EQUALITY IN THE CARTESIAN PLANE

A fourth, more mathematical approach for investigating restrictions, is through graphing equations, and possibly inequalities, in the Cartesian plane. Students need opportunities to explore combinations of graphs when solving systems of equations so they can have a visual referent for how different systems involving linear functions can produce infinite solutions when the functions are equivalent or no solutions when the graphs do not intersect. However, there are also methods that can be used beyond simply graphing and identifying points or regions of intersection. For example, how might changes to the slope of a given function (or the rate of change in a situation) change the point of intersection?

The Cartesian plane can also be used, as part of a mapping context, to explore the use of inequalities to describe a situation. In contrast to the solution of linear functions being represented by lines in the Cartesian plane, inequalities are represented by regions bordered by one or more lines.

Using the context of a forest fire, as elaborated in the *Mathematics in Context* unit Graphing Equations (Kindt, Wijers et al., 2006) the sightings of a fire from different stations can suggest (vision) lines on a map (see Figure 7). These lines could be described in terms of angle measures or slope from particular points on the y-axis (North-South line).

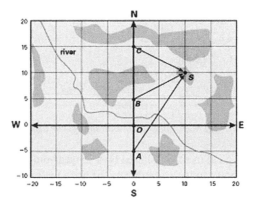

Figure 7. A Cartesian plane problem

Regions on a map or estimated regions for the location of a fire can further motivate the use of informal descriptors such as 'above' or 'north of', which relate to more formal mathematical language such as $y > -5$ or $3 < x < 6$. In Figure 8 (from Webb, Krusi, Wijers & de Haan, 2006), the region that is marked could be described as $6 < y < 10$ and $-6 < x < -3$.

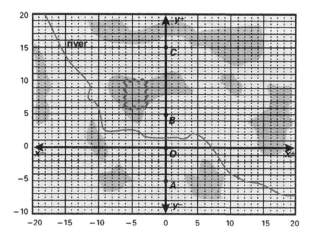

Figure 8. Inequalities as region in the plane

In elaborating further on the mapping context, there are times in which an exact location is required and other situations in which a region is needed. Having students explore the mathematical equivalents to these situations reinforces the difference between the singularity of solutions offered with systems of equations and the necessity of a visual representation to adequately represent systems of inequalities.

Returning to the theme of this chapter, the barter and balance contexts beg the question: What is being restricted? In the case of bartering, the value of three commodities (goats, chickens and salt) is 'restricted' by indicating that one set is equal to the value of another set. In the second, the weight of three different fruit is restricted by showing that the weight of one set is the same as the weight of another set. By using combinations of these equal sets, different relationships can be found without ever using a specific price or weight. When graphs are used to represent a situation with two variables, one line in the Cartesian plane suggests an infinite number of solutions – i.e., all coordinate pairs on the given line. But when a second line intersects the first line, the number of solutions shifts – an infinite number of possible solutions is restricted to just one solution.

FROM INFORMAL AND PRE-FORMAL REPRESENTATIONS TO FORMAL STRATEGIES

Ideally, a learning trajectory of solving sets of linear equations should go from informal, to pre-formal to formal. As articulated by Gravemeijer (1994) in his discussion of emergent modelling, the situational models (informal) are closely related to particular situations. Pre-formal models can be derived by students or introduced by the teacher to students; some models are derived from problem contexts that suggest the structure of the model – e.g., consider how the combination of pencils and erasers in the student store suggests the need for a combination chart. Pre-formal models provide greater mathematical structure: they are used to model and solve a wide range of problems. As the need for a more generalizable, inclusive strategy emerges, formal strategies can be introduced and related to students' experiences with the informal strategies and pre-formal models. The underlying issue when designing algebra education according to this principle is what representations and strategies are accessible for students who do not yet have experiences with formal algebra, but help develop their thinking in this direction.

An introduction can be offered to students using problems that involve situations with variable amounts that could be expressed, eventually, by equations. However, instead of giving students equations, we recommend that such problems include pictures of easy to imagine contexts, so that students can invent their own strategies (Meyer, Dekker & Querelle, 2001). In the beginning, no formal algorithms are introduced since the focus is on informal methods such as guess and check, combining quantities, and looking for relationships between prices. In this section, examples of these mostly situation specific, informal approaches are described.

Monica and Martin are responsible for the school store. The store is open all day for students to buy supplies. Unfortunately, Monica and Martin can't be in the store all day to take students' money, so they use an honor system. Pencils and erasers are available for students to purchase on the honor system. Students leave exact change in a small locked box to pay for their purchases. Erasers cost 25c each and pencils cost 15c each.

Figure 9. Eraser-pencil task

The first example, shown in Figure 9, is a problem that invites the use of informal methods (Kindt, Abels et al., 2006). The prices of each item and their combinations are easy for students to work with mentally, allowing students to showcase their number sense. At this point, though, there is no specific problem to solve. This a context that is accessible for students, to begin a discussion of possible amounts that could be in the cashier box.

Students are later asked to figure out how many erasers and pencils were sold if a particular amount was left in the cashier's box. Some amounts, such as $0.75 or $1.50, result in multiple solutions. Students typically solve the problem using 'guess-and-check,' and as an introduction to the problem they are encouraged to do so. Students will soon notice, however, that some method of organization is called for to account for all of the different combinations. One such method is to create two lists of the prices of each item as shown in Figure 10 (from Kindt, Abels, et al., 2006).

Erasers	Price
0	$0.00
1	$0.25
2	$0.50
3	$0.75
4	$1.00
5	$1.25
6	
7	

Pencils	Price
0	$0.00
1	$0.15
2	$0.30
3	
4	
5	
6	
7	

Figure 10. Price table for the eraser-pencil task

A different approach is the use of a combination chart. Figure 11 shows such a chart, which combines the two lists above to show the total cost of a variety of combinations of erasers and pencils.[i] This is a pre-formal model that, in contrast to the fair exchange method, adds a new way to see the mathematical structure of the problem. Each cell can represent an equation – e.g., 2E + 1P = 65 – even though students do not refer to such equations[ii] when using this chart. The context and representation work together to remind students that two erasers and one pencil costs 65 cents. The purpose of introducing the combination chart supports a search for numerical *and* visual patterns.

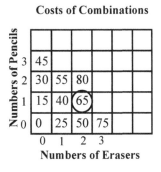

Figure 11. Combination chart

The number patterns found in the beginning of the chart helps students complete the rest of the chart. In addition, these number patterns also support the exploration of the *exchange strategy* (Figure 12).

Costs of Combinations

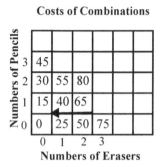

Figure 12. Exchange strategy in combination chart

A horizontal move from right to left can be interpreted as one less eraser, the price drops by 25 cents. Using formal algebra notation, this 'move' can be represented as follows:

$2E + 1P = 65$

$1E + 1P = 40$

With one more move to the left, $1P = 15$.

Costs of Combinations

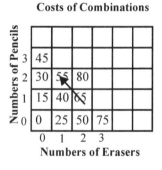

Figure 13. Diagonal 'move' in the chart

The diagonal movement up and to the left can be interpreted as if you exchange one eraser for a pencil, the price drops by 10 cents (see Figure 13). Using equations, this "move" can be represented in the following way:

$2E + 1P = 65$

$1E + 2P = 55$

One more move up and left, 3P = 45.

This type of diagonal movement through the combination chart models an exchange of one item for the other, a trade of one eraser for one pencil. The price drops by 10 cents with this exchange because the price of a pencil is 10 cents less than the price of an eraser.

This type of exchange strategy is also modelled in a more informal exchange strategy that involves a visual comparison of combinations of items with a total price. The advantage of this representation is the visual rendering of item combinations. There are few words for students to read, although they have to be able to interpret the picture.

The example in Figure 14 from Van Reeuwijk (1995) shows two T-shirts and two sodas that cost $44. The second combination shows one T-shirt and three sodas and a total price of $30.

Figure 14. T-shirt-soda problem

Even without explicitly phrasing the question, it might be clear what the problem is. Many people solve this problem using the more formal algebraic method shown below, even though it is accessible to multiple, less formal, and in this case even more efficient strategies:

$$\begin{cases} 2x + 2y = 44 \\ x + 3y = 30 \end{cases} \rightarrow \begin{cases} x + y = 22 \\ x + 3y = 30 \end{cases} \rightarrow \begin{cases} x = 22 - y \\ 22 - y + 3y = 30 \end{cases} \rightarrow \begin{cases} x = 18 \\ y = 4 \end{cases}$$

Using different informal and pre-formal strategies shown by the examples in Figures 15 and 16 students can find the price of each item. The guess and check strategy is an example of an informal approach since it is based on specific features of this particular problem context. The exchange strategy is also informal, although it is a slightly more generalizable, structured strategy that can be used with other problems of the same type. Note that in addition to the different strategies used by the students, their work also shows each student's preference for a specific notation.

Guess and check

In the student work shown in the left part of Figure 15, taken from Van Reeuwijk (1995), values are verified using the second picture (TSSS). Because these values for T and S give an amount that is too high, lower values are used next. Although T = 15 and S = 5 work for the second picture equation, the values T = 18 and S = 4 are selected as the answer. Again, because of the close relationship of this strategy to the problem context, this is an example of an informal strategy.

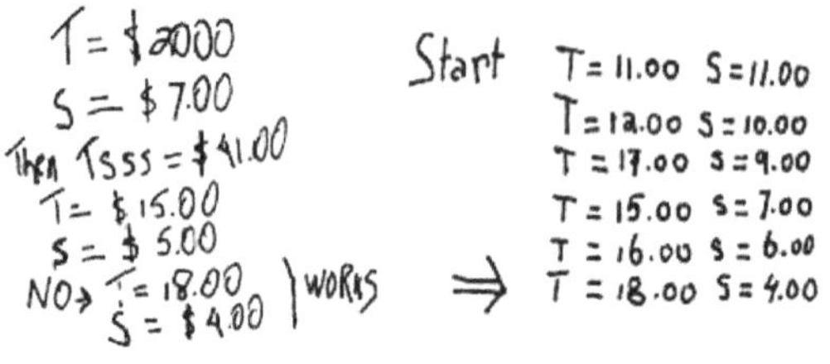

Figure 15. Two students' work on the T-shirt-soda task

The work at the right of Figure 15 shows a more organized way to guess and check. This student's choice to start with T = 11 and S = 11 can be explained by looking at the first picture equation: assume the four items are the same price with a total cost of $44. The student mentally verified these values in the second picture equation. This process is continued by increasing the value of the T-shirt and decreasing the value of the soda, verifying these values with both the first and second picture. This could be considered a more strategic guess and check, but still an informal strategy.

Exchange

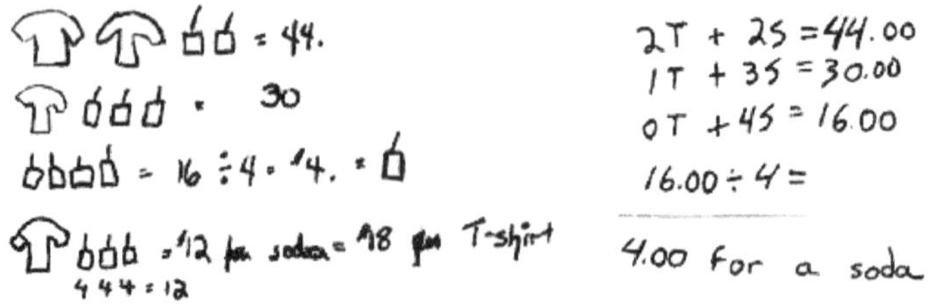

Figure 16. Two students' exchange strategies

The two students whose work is shown in Figure 16 compared the two picture equations and noticed that when you exchange one T-shirt for a soda, the price decreases by $14. They exchanged one T-shirt for a soda again and arrived at an equation that shows the price of four sodas. In each case, the cost relationship between increasing one quantity and decreasing the other is essential to finding a solution.

All previous strategies can be used to solve a problem where a set of two linear equations with two unknowns is involved. To solve a set of equations with three or more unknowns, a different approach is needed.

Using historical developments in mathematics: another pre-formal model

Following Aad Goddijn's suggestion in Chapter 2, we can often look to historical developments in mathematics to identify useful models and strategies to support student learning. If we look at mathematics developed in China, we find a method developed in the period 300 BC to 200 AD. It is described in the *Nine Chapters on the Mathematical Arts* of Chiu Chang Suan Shu.

To solve a system of linear equations Chiu Chang Suan Shu used what we now call 'matrix notation'. He only used the coefficients of the unknowns, represented by counting rods. Red rods were used for positive coefficients and black rods for negative coefficients. The counting rods were placed in columns in such a way that each column represents one equation. Figure 17 shows an example taken from Joseph (2000).

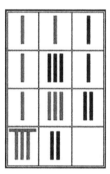

This diagram represents the following system of equations in three unknowns. Each column represents one equation and should be read from right to left:

$$-x - y - 2z = 0$$
$$x - 3y + 3z = -2$$
$$x + y + z = 8$$

Figure 17. Chinese 'matrix notation'

This type of diagram is the first example of the use of a matrix to solve a system of three equations with three variables. Given the placement of the values, column operations were used to solve the system which is mathematically consistent with the row operations that are used to solve matrices in modern mathematics.

ORDER	TACO	SALAD	DRINK	TOTAL
1	1	—	2	$3.00
2	2	1	4	$8.00
3	—	4	4	$11.00
4				
5				
6				
7				

Figure 18. 'Notebook notation'

Inspired by the Chinese counting rods, in the *Mathematics in Context* unit *Comparing Quantities* (Kindt, Abels et al., 2006), the Chinese approach is adapted to produce a new pre-formal model referred to as *notebook notation* (see Figure 18).

The notebook notation is less formal from a symbolic point of view, but is very close to the Row Echelon Form used with a matrix representation of a system of equations. In the case shown here, the context is taking food orders at a restaurant. The quantity of items in each order is noted along with the total price of the order. This same situation could also be represented by the following system of three equations or its related matrix:

$$\begin{cases} 1T + + 2D = 3 \\ 2T + 1S + 4D = 8 \\ + 4S + 4D = 11 \end{cases} \qquad \begin{bmatrix} 1 & 0 & 2 & 3 \\ 2 & 1 & 4 & 8 \\ 0 & 4 & 4 & 11 \end{bmatrix}$$

The method of solution proceeds in a manner similar to working with a 3×4 matrix, except the complete system does not have to be rewritten again and again. The focus instead is on reducing and eliminating items so that the price of one item is found.

In the example shown below (from Webb, Hedges & Abels, 2006), Order #1 is doubled to get Order #4. Then Order #4 can be subtracted from Order #2 to find the price of one salad. This information can be used with order #3 to find the price of one drink, and then the price of one taco.

ORDER	TACO	SALAD	DRINK	TOTAL
1	1	--	2	$ 3.00
2	2	1	4	$ 8.00
3	--	4	4	$ 11.00
4	2	--	4	$ 6.00
5	--	1	--	$ 2.00
6				
7				

×2

Figure 19. Strategy in notebook notation

Notice that in many of the strategies discussed so far – guess and check, exchange, combination chart, notebook notation – the use of a monetary context and whole number combinations of different items are used. The context and use of whole number items reduce the arithmetic demands on students to solve the problem, which seems appropriate for students who are novices in algebra. This approach elevates the focus on algebraic reasoning, patterns and relationships. To motivate students to consider more formal algebraic methods, other contexts, numbers and values can be used. For example, when equations with whole number coefficients are replaced with decimal or fraction coefficients, students are more inclined to use numerical rather than pictorial representations. When quantities and prices are 'less friendly' to mental arithmetic, students are more inclined to use symbolic notation to solve a problem. Even with this shift to more formal representations, however, the initial context continues to serve as a concrete reference for students to recall related strategies and provide informal justification to explain why related strategies with equations and matrices work.

Even though guess and check, exchange, combination chart, and notebook notation are all useful strategies that use a monetary context (informal), the combination chart and notebook notation are mathematical tools that offer greater structure to solve problems (pre-formal). When students use guess and check strategies, the choices they make to select and compare quantities depend on their strategic competence (Kilpatrick, Swafford, & Findell, 2001). This strategy provides no inherent guidance for solving the problem. In contrast, the combination chart and notebook notation require the organization of key values that set up a generalizable solution strategy – e.g, when using the combination chart follow a diagonal pattern to the horizontal or vertical edges to reduce the quantity of one item to zero. As noted earlier, the solution strategy for notebook notation – a pre-formal tool that suggests a restaurant context – is very similar to the formal Row Reduction Elimination Method used with matrices.

In comparing these two preformal models, the notebook notation has a clear advantage over the combination chart in that the notebook can be expanded to include as many columns and rows as needed for the respective number of variables and equations. With the combination chart the horizontal and vertical axes are defined by two variables; it cannot be used with situations that have three or more variables – i.e., a situation with three variables would require a combination cube!

PREPARING TO APPLY INSTRUCTIONAL DESIGN PRINCIPLES

The strategy-building contexts and pre-formal models discussed in this chapter have a role in developing student understanding of algebra. As with the formal strategies – namely, the substitution and elimination methods for systems of equations, student learning must be supported with instruction that emphasizes the essential features of the model or strategy that is being developed. Rather than having students 'discover' these models on their own, the teacher has an instrumental role in supporting students' guided reinvention of the models through the use of questions, examples, and counterexamples that can clarify how the model could be used (Webb, 2008).

We have found that a useful activity for teachers to engage in when planning for instruction is to review their available instructional materials for examples of useful contexts (e.g., bartering, balance, mapping, and consumer situations) and pre-formal models that support student sense-making (e.g., fair exchange, combination charts, notebook notation, frog jumping, etc.). As part of a research project with middle school teachers in the United States (Webb, 2009), small groups of teachers engaged in collaborative planning to identify learning lines in their own instructional materials that included informal, pre-formal and formal representations based on their collective knowledge about a mathematics topic (Webb, Boswinkel & Dekker, 2008). One group of teachers who selected systems of equations as their topic, was able to develop an online, interactive guide[iii] that illustrated how different activities and representations could be used to develop student understanding of the formal mathematics for the domain. This type of planning activity could be used to identify where their instructional resources include important informal and pre-formal representations. It is also important to know which representations are not part of available instructional materials, so that the introductory contexts and preformal models discussed in this chapter can be included as instructional activities to strengthen the learning experience for students.

CONCLUSION

We hope that we have conveyed that the mathematical domain of restrictions includes important meaningful representations that promote students' understanding of equality and equations. The basic relationships described in equations can be explored in a deeper, more thought provoking manner if the equations are not viewed as something to solve. Rather, equations should also be understood as a representation of a restricted relationship.

Systems of equations can then be viewed as a binding combination of relationships that describe a situation – multiple equations or inequalities that work together to describe different aspects of a whole. One of the common errors that students make when they are first introduced to a system is to focus on the solution of one part (or find a solution that works for only one equation) without reconciling if that solution holds true in the other equations or inequalities used to describe the system.

An approach that embodies principles of progressive formalization (Van Reeuwijk, 2001; Webb & Meyer, 2007) will likely be initially more accessible to students and invite alternative ways of reasoning algebraically about the problem. The contextual referents can serve as reminders of why more formal approaches work as they explore more formal, symbolic representations devoid of context (Gravemeijer, 1994).

NOTES

i   The figures on this page are adapted from solutions given in Webb, Hedges & Abels, 2006, p. 8A.
ii In this case, the letters in the equation are not variables since they represent a set price for each item. Rather, they are abbreviations for the items being sold. If the prices for each item were dynamic or optional, then E and P could be considered variables.
iii This guide can be found at http://tinyurl.com/bpeme-systems

REFERENCES

Amerom, B. van (2002). *Reinvention of early algebra*. Utrecht: CD-beta press.

Carpenter, T.C., Franke, M.L., & Levi, L. (2003). *Thinking mathematically: integrating arithmetic and algebra in elementary school*. Portsmouth, NH: Heinemann.

Faulkner, K., Levi, L., & Carpenter, T. C. (1999). Children's understanding of equality: a foundation for algebra. *Teaching Children Mathematics, 6*, 232-236.

Gallistel C.R., & Gelman R. (2000). Non-verbal numerical cognition: from reals to integers. *Trends in cognitive sciences, 4*(2), 59-65.

Gravemeijer, K.P.E. (1994). *Developing realistic mathematics education*. Utrecht, the Netherlands: CD-Beta press/Freudenthal Institute.

Joseph, G.G. (2000). *The crest of the peacock; the non-European roots of mathematics*. Princeton NJ: Princeton University Press.

Kilpatrick, J., Swafford, J., & Findell, B. (Eds.) (2001). *Adding it up: helping children learn mathematics*. Washington, DC: National Academy Press.

Kindt, M., Abels, M., Dekker, T., Meyer, M.R., Pligge M.A., & Burrill, G. (2006). Comparing quantities. In Wisconsin Center for Education Research & Freudenthal Institute (Eds.), *Mathematics in context*. Chicago: Encyclopædia Britannica, Inc.

Kindt, M., Wijers, M., Spence, M.S., Brinker, L.J., Pligge, M.A., Burrill, J., & Burrill, G. (2006). Graphing equations. In Wisconsin Center for Education Research & Freudenthal Institute (Eds.), *Mathematics in context*. Chicago: Encyclopædia Britannica, Inc.

Meyer, M.R., Dekker, T., & Querelle, N. (2001). Context in Mathematics Curricula. *Mathematics Teaching in the Middle School, 6*(9), 522-527.

Reeuwijk, M. van (1995). *The role of realistic situations in developing tools for solving systems of equations*. Paper presented at the Annual Meeting of the American Educational Research Association, San Francisco, CA. Retrieved April, 8th, 2010 from http://www.fisme.uu.nl/publicaties/literatuur/3781.pdf.

Reeuwijk, M. van (2001). From informal to formal, progressive formalisation: an example on solving systems of equations. In H. Chick, K. Stacey, J. Vincent & J. Vincent (Eds.), *Proceedings of the 12th international commission on mathematical instruction (ICMI) study conference 'the future of the teaching and learning of algebra', Vol. 2* (pp. 613-620). Melbourne: University of Melbourne.

Starkey P., Spelke E., & Gelman R. (1990). Numerical abstraction by human infants. *Cognition, 36*(2), 97-127.

Webb, D. C. (2008). Design Principles for Professional Development: What Should Teachers Know about Mathematics in Context? In M.R. Meyer, C. Langrall, F. Arbaugh, D.C. Webb & M. Hoover (Eds.), *Lessons Learned in Implementing Mathematics Curricula: Ten Years of the ShowMe Project* (pp. 161-171). Charlotte, NC: Information Age Publishing, Inc.

Webb, D. C. (2009). Designing professional development for assessment. *Educational designer, 1*(2), 1-26. Retrieved April, 8th, 2010 from: http://www.educationaldesigner.org/ed/volume1/issue2/article6.

Webb, D.C., Boswinkel, N., & Dekker, T. (2008). Beneath the tip of the iceberg: using representations to support student understanding. *Mathematics teaching in the middle school, 14*(2), 110-114.

Webb, D.C., Hedges, T., & Abels, M. (2006). Comparing quantities, teacher guide. In Wisconsin Center for Education Research & Freudenthal Institute (Eds.), *Mathematics in context*. Chicago: Encyclopaedia Britannica, Inc.

Webb, D.C., Krusi, J., Wijers, M., & de Haan, D. (2006). Graphing equations, teacher guide. In Wisconsin Center for Education Research & Freudenthal Institute (Eds.), *Mathematics in context*. Chicago: Encyclopaedia Britannica, Inc.

Webb, D.C., & Meyer, M.R. (2007). The case of mathematics in context. In Christian Hirsch (Ed.), *Perspectives on design and development of school mathematics curricula* (pp. 81-94). Reston, VA: NCTM.

MICHIEL DOORMAN, PAUL DRIJVERS

6. ALGEBRA IN FUNCTION

The function is a special kind of dependence, that is, between variables which are distinguished as dependent and independent. (...) This – old fashioned – definition stresses the phenomenologically important element: the directedness from something that varies freely to something that varies under constraint. (Freudenthal, 1983, p. 496).

INTRODUCTION

The teaching and learning of the concept of function is strongly related with symbol sense and algebraic skills. Dealing with functions depends on and supports understanding variables, manipulating formulas and relating representations such as tables, graphs and formulas. Lack of algebraic awareness makes reasoning with functions very difficult if not impossible.

The example shown in Figure 1 illustrates the relationship between functions and algebra. The task for the students is to compare and to reason with two cell phone offers. This activity is part of an introduction to the function concept through a series of open ended activities supposed to reveal the students' thinking, to evoke the need for organizing series of calculations and to provide opportunities for the teacher to introduce aspects of dependency relationships.

Two offers from a cell phone company
Tom Often: monthly subscription charge € 7.50, plus 25 cents per minute. The first 30 minutes are free.
Tom Seldom: monthly subscription charge € 22.50, plus 15 cents per minute. The first 80 minutes are free.
> Suppose you call 100 minutes each month. Which offer would you choose?
> When would you change from one offer to the other?

Figure 1. Cell phone task

In a teaching experiment, this task invited the students' situational reasoning, in which functions emerged as algebraic generalizations of input-output calculations. The variety of solution strategies and uses of representations students came up with illustrate their attempts to invent ways to organize the situation mathematically, i.e., to organize repeated calculations, define variables and use various representations. Some students tried to organize their repeated calculations by systematically writing

P. Drijvers (ed.), Secondary Algebra Education, 119–135.

them in a list (poster on the left in Figure 2). This helped them to see the pattern in the calculation, and to apply this pattern to a new situation. In fact, the way in which these students listed their calculations already resembles an input-output relationship (the first number varies over the input values). However, calculations on other posters were less structured and the input-output pattern was less clear. The students' attempts to use formulas to describe the calculations for the two cell phone offers are shown in the poster on the right in Figure 2. Although the formulas are not in conventional notation, they show that these students identified the two variables of the dependency relationship (m for minutes and b for costs).

Such strategies can be used by the teacher to build upon the students' intuitive ideas. In a teaching experiment, the teacher discussed the results and compared the different solution strategies. New mathematical goals emerged in this discussion: repeated calculations are time consuming, general patterns can be found in the calculation procedures, these patterns can be described with input-output machines, different representations are useful for different purposes. The discussion served as an introduction to the emerging function concept, and invited the understanding of the variable concept and the methods for constructing and manipulating formulas.

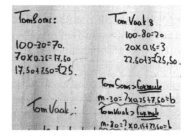

Figure 2. Posters of students' calculations

In this chapter we will first address the function concept: what is a function and which faces does this mathematical concept have? Next, attention is paid in more detail to the different notations and representations of functions. After this, we address the relationship between the function strand and other strands within algebra education.

An affordance of the function concept is grasping change. Studying change and variation will eventually lead students into calculus. The next section, therefore, addressed the function as a bridge between algebra and calculus.

Traditionally, curricula are aligned from linear functions to quadratic to polynomials, and after that include other types of functions such as trigonometry, exponential and logarithmic functions. Along such a function line students have to master the algebraic skills that are related to dealing with the corresponding formulas. As an alternative, the final section discusses a tilted approach to teaching functions and its consequences for algebra.

WHAT IS A FUNCTION?

In order to investigate the role of the function concept within algebra education, and its particular relation to the patterns and formulas strand and the restriction strand described in earlier chapters, a further analysis of the essence of the concept is needed. In this section, therefore, we explore different views on the concept of function.

The word 'function' in its mathematical sense was first used by Leibniz in 1673 (Eves, 1990; Ponte, 1992). It was derived from the Latin word 'fungor', which means 'I carry out a task'. Later, in 1718, Bernoulli defined a function as 'a quantity composed of variables and constants'. In the 1750s, Euler described a function as 'an analytical expression' and as a quantity being a function of another quantity, if the value of the first is determined by the value of the latter. In other words: if x stands for an independent, variable quantity, then all quantities that depend on x, or are determined by x, are seen as functions of x.

Nowadays, set theory forms the basis of the function concept: A function links one set to another, and is seen as a set of ordered pairs. This is clearly expressed in the Dirichlet-Bourbaki definition, formulated in 1934:

> f is a function from one set to another, say A to B, if f is a subset of the Cartesian product of A (the domain) and B (the range or codomain), such that for every $a \in A$ there is exactly one $b \in B$ with $(a, b) \in f$.

Even if the Dirichlet-Bourbaki description is the currently used mathematical definition, one may wonder how useful it is for pedagogical purposes at the level of secondary mathematics education. We all know that there can be a gap between formal definitions of mathematical conceptions and the images that students have (Vinner & Dreyfuss, 1989). Freudenthal considers the Dirichlet-Bourbaki definition as not very appropriate for teaching: "It obscures the essential action of assigning directed from A to B". As the introductory quote of this chapter already witnesses, Freudenthal stresses the causal dependency character of a function:

> Indeed, the very origin of function is stating, postulating, producing, reproducing dependence (or connection) between variables occurring in the physical, social, mental world, that is, in and between these worlds.
> (Freudenthal, 1983, p. 494)

Examples of dependency relations in which time is the independent variable are dynamic processes such as motion, growth, decay, and trend. Speed usually is a function of time as well. But time is just one of the possible independent variables:

- The light intensity of a lamp at a certain position is a function of the distance from that position to the lamp; in fact, the intensity is proportional to the inverse of the square of the distance:

$$I = \frac{c}{d^2}$$

- The area of a circle is a function of its radius; $A = \pi \cdot r^2$

- In the lens example presented in Chapter 1, the image distance b depends on the object distance v, provided that the focal distance f of the lens is fixed. This functional relationship is described algebraically as

$$v \to \frac{f \cdot v}{v - f}$$

- In the V-pattern example in Chapter 3, the n-th V-number can be described by
$$V(n) = 2n + 1$$

The nice thing about these algebraic representations is that you can easily put in a numeric value for the independent variable, to calculate the corresponding output value. In such an activity, the concept image of the function is the input-output view, in which the 'function machine' calculates output values according to a stepwise procedure. If we are interested in how the intensity of the lamp changes as we move away from it, the concept image includes a dynamic, co-variance view. Finally, if we consider the lens example and study properties of the functions for different values of the focal distance f, we see each of the functions as a mathematical object which is a member of a class of similar objects.

These considerations lead to the distinction of three main elements in the students' concept image of function (Drijvers et al., 2007; Oehtrman et al., 2008; Ponce, 2007; Vinner & Dreyfuss, 1989):

1. The function as an input-output assignment
   The function is an input-output assignment that helps to organize and to carry out a calculation process. This initially somewhat vague notion gradually gets more nuances: how does the output depend on the input, how does the input determine the output?

2. The function as a dynamic process of co-variation
   This concerns the notion that the independent variable, while running through the domain set, causes the dependent variable to run through the co-domain. The dependent variable co-varies with the independent. Initially, the linked change may be noticed in a somewhat phenomenological way. Next, the question emerges of how and why this process of joint dynamics takes place.

3. The function as a mathematical object
   A function is a mathematical object which can be represented in different ways, such as arrow chains, tables, graphs, formulas, phrases, each providing a different view on the same object. The concept image is an integrated function notion, which allows for reasoning with functions on a global level.

These three elements of the function concept can be linked to the process-object duality, which was identified in Chapter 1 as one of the difficulties of algebra. The input-output assignment view and dynamic co-variation view stress the process character of the function: it is an action, it takes the input value and processes it to find the output. The mathematical object view clearly relates to the object character of the function: it is a 'thing', which can be a member of a family, or can be subjected to higher order processes such as differentiation, or may even act as unknown in a differential equation. In line with Sfard's claims on the procedural preceding the structural (Sfard, 1991), we suggest that the three elements should be addressed in the above order. Furthermore, the three different views on functions affect the representations that are appropriate in problem solving processes, which is the topic of the next section.

FUNCTION NOTATIONS AND REPRESENTATIONS

Function notations

Reasoning and communicating about functions require notations. To denote a function, different notations are used, each highlighting specific aspects of the function concept and its use in the particular situation. One of the most common notations in mathematics is the 'equation notation', as for example in $f(x) = (x-3)^2 + 5$. In this notation, which was introduced by Euler, the meaning of the equal sign can be ambiguous. It is unclear if the above formula is a definition of a function f, or if f has already been defined earlier and the equal sign indicates an equation: for which value of x is $f(x)$ equal to $(x-3)^2 + 5$? Usually, this ambiguity does not lead to confusion in the context of the problem situation. The ambiguity can be avoided by using ':=' for definitions and '=' for equations, but this may be too formalistic.

Another, related function notation is the '$y =$' notation: $y = (x-3)^2 + 5$. Compared to the previous one, this notation obscures the distinction between independent and dependent variables: even if it is likely that y is considered a function of x, this is not made explicit by adding an argument to y, as was the case in the '$f(x) =$' notation. Furthermore, the letters x and y may be associated with the axes in the Cartesian plane, and as such this notation has a strong association with the graphical representation of a function. The '$y =$' notation may be transformed into an implicit form as well, such as $(x-3)^2 + y = -5$. In the latter notation, it is still open which variable will get the role of the independent, and which one is considered as dependent. In these notations, different functions can be distinguished through different names or subscripts, such as f, g, h, or f_1, f_2, f_3, or, as is common on some graphing calculators, $y_1, y_2, y_3, ...$

The above notations share a somewhat structural, static character, which does not stress the input-output process character of functions. This is different for the arrow notation: $x \rightarrow (x-3)^2 + 5$. This notation highlights the operational input-output character of the function, and as a consequence its co-variation aspect. It can be preceded by a function name, and to put in a slightly tautological way, we could even write $f : x \rightarrow f(x)$. This is not very informative for students, but it does shows the difference between f as the name of the function, and $f(x)$ as the output value of the calculation procedure for an input x.

Educational systems show different preferences and choices concerning function notations. Also, mathematics and science have different function notation traditions (Freudenthal, 1983). In mathematics, characters such as f, g, h, ..., are used as function names, while x, y, a, b, c, ..., represent input and output variables, and parameters, which often are detached from meaning. In science domains such as kinematics, s, v, and a are physical quantities that implicitly represent functions, i.e. functions of time. Students need to be aware of the different conventions, and be alert for possible confusion. For example, in a mathematics course $d(m)$ may refer to a function d of m, whereas in science $d(\text{m})$ may denote a distance d expressed in meters as length unit.

We do not claim that one particular function notation or convention is to be preferred above others. We just want to point out that there are different notations and traditions, which may be good to address explicitly in order to avoid confusion and to strengthen the general features of the function concept.

Function representations

Besides different notations, functions have different representations. The main function representations are verbal descriptions, tables, graphs and the algebraic formulas. Additional representations may be arrow chains, nomograms, flow charts, ... Ideally, all these representations are part of students' concept image; together, the representations form an integrated, versatile and rich function concept. In Figure 3, possible successive representations of the calculation recipe of the earlier cell phone example (Figure 1) are shown. These subsequent representations suggest a possible progressive mathematization trajectory for functions, and reflect the three aspects of the function concept image outlined in the previous section.

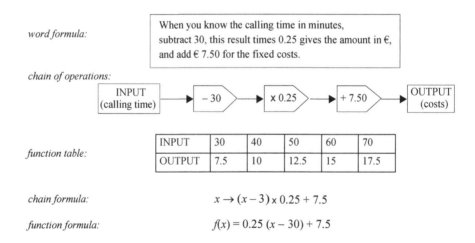

Figure 3. A chain of function representations

An important aspect of a rich function concept is the ability not only to understand and use each of the function representations, but also to relate them, to translate properties of one representation into properties of another, and in this way to connect the different representations (Janvier, 1987, 1996; Van Streun, 2000). In order to acquire such a versatile understanding of function and the affordances and constraints of the representations, tasks have been designed that specifically focus on relations between representations (e.g. Swan, 2008). Figure 4 shows such a task, in which cards contain function representations, some of which created by a computer tool which students used before (Boon et al., 2008). The task for the students is to match corresponding representations and to explain how one can be sure the match is correct.

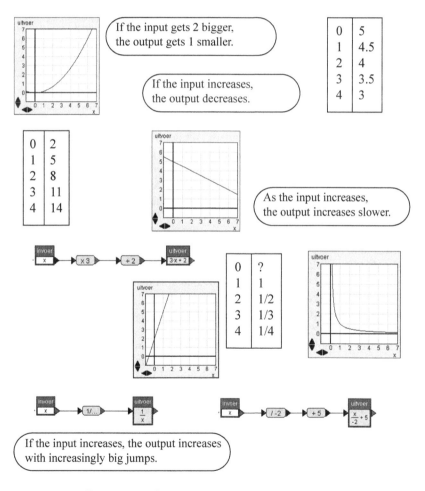

Figure 4. Matching representations (Boon et al., 2008)

In this section, we saw a variety of function notations and representations, that each afford specific views on the function concept. As mathematics teacher or educator, it is good to be aware of these connotations and to design algebra education so that students become equipped with a repertoire of notations and representations, with the ability to make appropriate choices and to relate the different notations and representations to each other.

FUNCTIONS AND ALGEBRA

Functions in relation to algebra strands

In Chapter 1, we distinguished three main strands within secondary algebra education, namely patterns and formulas, restrictions, and functions. The two preceding chapters address patterns and formulas and restrictions, respectively. How does the function strand relate to the two others, and which particular role plays the function strand within algebra at school?

In the patterns and formulas strand, the patterns can be described by formulas. In the dot pattern example in Chapter 4, the number of dots is represented by $(N-1)^2$, with N being the rank order of the pattern. While this may seem to be a somewhat static algebraic expression, its values are calculated by substitution of values for N, and as such the number of dots is a function of the rank order of the pattern. If we consider the change of the number of dots while N increases, the character of N changes from placeholder to an independently changing quantity, and the number of dots becomes *a function of* the rank order N.

As an illustration of the restrictions strand, Chapter 5 gives an example with prices of erasers and pens, which lead to a system of equations: $2 \cdot E + P = 65$, $E + P = 55$. The variables E and P are unknowns here, and once a value for one of the two is substituted, the other can be calculated. If there is a reason to investigate how the number of erasers *depends on* the number of pens, the functional aspect comes into view, and the first equation might be better represented in an explicit notation: $E = (65 - P)/2$.

These brief examples from other algebra strands show that algebraic problem situations may invite a functional view. If the situation can be described in terms of input-output processes, of dependency relationships in which the independent variable changes and evokes co-variance, the functional view is connected to the patterns and formulas and restriction strands. Even if algebraic expressions and formulas are important ways to represent functions, the function perspective is different because of its dynamic dependency perspective and its representational tools.

Functions as a motive for algebra

As formulas and expressions are important ways to represent functions, the use of functions may provide interesting opportunities for algebraic work. We present three short examples. The first example refers to the 'multiplying lines' task in Chapter 8, in which the graphs of two linear functions and their product function are drawn. Questions about specific properties of the 'product graph' and the two lines are: Which relations exist between the zeros? What can you say about the vertex of the parabola? Which conditions do the linear functions need to fulfil in order for the parabola to touch the *x*-axis? Is each parabola the 'product graph of two lines'? Answering these questions requires algebraic reasoning. This type of task with graphs as the starting point for manipulations with formulas can easily be extended to sums and quotients of graphs (Figure 5).

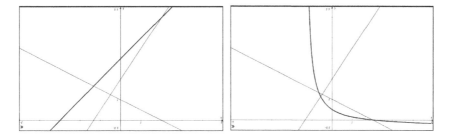

Figure 5. Sum and quotient graphs of two linear functions

A second example of algebraic activity while working on functions has a more theoretical character and concerns the derivation of the product rule for differentiation from the chain rule. It is more than just an algebraic exercise, as it also provides insight in the relationships between the rules for differentiation. The idea is to differentiate $(f+g)^2$ as well as its expanded form. To shorten notations, we write *f* and *g* for $f(x)$ and $g(x)$, respectively.

$$(f+g)^2 = f^2 + 2f \cdot g + g^2$$

Differentiation of left and right hand side with the chain rule leads to:

$$2(f+g) \cdot (f'+g') = 2f \cdot f' + 2(f \cdot g)' + 2g \cdot g'$$

Expanding the brackets in the left hand side leads to terms that are cancelled out. After division by 2, we end up with the product rule for differentiation:

$$g \cdot f' + f \cdot g' = (f \cdot g)'$$

The third and final example shows that analytic geometry, and graphs of parametric curves in particular, may invite algebra (Drijvers & Kindt, 1998). In the first task shown in Figure 6, the graphical suggestion that the Lissajous curve indeed is a parabola in case $t = 0$ begs for algebraic verification:

$$y = \cos(2t) = 2 \cdot (\cos t)^2 - 1 = 2x^2 - 1$$

An interesting follow-up question would be to find other values for parameter a so that the curve is a parabola. The second task in Figure 6 is to verify that the parametric curve has the given equation, which appeals for algebraic skills with trigonometric functions. Parametric curves such as the Lissajous family, which students can explore graphically with technological means such as computer software or the graphing calculator, provide an inspiring and natural source for the use, development and maintenance of algebraic skills.

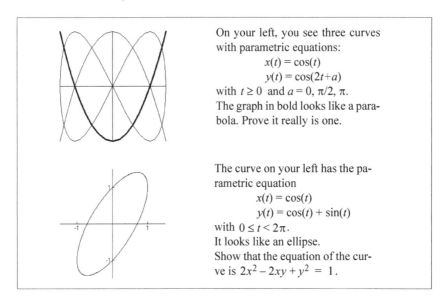

On your left, you see three curves with parametric equations:
$$x(t) = \cos(t)$$
$$y(t) = \cos(2t+a)$$
with $t \geq 0$ and $a = 0, \pi/2, \pi$.
The graph in bold looks like a parabola. Prove it really is one.

The curve on your left has the parametric equation
$$x(t) = \cos(t)$$
$$y(t) = \cos(t) + \sin(t)$$
with $0 \leq t < 2\pi$.
It looks like an ellipse.
Show that the equation of the curve is $2x^2 - 2xy + y^2 = 1$.

Figure 6. Parabola and ellipse as Lissajous figure

To summarize this section, we notice that on the one hand, the function view adds dynamic dependence to the more static patterns and restriction views within school algebra. On the other hand, working with functions and their algebraic representations leads to the development and practice of algebraic manipulation skills.

The above examples, which aim to make these claims more concrete, have an analytical character. The role of the function as a main concept in both algebra and calculus will be explored in more detail in the next section.

ALGEBRA AND CALCULUS

The relationship between algebra and calculus has a dual nature. On the one hand, algebraic competence is needed to solve problems within calculus. For instance, it is necessary to recognize structures of formulas for identifying the appropriate differentiation rules, and for applying these rules correctly. Moreover, a strong and flexible understanding of the variable concept is needed for reasoning with expressions such as $f(x + \Delta x)$. On the other hand, the algebraic procedures for computing a derivative may also disguise the underlying concepts of instantaneous change and difference quotient. This two-sidedness of the role of algebra in calculus requires careful considerations of both teaching and learning trajectories and of the underlying models and representations.

As a means to bridge algebra and calculus, we argue in this section that students take the history of this topic into account and deal exhaustively with discrete sums and differences before entering into continuous calculus techniques (Kindt, 1997). This will enable them to develop understanding of the relationship between differences and sums as a preparation for differentiation and integration, and to understand current notational conventions and graphs.

Calculus is a theory about change and has largely been developed in the context of understanding motion. This context forms one of the basic motives for calculus: to establish the relationship between distance travelled and displacement or velocity. A first example of the algebraic reasoning, therefore, concerns the discrete relationship between taking sums and differences in this context. Suppose $s_0, s_1, s_2, \ldots$ is a sequence of distances travelled, and d is the sequence of corresponding displacements:

$$d_0 = s_1 - s_0, \; d_1 = s_2 - s_1, \ldots d_{n-1} = s_n - s_{n-1}$$

Combining the two results in

$$d_0 + d_1 + \ldots + d_{n-1} = s_n - s_0$$

This equality represents a rather obvious fact: the addition of consecutive displacements results in the final distance covered. In general, a similar mathematical relationship between sums and differences holds. Let a graph of a quantity S be given. Define successive differences $D(k) = S(k+1) - S(k)$. From the graph it can be seen that the sum of all differences $D(0) + D(1) + \ldots + D(n-1) = S(n) - S(0)$ (see Figure 7).

In chapter 4 (Patterns and formulas) we have seen a special case of this general relationship between sums and differences. The differences between successive squares are successive odd numbers: $1 - 0 = 1; 4 - 1 = 3; 9 - 4 = 5; \ldots$ Consequently, the sum of these odd numbers is a square, or more formally: $\Sigma(2k+1) = n^2$.

With this sum-difference property various mathematical relations come within reach. A nice algebraic task is, for example, to prove that $3^{k+1} - 3^k = 2 \cdot 3^k$. Applying the sum-difference property results in the sum formula $\Sigma 3^k = 1/2 \cdot (3^n - 3^0)$. This approach is elaborated in Kindt (1997).

Algebraic activities on relating sums and differences for understanding change prepare students for the relationship between integral and derivative function. This can easily be framed in the context of understanding motion and finding relationships between displacements D and total distance travelled S. In this way, algebraic reasoning and skill go hand in hand with conceptual development on the topic of calculus. Following this line of reasoning, the next step is to decrease time interval length and, finally, to take limits to reach the notion of instantaneous change.

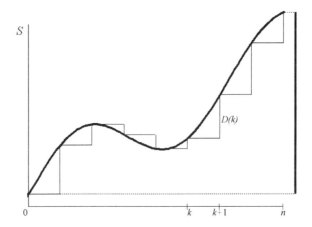

Figure 7. The sum of differences D(k) results in the total change $S(n) - S(0)$

This concept is far from trivial in intuitive reasoning about motion. Beth (1928) describes this in a paradoxical definition of instantaneous velocity:

> The velocity is what it would become if it remained what it was.
> (Beth, 1928, p. 54; translated from Dutch)

Around 1680 Leibniz invented a symbol system for calculus that codifies and simplifies the essential elements of reasoning about instantaneous change. The invention of a literal symbolism (e.g. the derivative of x^2 is $2x$) was essential for the rapid progress in calculus. It allowed for a straightforward algebraic treatment of the concept of change. Problems that once required the ingenuity of Archimedes now become doable for students: one can mechanically carry out the algebraic techniques, even without understanding the underlying principles (Kaput, 1994). As a result, calculus education typically has a strong routine aspect and is a rich source for algebraic work; meanwhile, one should be aware of the long history, including notational and graphical developments, that underpins these techniques.

It is useful to look into this history to gain insight into the conventions and to analyze how and why people tried to organize related problems without having any notion yet about the basic principles of calculus (Doorman & Van Maanen, 2008). For instance, motion graphs with horizontal time axes are used in education to explain the calculus methods. These graphs illustrate the relationship between distance travelled and velocity. In fact, in most mathematics classrooms, such time graphs are used as if they were the only way to express motion. However, history shows that one can also depict changing velocity in a graph with distance travelled along the horizontal axis (the position along a road). What do slope (a quotient of the two displayed variables) and area (a sum of products of the two displayed variables) mean in such a graph? Understanding that slope can be interpreted as velocity in a distance-time graph requires algebraic understanding of its measure.

The issue of the meaning of slope and area becomes even more manifest in the graph in Figure 8. This sports graph supports reasoning like 'it takes *y* seconds to arrive at position *x*'. The position – instead of time – appears as an independent variable displayed along the horizontal axis. Split times of a speed skating race are displayed vertically (with a reference to an average split time). An increasing graph means that the split times increase and that the velocity of the speed skater decreases.

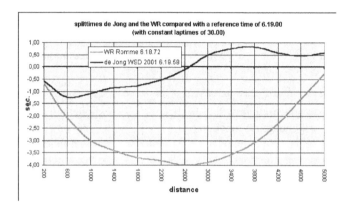

Figure 8. Speed skating graphs

In addition to the relationship between quantities in graphs and their quotients (when calculating slope) or products (when calculating area), Pence (1995) points out the need for an understanding of the variable concept in calculus. He notices that many students starting a calculus course do not realise that $2x$ is twice as far from 0 as x. They are not able to locate $2x$ on a number line when x is already positioned. These students do understand that $2x$ represents a multiplication, but are not able to interpret $2x$ as representing a quantity twice as large as x. Freudenthal (1983) also highlights the required understanding of variables. He argues that variables are often taught and understood as placeholders or letters to be manipulated, and as a result the kinematic understanding that the letters refer to something which varies is lost.

> The effort to suppress the kinematics of the variable goes hand in hand with the annexation of the term 'variable', stripped of its kinematics undertone. (Freudenthal, 1983, p. 493)

Comparison of present-day mathematics with older methods enables us to value our modern notations and conventions, and helps to establish more coherence between algebra, calculus and physics. Historical explorations and algebraic reasoning with sums and differences as support for learning calculus might prevent algebraic algorithms becoming disconnected from their roots (Doorman & Gravemeijer, 2009).

A TILTED APPROACH TO FUNCTIONS

As explained earlier in this chapter, there is a dual relationship between the function strand and the necessary algebraic skills. For instance, dealing with quadratic functions requires the ability to factorize and expand quadratic expressions.

Traditionally, function courses are structured along the increasing mathematical complexity of the objects of study, and the complexity of the corresponding algebraic techniques: first linear functions, solving linear equations, then quadratic functions and quadratic equations, etcetera. The left part of Figure 9 depicts such an approach, with the time as a vertical dimension. Often, much effort is spent on manipulations with variables and expressions. The danger of this approach, however, is that the algebraic manipulations, such as solving quadratic equations, are practiced in isolation and not as elements within a range of possible techniques.

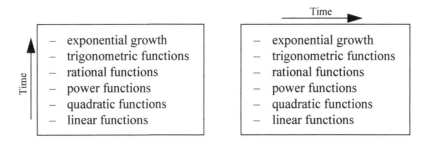

Figure 9. Two ways of structuring a function strand

The right part of Figure 9 shows an alternative approach, in which 'time is tilted'. According to this approach, the study of relationships remains important, but gets a different emphasis. These relationships are presented in contextual problems, and are not limited to linear and quadratic relationships as in traditional curricula: exponential, periodical and more complex relationships are explored in an early stage, and the relevant concepts are developed in parallel rather than sequential. Strategies and problem solving techniques are developed that flexibly can be applied in different situations for different types of relationships: numerical approximation techniques with formulas, graphs and tables, use of zoom tools, study of co-variation, and translations between representations.

To exemplify this tilted approach, Figure 10 shows a comparison task involving linear and exponential growth for 11-12 year olds. The following questions may emerge when the students work on this problem and may evoke more sophisticated representations such as tables and formulas:
– How do you organize your calculations?
– Is there a week in which both offers result in the same amount of money?
– Can you think of an offer that can compete with offer 1?

A pocket money agreement
Suppose you get two offers for pocket money for one year:
1) This week you receive € 0.01 and then every week this amount will be doubled: next week € 0.02, then € 0.04, € 0.08, etcetera.
2) This week you receive € 1.00 and then every week you receive an extra € 1.00.
> Which offer would you choose?

Figure 10. Comparing linear and exponential growth

This example illustrates how a contextual problem can involve linear and exponential growth, and can be used as a motive for needed algebraic skills. These skills are developed together with the problems where they are in use, and together with the representations that are involved: from dealing with word formulas, along intermediate models like arrow chains to graphs, tables and formulas.

In the Netherlands the longitudinal learning trajectory for functions was revised in the nineties of the last century. As a consequence, the algebraic methods and skills needed in this new trajectory were reconsidered and changed according to this tilted approach (Abels, 1996). This resulted in the following algebraic topics in the curriculum for students of age 12 to 16 (Team W12-16, 1992).

1. Manipulate with and translate between representations
   – investigate sum and difference relationships (see also calculus)
   – move and stretch graphs by manipulating parameters
   – transform formulas (including substitution)
2. Solve equations
   – invert arrow chains
   – cover-up methods
   – numerical methods with zooming, extrapolation and interpolation
3. Growth
   – compare relationships
   – analyze relationships (which part is most influential in which domain)
   – use formulas and patterns in tables (e.g. the additive pattern in linear relations and the multiplicative pattern in tables of exponential relations)

This tilted approach in the Dutch curruculum was successful in the sense that it enhances students' flexibility and problem solving skills; however, a danger of limited practice and maintainance of basic skills also became manifest. In the Mathematics in Context project a balance between the two approaches was searched for (WCER

& FI, 2006). Speaking in general, the two structures of the function strand, as presented here, should be considered as two extremes of possible approaches.

Recently, the local debate in the Netherlands shifted focus towards traditional basic skills (see also Schoenfeld, 2004). Students' lack of procedural skills, as experienced by higher education teachers, might be a result of the new curriculum, but may also be influenced by other factors, such as societal changes, national cuts in the expenses for education or a competency-based reform in upper secondary education. The debate led current text book series to restore isolated practice of basic skills at the expense of a more integrated approach. We hope that this recent development will converge towards a balanced algebra curriculum that serves both societal demands in the technological era, and students' further education.

REFERENCES

Abels, M. (1996). A shift in algebra, development and implementation: varia-abilities. In M. Kindt, M. Abels & L.M. Doorman (Eds.), *Working group 13: Curriculum changes in the secondary school* (pp. 3-7). Utrecht: Freudenthal Instituut.

Beth, H.J.E. (1928). Het experimenteel georiënteerde onderwijs in mechanica. [Experiment-oriented mechanics education.] *Euclides 5*, 49-60.

Boon, P., Doorman, M., Drijvers, P., & Gisbergen, S. van (2008). *Pijlenketting en functie. Een experimentele lessenserie over functies met het applet AlgebraPijlen voor klas 2 h/v.* [Arrow chain and function. An experimental lesson sequence on function using the applet AlgebraArrows for grade 8]. Retrieved April, 16th, 2010, from www.fi.uu.nl/tooluse/en.

Doorman, L.M., & Gravemeijer, K.P.E. (2009). Emergent modeling: discrete graphs to support the understanding of change and velocity. *ZDM The International Journal on Mathematics Education 41*(1), 199-211.

Doorman, L.M. & Maanen, J. van (2008). A historical perspective on teaching and learning calculus. *Australian Senior Mathematics Journal, 22*(2), 4-14.

Drijvers, P., Doorman, M., Boon, P., Gisbergen, S. van, & Gravemeijer, K. (2007). Tool use in a technology-rich learning arrangement for the concept of function. In D. Pitta-Pantazi & G. Philippou (Eds.), *Proceedings of the V Congress of the European Society for Research in Mathematics Education CERME5* (pp. 1389-1398). Larnaca, Cyprus: University of Cyprus.

Drijvers, P., & Kindt, M. (1998). *Differentiaal- en Integraalrekening deel 6: Trillingspatronen.* [Differential and integral calculus: oscillation patterns.] Utrecht: Freudenthal Instituut. Retrieved April, 19th, from http://www.fi.uu.nl/wiki/index.php/Profi.

Eves, H. (1990). *Foundations and Fundamental Concepts of Mathematics, Third Edition.* Mineola, NY: Dover.

Freudenthal, H. (1983). *Didactical phenomenology of mathematical structures.* Dordrecht, the Netherlands: Reidel.

Janvier, C. (1987). *Problems of Representation in the Teaching and Learning Mathematics.* Hillsdale NJ: Lawrence Erlbaum Associates.

Janvier, C. (1996). Modelling and Initiation into Algebra. In N. Bednarz, C. Kieran & L. Lee (Eds.), *Approaches to Algebra: Perspectives for Research and Teaching* (pp. 225-236), Dordrecht: Kluwer Academic Publishers.

Kaput, J.J. (1994). Democratizing Access to Calculus: New Routes to Old Roots. In A.H. Schoenfeld (Ed.), *Mathematical Thinking and Problem Solving* (pp. 77-156). Washington: Mathematical Association of America.

Kindt, M. (1997). Som en verschil, afstand en snelheid. [Sum and difference, distance and speed]. Utrecht, the Netherlands; Freudenthal Institute.

Oehrtman, M.C., Carlson, M.P., & Thompson, P.W. (2008). Foundational Reasoning Abilities that Promote Coherence in Student's Function Understanding. In M.P. Carlson & C. Rasmussen (Eds.), *Making the connection: Research and practice in undergraduate mathematics* (pp. 27-42). Washington, DC: Mathematical Association of America. Retrieved April, 2nd, from
http://mathed.asu.edu/media/pdf/pubs/carlson/Oehrtman-Carlson-Thompson_final.pdf

Pence, B.J. (1995). *Relationships between understandings of operations and success in beginning calculus.* Paper presented at the North American chapter of the PME, Columbus, Ohio.

Ponce, G. (2007). Critical Juncture Ahead: Proceed with Caution to Introduce the Concept of Function. *Mathematics Teacher, 101*(2), 136-144.

Ponte, J.P. (1992). The history of the concept of function and some educational implications. *The Mathematics Educator, 3*(2), 3-8. Retrieved April, 2nd, from http://math.coe.uga.edu/TME/Issues/v03n2/v3n2.html.

Schoenfeld, A. (2004). The math wars. *Educational policy, 18*(1), 253-286.

Sfard, A. (1991). On the dual nature of mathematical conceptions: Reflections on processes and objects as different sides of the same coin. *Educational Studies in Mathematics, 22*, 1-36.

Streun, A. van (2000). Representations in applying functions. *International Journal of Mathematical Education in Science and Technology, 31*(5), 703-725.

Swan, M. (2008). A Designer Speaks. *Educational Designer, 1.* Retrieved October, 22nd, 2009 from http://www.educationaldesigner.org/ed/volume1/issue1/article3.

Team W12-16 (1992). *Achtergronden van het nieuwe leerplan. Wiskunde 12-16: band 1.* [Backgrounds of the new curriculum Math12-16, Vol. I.] Utrecht / Enschede, the Netherlands: Freudenthal Instituut & Stichting LeerplanOntwikkeling.

Vinner, S., & Dreyfuss, T. (1989). Images and definitions for the concept of function. *Journal for Research in Mathematics Education, 20*(4), 356-366.

Wisconsin Center for Education Research & Freudenthal Institute (Eds.) (2006). *Mathematics in context.* Chicago: Encyclopaedia Britannica.

MARTIN KINDT

7. PRINCIPLES OF PRACTICE

Advocates of insightful learning are often accused of being soft on training.
Rather than against training, my objection to drill is that it endangers retention
of insight. There is, however a way of training – including memorization –
where every little step adds something to the treasure of insight: training integrated with insightful learning.
(Freudenthal, 1991, p. 114)

GOODBYE TO SKILLS

On 25 October 2005, an article titled *'Long division.. what is that?'* was published
on the front page of a Dutch newspaper (*NRC Handelsblad*); its subject was the
shortcomings of first-year students at one of the technological universities in the
Netherlands. At the beginning of their study, these students are given an entry test to
evaluate their basic algebra skills. The results from 2005 were pathetic: only 4% of
the first-year students earned a passing score. Of course, this result could stem directly from the test's authors being uninformed about current secondary education.
However, when constructing the test, an important role was given to a mathematics
teacher from secondary education. An analysis of the problems in the test (partly in
multiple-choice form) shows that the type of problem certainly did not link up seam-
lessly with the content of the current mathematics textbooks; nevertheless, one
would expect a much better – if not completely opposite – result from graduates of a
pre-academic programme. The students who failed the test were required to take a
brush-up course. One of the conclusions about this course was the following: "Focus
especially on adding and simplifying fractions." This obviously indicates a serious
weakness in secondary education.

Of course, we should realize that complaints about the algebra skills of secondary
school students and university students are nothing new. Unfortunately, the serious-
ness and number of complaints have increased strongly in recent years. This applies
not only to observers outside secondary education, but also to those within. Some observers attribute the problematic algebra skills to the spirit of the time: accuracy and
concentration – to put it mildly – no longer enjoy their former status. Others blame
the current mathematics programme, which pays only limited attention to symbolic
manipulation or the permanent availability of advanced computation aids, such as
the graphing calculator. Still other people claim that it is precisely these electronic
aids that make algebra skills – with the accompanying ready knowledge – more or
less obsolete.

P. Drijvers (ed.), Secondary Algebra Education, 137–178.

Regardless of the cause, the lack of basic skills and self-confidence in the area of algebra is a fact we can no longer ignore. Of course, the question is, should we do anything about it, and if so, what? In any case, it is clear that practice plays a role in this process. But what kind of exercises should be used and how should they be applied? While some observers see promise in the reintroduction of drill-and-practice, without all that didactical gobbledygook, others are wary because that would push insightful action into the background, leading to what Van Dormolen (1975) called 'routine based on tricks'. Instead, Van Dormolen proposed 'routine based on insight', where problems are not only approached adequately and intentionally, but can also be solved within a reasonable length of time. In fact, this was his definition of 'skill', and this description is highly compatible with our ideas about the desirable orientation of practice in algebra.

WHY SKILLS ARE IMPORTANT AFTER ALL

An entry test, like the one given at the technical university mentioned above, is specifically intended to test only 'procedural skills'. Virtually all questions can be answered 'mechanically', i.e. with a symbolic calculator. However, such an apparatus is only worthwhile if the user is capable of reading the problems and converting them into a language that can be entered on the calculator. This requires a certain degree of knowledge about the grammar of algebraic language, which can only be obtained through practice.

The mastery of procedural skills, as measured by the test, is certainly not a goal that stands on its own. If the practiced techniques are not used for other purposes or are not linked to other topics, doing countless exercises leads to short-term success at best. If the techniques are forgotten and/or cannot be applied in the appropriate situations, then this practice is a waste of time. This is why many algebra techniques and rules have disappeared from the Dutch curriculum, beginning around 1960.

Many techniques and rules have been thrown overboard as useless ballast, such as long division of polynomials, manipulating surds, rationalizing the denominator and the formula for sum and product the roots of a quadratic equation, to name only a few. However, people perhaps neglected the fact that a number of these discarded topics can provide an opportunity to maintain or improve skills that were acquired previously. After all, without repeated practice, no actual skills in working with formulas can be acquired.

We will now use several examples to demonstrate why we continue to value the mastery of basic algebra skills, in any case for students at the pre-academic level.

First, we will describe a recent experience with a selected group of students at Utrecht University's Junior College, who were studying algebra at the pre-academic level. While addressing iterative processes, the recursion formula

$$x_{n+1} = ax_n + b$$

came up for discussion. An essential and sufficient precondition for the existence of a stable equilibrium in the process represented by such an equation is $-1 < a < 1$. This can be understood at an intuitive level with the aid of graphs (Figure 1).

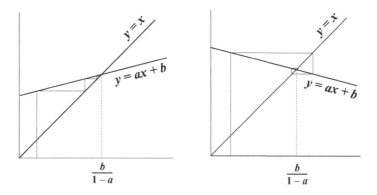

Figure 1. Graphing an iterative process

A question that arises naturally from this situation is to ask the students to express the equilibrium value in a and b, which amounts to solving the equation for x:

$$x = ax + b$$

But this was asking too much of these students. The teacher saw an opportunity to use a Socratic discussion to find the answer

$$\frac{b}{1-a}$$

But he didn't stop there; he put the students on the spot:
Check this solution with substitution by showing that $a \cdot \dfrac{b}{1-a} + b$ is equal to $\dfrac{b}{1-a}$.

This step also took place with the greatest difficulty; it became painfully obvious that algebraic fractions were scarcely practiced in the lower grades of secondary school.

   Although a skilled teacher should be able to make ad hoc repairs of such deficiencies, such interruptions can obviously stall the learning process if they occur too often. After all, when introducing new concepts and techniques and when applying mathematics, teachers continually make assumptions about the knowledge and skills of the students. If such knowledge or skills are lacking, the possibility of reaching a higher level is severely limited, if not blocked entirely. In short, it is only when students have mastered the previous material with insight and technical skill that the focus can shift entirely to a new concept and the corresponding new skill. Stated another way:

   Mastery of skills is an essential precondition for going to a higher level.

139

When practicing techniques, there is always the danger that students will start using 'recipes', which will cause them to lose previously acquired insights. Dijksterhuis (1934) identified this problem. He argued that *students should always be able to account – to themselves and others – for the meaning of the terms that they use and the methods that they apply*. We believe that Dijksterhuis' proposition, although rather utopian, is still a valuable ideal that should be pursued in mathematics education.

Let us illustrate this with a simple example: *why is $(5x)^2$ equal to $25x^2$?* Well, this is because $(5x)^2$ means $5x$ times $5x$, and that is the same as 5 times 5 times x times x, or 25 times x^2. The latter is based on the associative and commutative properties of multiplication, but due to the students' experiences with arithmetic, these properties are self-evident and can be used intuitively.

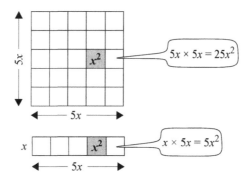

Figure 2. Why is $(5x)^2$ equal to $25x^2$?

This can best be explained with an illustration such as the one shown in Figure 2. The illustration also emphasizes the difference between $(5x)^2$ and $5x^2$, where it should be noted that the interpretation of the latter form is based entirely on a priority rule.

Students must be able to give such simple explanations when they are asked or when they have doubts... let's see, how did that go? To this end, teachers and authors of textbooks should frequently ask the 'why' question. When practicing skills, it is essential that insight should not be submerged, but should indeed be pulled to the surface as regularly as clockwork. This was beautifully formulated by Freudenthal:

> It is most often necessary but not sufficient that algorithms and automatisms are acquired by insight. The learning process must be steered in such a way that sources of insight are not clogged during the process of algorithmization and automatization. This can be achieved, in my view, by returning again and again during the process of algorithmization and automatization, and even afterwards where it fits, to the sources of insight. This process aims at an ever greater consciousness of what initially was subconscious and an ever sharper verbalization

of what initially was not verbalized at all.
(Freudenthal, 1983, p. 209)

We can summarize the above in a unequivocal proposition:
Without insight, there is no skill, and without skill, there is no insight

The applicability of basic algebra, for example to other school subjects or daily life, lies primarily in creating, understanding and using simple algebraic models.

For instance, consider the lookout tower and the panoramic view. Everyone knows from experience that the higher the tower, the further you can see (with an unencumbered view). If a tower is 20 meters tall, the view distance is approximately 16 km. A naïve thought (the illusion of linearity) is that you could see 32 km from a 40 meter high tower. This turns out to not be the case; the view distance is only increased by around 40%. Nevertheless, there is still a kind of proportionality.

The following example is one way you could address this problem in a class.
Imagine an apartment building on the coast with 25 floors.
How far out you can see towards the ocean depends on the number of the floor.
The table below gives the viewing height per floor (in m) and the viewing distance (in km).

story	1	2	3	4	5	6	7	8	9	10	11	12	....
viewing height (m)	3	6	9	12	15	18	21	24	27	30	33	36	....
viewing distance (km)	6.2	8.7	10.7	12.4	13.8	15.1	16.4	17.5	18.6	19.6	20.5	21.4	....

The question is then to find a relationship between the viewing height h and the viewing distance d. A hint would be to look at the internal proportions in the h and d rows. For example, in the table it turns out that '4 times as high' corresponds with '2 times as far', and '9 times as high' corresponds with '3 times as far' and that can lead to the assumption that d^2 is proportional to h or that d is proportional to $\sqrt{h}$. After this, the proportionality factor can be estimated from the table, and the assumption can be checked for various values in the table. This type of thinking in terms of proportionalities is of practical importance in the natural sciences, as well as in fields such as economics.

An advantage of this situation chosen here is that the relationship between d and h can be clearly understood by means of geometry. An introductory question to this topic could be: what should be the relationship between height and viewing distance on the moon? This could perhaps bring the students closer to the idea of relating the problem to vision lines that are tangent to a sphere. The approximation formula that expresses the view distance d in terms of the height h of the viewpoint and the radius r of the sphere is: $d \approx \sqrt{2rh}$. Understanding this formula requires both geometric and algebraic-analytic insight.

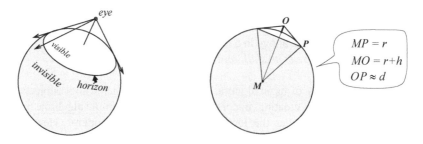

Figure 3. Sketch of the viewing distance problem situation

The height of the tower is relatively small with respect to the radius of the earth or the moon; consequently, the viewing distance d will be nearly the same as the length of the tangent OP (see Figure 3). Applying the Pythagorean theorem to the triangle OMP results in:

$$d^2 \approx OP^2 = OM^2 - MP^2 = (r + h)^2 - r^2 = 2rh + h^2$$

Now, it turns out that

$$\frac{d^2}{h} \approx \frac{2rh + h^2}{h} = 2r + h$$

Because the value of h is negligibly small relative to $2r$, this ultimately leads to the proposed formula.

If we measure the viewing height in meters and the viewing distance in kilometers, then the proportionality factor on the earth is approximately equal to 3.6; this leads to the rule of thumb

$$d \approx 3.6\sqrt{h}$$

This rule can then be used in a problem such as:

> Assume that someone in France wants to build a tower that is high enough that they can see the coast of England from the top, what is the minimum height of such a tower?

We also want to emphasize that the relationship between height and viewing distance is a very rich example; to solve such problems, students not only use vision geometry and perform the algebraic reduction of $(r + h)^2 - r^2$ to $2rh + h^2$ or $h(2r + h)$, they also reason by using approximations.

In addition, we have observed that practicing operations where one quantity is proportional to a rational exponent of the other is very important for algebraic applications. It goes without saying that computational and algebraic skills also play a role in this process.

Good skills in arithmetic and basic algebra have practical benefits.

According to the standard book *Guidelines for Teaching Mathematics* (Johnson & Rising, 1967), one of the aims of computational skills is:

'to promote productive thinking in problem solving, research, and other creative activities.'

We would like to add: to promote self-confidence.

Students who have a certain repertoire of practical computational facts, smart computation methods, algebraic rules and algebraic skills will be less reluctant to tackle standard situations and will have better judgement about whether and how to use a calculator. In that case, the actual brain work consists of fathoming the situation and choosing a suitable strategy. Students who have achieved such an attitude no longer have to shrink from the technical completion of a problem.

Such students, who have acquired a certain degree of mathematical self-confidence, can focus entirely on matters such as:
– How can you tackle the problem?
– What aids are available?
– Does the result agree with your previous estimate or computation?
– After you find a formula, what are the effects on special cases?
– Can you generalize any further?
– Can you relate the result to similar problems?
– ...

In short, students are given the possibility of independently doing mathematics and independently tackling problems. All energy can now be directed to productive thinking.

Good skills in computation and algebra create space for productive mathematics.

HOW WAS IT IN THE PAST, AND WHAT NOW?

Past algebra books contained extensive collections of exercises, but their purpose was also to give teachers a broad assortment of material to choose from. This is obvious when you read the forewords, prefaces, introductions, etc. Not every student had to solve every problem, and the teachers could base their selection on the progress of the class and whether or not they could skip certain sections with complicated reductions of algebraic formulas entirely. These books were characterized by a clear separation between the theory (with examples) and the sections with problems. Contemporary schoolbooks rarely make this distinction, and many problems are actually used to explore or develop a new area of subject matter. If you thumb through the old textbooks, the uniformity of the exercises is very striking. You find long lists of exercises with equations, factorizations, rational expressions, etc., based on the idea of *progressive complexity*. Renowned for their sheer quantity of exercises, the textbooks by Alders (e.g., Alders, 1953) were best-sellers in the 1950s and were reprinted for many years. It was what you could call a 'no-nonsense' textbook series: the sections with theory were extremely brief in comparison to the sections with problems. If there was a didactical approach, it was hidden in the sequence of examples and problems. To illustrate his methods, Figure 4 shows a section on adding and subtracting fractions from Alders (1953):

> Property IV. The sum of like fractions is equal to the sum of the numerators divided by the common denominator.
>
> $$\frac{a}{p} + \frac{b}{p} + \frac{c}{p} = \frac{a + b + c}{p}$$

This is because if you multiply both terms by p, you get $a + b + c$. Of course, a corresponding property also applies to the difference of two like fractions.

Therefore: $\dfrac{a}{x} - \dfrac{a-b}{x} + \dfrac{b}{x} = \dfrac{a-(a-b)+b}{x} = \dfrac{2b}{x}$

If you have to add or subtract unlike fractions, you must first convert them into like fractions. The simplest ways to do this is to find the least common multiple of the denominators of the fractions that must be added or subtracted.
For example:

1. $\dfrac{1}{a} + \dfrac{1}{b} = \dfrac{b}{ab} + \dfrac{a}{ab} = \dfrac{b+a}{ab}$

2. $\dfrac{a}{b} - \dfrac{b}{a} = \dfrac{a^2}{ab} - \dfrac{b^2}{ab} = \dfrac{a^2 - b^2}{ab}$

3. $2a - \dfrac{2a^2}{a+b} = \dfrac{2a(a+b) - 2a^2}{a+b} = \dfrac{2a^2 + 2ab - 2a^2}{a+b} = \dfrac{2ab}{a+b}$

4. $\dfrac{x}{x+1} - \dfrac{x}{x+2} = \dfrac{x(x+2) - x(x+1)}{(x+1)(x+2)} = \dfrac{x}{(x+1)(x+2)}$

5. $\dfrac{x}{x-1} - \dfrac{1}{1-x} = \dfrac{x}{x-1} + \dfrac{1}{x-1} = \dfrac{x+1}{x-1}$

6. $\dfrac{a}{b^2 - ab} - \dfrac{b}{a^2 - ab} = \dfrac{a}{b(b-a)} - \dfrac{b}{a(a-b)} = \dfrac{a^2}{ab(b-a)} + \dfrac{b^2}{ab(b-a)} = \dfrac{a^2 + b^2}{ab(b-a)}$

7. $\dfrac{1}{x^2 + xy} + \dfrac{1}{y^2 + xy} = \dfrac{1}{x(x+y)} + \dfrac{1}{y(x+y)} = \dfrac{y+x}{xy(x+y)} = \dfrac{1}{xy}$

Figure 4. A section from Alders (1953)

The section with theory shown here appeared halfway into the first part of the textbook, which was intended for grades 7-9 in pre-academic education. The teacher was expected to provide the explanation, and we can imagine that in this case there must have been a didactical approach of some sort. This was followed by a section with twenty problems, some of which were reasonably similar to the initial examples. Many of the problems were actually at a higher level than those from the previously mentioned entry test of the Dutch technical university. The miscellaneous problems at the end of the chapter were even more difficult. So that is how it was in the 'old days'.

With every change of the Dutch curriculum after 1950 (in 1958, 1968 and 1993), school algebra was significantly simplified, usually under protest from a number of teachers. The most rigorous change took place in 1992. Progressive complification became progressive formalization, a didactical principle that we fully support. However, one could state that in some textbooks the formal manipulations were spread out too far, and algebra chapters provided very little challenge, especially for students at pre-academic levels.

In the newest editions of the textbooks, some changes are apparent, but compared with the 'old days' the algebra remains at a very low level. A survey of experienced mathematics teachers has shown that a number of them need additional practice material for algebra (see Figure 5). The teachers explained that concrete events in the class caused the setting up of separated, additional practicing lessons. Meanwhile, a few arguments emerged from this small-scale survey that reveal intrinsic motivation for mastering algebra by means of drill-and-practice; or as one of the respondents claims, the teachers should be able to transfer their own intrinsic motivation for mathematics to the students. If teachers decided to use additional material, this almost always concerned 'old-fashioned' straightforward algebra exercises. In modern textbooks as well, this phenomenon of purely reproductive exercising is discernible. We previously referred to the dangers of this approach, and we can state it is often counterproductive. Sterk and Perrenet (2005) conclude that making students familiar with computational techniques must go hand-in-hand with allowing them to experience the usefulness of the technique and the usefulness of having a certain repertoire of manipulation skills. This is because more serious problems require targeted manipulations that often deviate from the traditional computation exercises (such as expanding or simplifying expressions).

MARTIN KINDT

Teacher A uses supplementary practice material in the hope that it will help the students do the sums in the book. The practice takes place only during the lesson, in 10-minute sessions to break the monotony of the double period.

Substitute $a = 3$ and $b = 2$ in:

a. $2a^2b$

b. $2a^2b^2 - 2ab$

c. $-3a^2b^3 + 2ab^2$

d. $2a^3b - 3ab^3$

e. $-5ab^2 - 2a^2 + 3b^3$

Teacher B believes that computational and algebraic skills receive insufficient attention in the current programme and are therefore learnt too superficially. He uses his own practice material to replace the exercises from the book.

Compute and simplify:

a. $\frac{2}{3} \times \frac{1}{5}$

b. $\frac{2}{3} \times \frac{4}{9}$

c. $\frac{2}{3} \times \frac{3}{7}$

d. $\frac{3}{8} \times \frac{2}{3}$

e. $\frac{5}{9} \times \frac{9}{25}$

According to teacher C, mathematics is more enjoyable if students do not continuously feel uncertain due to their lack of technical algebra skills. He practices with his students in grades 10 and 11, and develops skill tests for this purpose.

Teacher D once noticed that a student thoughtlessly computed 6×0 with his calculator. This led him to develop a brush-up programme for arithmetic and algebra. It became a type of dictation exercise: 'the Rambam computation contest'. A few gems from this excellent programme are shown below.

Factor the following expressions (also consider special products):

$1 + 2b^2 + b^4$

$x^2 + 4 - 4x$

$-x^2 + 64$

$x - y + z + xy - y^2 + yz$

Compute:

$2a \times 3b = \dots\dots$

$2a + 3b = \dots\dots$

$(a - c)(b - c)(c - c) = \dots\dots$

$\dots\dots \times 10a = 5$

$abc : bc$

Figure 5. Four examples of additional activities provided by mathematics teachers

THE ART OF PRACTICE

(...) And then on the board we wrote the numbers from 1 to 100. And then we joined forces to find the numbers that were not in the multiplication tables, such as 7, 11, 13 etc. I helped them a great deal ... we erased all those numbers, and with great relief we noted that not that many were left. The ones that remained, we tackled those combatively. There were four of us: if one of us didn't know something, the other one did. "Twenty is 2 times 10," said Fok with a grin, and then Leentje Roos called out eagerly, "Or 10 times 2." So I said, "And 4 times 5." To which Leentje again replied, "Or 5 times 4." And then I tried, "And 3 times 7." But that caused Kootje Kuiper to protest, "No, it isn't!" And then we started summarizing what we should remember about 20 in the future...
(Thijssen, 1925)

This is a fragment from *Schoolland* by Theo Thijssen (1925). At the beginning of the course, the teacher, Mr Staal, realizes that three of his students have not yet mastered the multiplication tables, and decides to practice with this group for an hour after school. During this process, he has the inspiration to look at the situation from the other side: start with the result, and ask the students to find the tables in which the result appears. This appears to work. Besides the three students who are brushing up on their multiplication tables, another student has to stay after school and do additional work for punishment. While doing her work, she listens to everything, and the next morning she hands the teacher a sheet of paper with the following:
$4 = 2 \times 2$, $6 = 2 \times 3$ or 3×2, $8 = 2 \times 4$ or 4×2, ... till $100 = 10 \times 10$.

"I can also do problems like that," she boasts. And during the next few days, it turns out that the other students have also acquired the taste for doing 'reverse tables'; during the fifteen minutes before school begins, they are all working at the blackboard. Mr Staal writes in his diary:

> This seems to be contagious. They seem to be unable to tolerate that I reserve this scholarship for my separate hours with the three stragglers.

This fragment from *Schoolland*, which, together with *De Gelukkige Klas* ('*The Happy Class*', 1926) should be mandatory reading for every prospective teacher, shows an example of the approach that is emphatically promoted by Treffers and others, which they call *'own productions'*. This simple idea of challenging the students to independently construct 'exercises' could be, or should be, an important aspect of 'modern' algebra teaching.

'Own productions' is not the only didactical theme that emerges from Thijssen's brush-up lesson. His primary idea – 'turn the situation around' – is acknowledged as a valuable principle in practice. Strictly speaking, Thijssen was asking the students to factorize numbers, but he did this long before there was a systematic treatment of factorizing. This is precisely the core of this principle. Although the reversal of an operation will later on be given the status of an algorithm, the students are now given the chance to spontaneously take this step themselves.

Such anticipatory *reverse questions* can, especially due to their puzzle-like character, be stimulating to the students and promote a certain degree of flexibility.

A third principle, which the designer of practice material must always keep in mind, and which is also illustrated in the fragment from *Schoolland*, is to create ***variation in practice formats***. Thijssen first wrote all natural numbers through 100 on the blackboard; he probably made ten rows of ten numbers. Today, we call this the 'hundred field', and the teacher would probably make photocopies and hand them out to the students. In mathematics didactics, the hundred field is one of a variety of practice formats. The didactics of algebra also offers many possibilities for variation: number strips, tables, operation trees, arrow chains, rectangular multiplication models, etc. make it possible to break through the template of monotonous lists of tasks.

Since the implementation of the curriculum for children age 12-16 in the 1990s, an old didactical discovery has re-emerged in many textbooks: ***the cover-up method***; This amounts to covering up a fragment of an algebraic equation, which clarifies the structure. It is worthwhile to practice this method – which also has a larger scope than solving equations – somewhat more systematically.

In the above text, the word 'list' appeared several times. This term is often used in somewhat contemptuously to mean lists of very similar exercises. But we can also use a sequence of exercises in a more positive way by getting away from lists with no mutual coherence. In this regard, we suggest constructing sequences of exercises so that the second exercise in the row is derived from the first, the third from the second, and so on. In this way, the students can make connections between them and reason logically about them. Here, we call these ***'strings'*** of exercises.

Another possibility is to present a string with a fixed ***pattern***; besides solving individual problems, the students can then be asked to generalize.

Up to now we have primarily referred to a number of aspects that concern the style of practicing. In the following sections, based partly on examples, these form aspects will be addressed in greater detail. Form and content belong together in the same way as body and spirit. This is why we will now discuss several topics that we believe are given too little attention in prevailing algebra education.

Universities have complained for years about the first-year students' lack of skill in operating with numerical and/or algebraic ***fractions***. In the past, algebraic factions were intensively practiced (perhaps too intensively), this is now almost completely absent from the first years of secondary education. In a digital newsletter for math teachers, a university teacher wrote about the entry test for mathematics and physics students at the University of Amsterdam: *almost no one could solve the problem*: $1/(\frac{1}{2}+\frac{1}{3})$.

In the current programme, these deficiencies are apparently not remedied in the teaching of calculus for students in the final two or three years of pre-academic education. Considering experiences in recent years, we would strongly recommend that continuous attention be paid to operations with numerical and algebraic fractions, especially for students in the first years of pre-academic education.

As a second point of attention for the content of algebra, we refer to *formal substitution*, which concerns replacing single variables with expressions, and the reverse. This approach also includes the use of the cover-up method, but at a certain point it becomes desirable for students to use more adult algebraic language. Formal substitution helps to simplify complicated expressions or equations to more recognizable or more familiar formats.

The idea of using formal substitution to solve equations can be traced back to the Babylonian mathematicians who were able to solve every quadratic equation. In the textbooks of today, the treatment of this classical topic unfortunately amounts to nothing more than teaching – usually without proof – the recipe known as the *quadratic formula*. This treatment also disregards the characteristic algebraic technique known as *completing the square*, which not only has a greater scope of application than the quadratic formula, but is also very suitable for practicing algebraic manipulation.

Formulas in physics and economics usually contain more than one variable. Exercises for algebra must therefore also focus – much more than is now the case – on operations with expressions having multiple variables. In addition, the 'distillation' of new formulas (equations) from *combinations* of formulas is important. This often amounts to *eliminating* one or more variables (or parameters), once again by using formal substitution. These activities. i.e. 'brewing' formulas from other formulas, require a certain repertoire of procedural skills and should be given adequate attention at least beginning in the third year of pre-academic education (grades 9-10).

The development of algebraic skills was formerly a continuous process (there were two or three hours of algebra lessons every week) Due to the expansion of the mathematics programme and the reduction in the number of weekly lesson hours, today it is a discontinuous process, with all inherent disadvantages. The only remedy to this situation is to also work on maintaining and using algebra skills in non-algebra subjects. The ideal situation, of course would be if algebra could be more or less integrated into other subjects, but sometimes this is not very easy. Nevertheless, we believe that there are many more opportunities here than are currently being utilized, especially in *geometry*.

For example, the Pythagorean theorem and computations of areas and volumes offer plenty of handholds for the useful practice of algebra.

The words in bold in the above sections indicate the themes that will be addressed in greater depth in the following sections.

REVERSE QUESTIONS

The principle of asking suitable reverse questions can be applied at every level, from primary school to university. Figure 6 shows seven examples.

1. *Find two fractions with different denominators of which the sum is equal to $\frac{14}{15}$.*
2. *Find two fractions with different denominators of which the product is equal to $\frac{14}{15}$.*
3. *Fill in suitable multiples of x or y:*

   (..... + ...) + (.... + ...) = 12x + 5y

4. *Fill in suitable numbers:*
$$(x + 8)(x + ...) = x^2 + 19x + ...$$

   Think of an equation for which 9 and -10 are the only solutions.
5. *This parabola appears on a computer screen.*

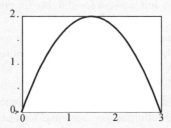

   Find a formula that goes with the graph.
6. *Find a function of which $x \rightarrow x^3 + 2x$ is the derivative*
7. *Find a function y of x so that $y' = 2y$*

Figure 6. Seven examples

Reverse questions often allow more than one answer. During a class discussion, this gives students who did not respond immediately a second chance; from a pedagogic point of view, this is obviously an advantage. In addition, the possibility of multiple answers also provides an immediate handhold for reflection and exploring the problem in greater depth: have we addressed all the possibilities, and how do we know that for sure?

A few remarks about the chosen examples. With example 1, a systematic investigation of all possibilities can be easily performed. It turns out there is only a single solution where both denominators are unequal to 15.

Example 4 could be used at the initial stage when practicing the multiplication of simple binomials. Such questions can make students aware of the 'sum and product method' with second-degree polynomials, which is very useful later on for factorization.

Example 6 indeed has only a single solution, but the function that is being sought can be designed in different ways. The two formulas that immediately throw a light on the chosen approach are:

$$y = -\tfrac{8}{9}x(x-3) \text{ and } y = -\tfrac{8}{9}(x - 1\tfrac{1}{2})^2 + 2.$$

Question 7 could, for example, be asked in grade 10 soon after the students learn how polynomial functions can be differentiated, although integral calculus is not part of the subject matter. In that case it is a puzzle-like question, where the role of a constant (as a factor and as a term) emerges during the differentiation. In the same way, question 8 can be asked when the students have learned how exponential functions can be differentiated, also if differential equations are not addressed later. Such questions compel the students to think instead of imitate, and give them the opportunity to make discoveries themselves.

COVER-UP METHOD

A well-known and widely used example of the reverse principle in primary education are the composed 'fill-in-the-blank' exercises; these are called equations in the algebraic context. Nowadays some textbooks initially use the 'cover-up' method. For example: what value of x makes $3x + 7$ equal to 19? Solution with the cover-up method:

$$3x + 7 = 19$$
$$\textcircled{12} + 7 = 19 \quad \rangle \quad 3x = 12 \rightarrow x = 4$$

You could call this a 'multiple fill-in-the-blank' exercise

$$(\dots + 7 = 19 \text{ and } 3 \times \dots = 12).$$

The cover-up method is actually a simple search strategy, not based on an artificial solution procedure, and is therefore very suitable to use and practice at the initial stage of solving equations. Moreover, even with young students, the teacher can confidently push on to more complicated equations, which lead to two, three or four step solutions, such as the ones given in Figure 7.

$$12 - \frac{300}{x} = 7$$
$$12 - \boxed{5} = 7 \quad \rangle \quad \frac{300}{x} = 5 \; , \; \frac{300}{\boxed{60}} = 5 \quad \rangle \rightarrow x = 60$$

$$\frac{300}{2+3x} = 6$$
$$\frac{300}{\boxed{50}} = 6 \quad \rangle \quad 2 + 3x = 50 \; , \; 2 + \boxed{48} = 50 \quad \rangle \quad 3x = 48 \rightarrow x = 16$$

Figure 7. Cover-up method

151

MARTIN KINDT

If this solution method is kept up for a time (and is not limited to a single lesson!), and if sufficient variation is provided in terms of difficulty and complexity, this will lead not only to a better understanding of what an equation actually is, but will also give the students courage to first look for a solution using common sense, before applying a solution algorithm that they have been taught. Without much difficulty, many exercises can be designed to help develop the skill of 'looking through a formula'. As an example, Figure 8 shows a series of problems with square roots.

Use the cover-up method to solve for x in the following equations:

$$\sqrt{x} = 5 \qquad\qquad 4\sqrt{10-x} = 12$$

$$\sqrt{4+3x} = 5 \qquad\qquad \sqrt{10+\sqrt{x}} = 4$$

$$2+\sqrt{3x} = 5 \qquad\qquad \sqrt{30+\sqrt{30+x}} = 6$$

$$\sqrt{10+x} = 3 \qquad\qquad \sqrt{20+\sqrt{20+\sqrt{20+x}}} = 5$$

Figure 8. Problems with square roots

Note that an applet is available on Wisweb with which the cover-up method can be practiced interactively.[i]

VARIATION IN PRACTICE FORMATS

The following argument is often used to support practicing with series of similar exercises: students enjoy being able to accomplish something, without having to rack their brains too much, and it contributes to their self-confidence. There is not much to say against this argument, except that there is a large variation between individuals. For example, when presented with sequences of stereotypical exercises, some students immediately try to solve the last problem in the list. If they can, they simply skip all the rest. To prevent this from happening, the teacher should aim for more variation and surprise in the task series.

As an example of a list of varied algebra problems, we use the multiplication of (non-homogeneous) binomials, such as $a+2$ and $a+7$, a skill which has withstood all simplifications of the algebra curricula during the past 50 years, and is still being taught. We assume that this multiplication has been made in an insightful fashion. A proven method here is to use the rectangle model, a classical approach which is still very productive.[ii]

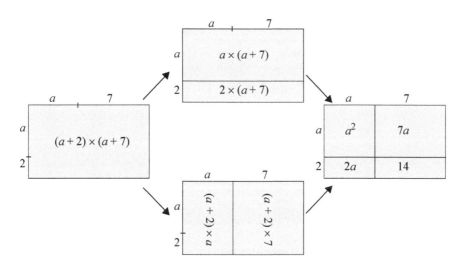

Figure 9. Rectangle model of multiplication

Figure 9 visualizes the solution procedure. The middle step (either the upper or lower box) is usually skipped, but it does provide a good illustration of the principle of 'double distribution'. At a certain point, the students will practice without the geometric representation; as a result there will be more opportunities for variation than are used in present-day textbooks.

For instance, there are almost no examples of 'vertical multiplication'. This method, which is analogous to vertical multiplication of concrete numbers, is very instructive and has the advantage over the linear method of being more easy to handle with products of polynomials with more than two terms, or products with more than three factors.

$$
\begin{array}{r}
a + 7 \\
a + 2 \\
\hline
2a + 14 \\
a^2 + 7a \\
\hline
a^2 + 9a + 14
\end{array}
\begin{array}{l}
\\ \times \\ \\ \\ + \\ \\
\end{array}
$$

When using the linear method of multiplication, the convention on the sequence of operations plays a role, and a notation method is needed to manage this sequence. The usual method is to use parentheses. Generally speaking, only the passive use of parentheses is practiced, but we believe it is important for students to also be challenged to actively use parentheses, or perhaps alternative 'aggregation operators' such as circles or horizontal lines (see Figure 10).

MARTIN KINDT

*Place parentheses in the four expressions to the left of the equal
sign to create an equality:*

$$a + 2 \cdot a + 7 = 3a + 7$$

$$a + 2 \cdot a + 7 = 3a + 14$$

$$a + 2 \cdot a + 7 = a^2 + 2a + 7$$

$$a + 2 \cdot a + 7 = a^2 + 9a + 14$$

Figure 10. Actively position parentheses

An advantage of working with operation trees (of which there are many variations in appearance) is that it is very easy to visualize more composed computations and reverse questions. Figure 11 provides some exemplary tasks.

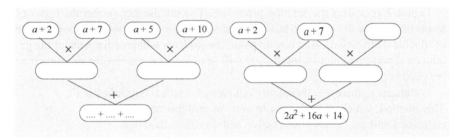

Figure 11. Tasks on operation trees

Uncountable variations of larger trees are conceivable, where the students must first decide where to start filling in the trees. In this way, the material can also be given a certain puzzle-like character, and practical experience has shown that these types of problems are experienced as more challenging than monotonous lists of problems, which primarily lead to imitation behaviour.

The multiplication table is another suitable format, which is currently being used in many textbooks as the successor to the rectangle model, for example to multiply two binomials. In this way, it can be derived from the adjacent table that the product of $a + 2$ and $a + 7$ is equal to $a^2 + 9a + 14$. It is simply a question of adding up the terms after they have been filled in. This property of the multiplication table: i.e. '*the sum of the products in the*

×	a	7
a	a^2	$7a$
2	$2a$	14

154

table is equal to the product of the sums of the marginal numbers' can be used in a problem, as in the example shown in Figure 12.

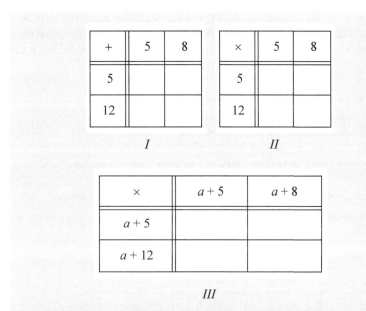

+	5	8
5		
12		

I

×	5	8
5		
12		

II

×	$a + 5$	$a + 8$
$a + 5$		
$a + 12$		

III

a. *Fill in the empty cells on addition table I and multiplication table II.*
b. *Use these tables to fill in the empty cells in multiplication table III.*
c. *Add the products from table III together.*
d. *This final expression is the product of two expressions. What are these expressions?*

Figure 12. Multiplication table task

While the first three questions are straightforward exercises, the fourth question is of a different calibre. To answer the latter question, the students have to think hard, and the teacher will have to return to this question in a class discussion. Once the polynomials $2a + 13$ and $2a + 17$ have been found, the teacher can, of course, assign another regular problem to 'prove' that the students have really learned something.

In passing, we note that the use of words such as 'sum', 'product', 'term', 'binomial' and 'factor', which are part of the jargon of algebra, can create obstacles for some students. However, algebra cannot exist without such language elements, and students should also practice somewhat more with this language than is generally the case today. As explained in Chapter 1, teachers can do this by verbally assigning tasks such as: 'expand the product of $a + 2$ and $a + 7$' or 'compute the square of the sum of a and 5'. Students can also be asked to describe algebraic formats in words.

Multiplication and addition tables are not only suitable for providing variation in practice formats, but they also provide their own structure on which interesting problems can be based. The example in Figure 13, adapted from De Moor and Schoemaker (1979) features a 'secret' addition table, where the marginal expressions have been left out. This explains why the result, regardless of the choice the student makes, is always the same. Here as well, this is initially a straightforward exercise, but it can have a surprising sequel in the students' thinking.

Select a cell from the table below and write down its contents.
Now cross out the row and column to which the cell belongs.
Choose a cell which has not yet been crossed out, write down its contents, and then cross out the row and column of this cell.
Do this two more times, and then add the four expressions you have written down.
Compare your answer with that of your classmates. What do you notice?

$2a$	$3a$	$a + 4$	$2a + 3$
$6a$	$7a$	$5a + 4$	$6a + 3$
$2a + 2$	$3a + 2$	$a + 6$	$2a + 5$
$2a - 3$	$3a - 3$	$a + 1$	$2a$

Figure 13. Tabular structure task

EXERCISES: ARBITRARY SERIES, COHERENT STRINGS AND PATTERNS

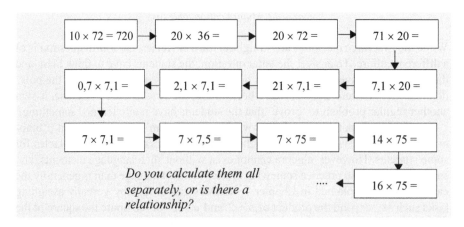

Figure 14. Calculation strings

A series of problems can be constructed in such a way that the students can independently discover relationships between them, and consequently achieve smarter solutions (de Moor & Schoemaker, 1979). Figure 14 contains an example. It is clear that mental arithmetic is required for this exercise. Of course, such strings can also be designed for algebra.

<table>
<tr><td>Solve for x from:</td><td>Write the following as simply as possible:</td></tr>
</table>

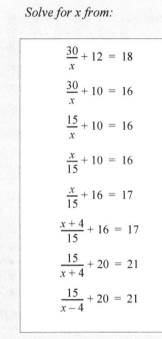

$\dfrac{30}{x} + 12 = 18$	$a \times a^2 = a^3$
$\dfrac{30}{x} + 10 = 16$	$(a + a) \times a^2 = \ldots\ldots$
$\dfrac{15}{x} + 10 = 16$	$2a \times a^2 = \ldots\ldots$
$\dfrac{x}{15} + 10 = 16$	$2a \times (a^2 + a^2 + a^2) = \ldots\ldots$
$\dfrac{x}{15} + 16 = 17$	$2a \times 3a^2 = \ldots\ldots$
$\dfrac{x+4}{15} + 16 = 17$	$\dfrac{6a^3}{2a} = \ldots\ldots$
$\dfrac{15}{x+4} + 20 = 21$	$\dfrac{6a^3}{3a^2} = \ldots\ldots$
$\dfrac{15}{x-4} + 20 = 21$	$\dfrac{3a^2}{6a^3} = \ldots\ldots$

Figure 15. Strings of tasks

Another type of list shows a certain type of pattern, where the students are challenged to discover this pattern and continue the sequence. After this, a generalized formula can be created, and with the aid of algebra rules, an adequate explanation can be sought. An example is presented in Figure 16.

Compute the following sequence: What do you notice? How could you continue this sequence? Can you explain the pattern by using algebra?	$15^2 - 10 \times 20$ $25^2 - 20 \times 30$ $35^2 - 30 \times 40$

Figure 16. Discovery and explanation of a pattern

The students will discover that the answer is always 25, and can continue the sequence with a few more examples. The next challenge is then to reason out or to prove that the discovered rule is generally applicable. This can take place in different ways, by means of observation with square and rectangle, or by computation of $(a+5)^2 - a(a+10)$.

Check the results of the adjacent sequence; what are the next three lines? Can you explain the pattern by using algebra?	$1 + 9 + 1 \times 9 = 19$ $2 + 9 + 2 \times 9 = 29$ $3 + 9 + 3 \times 9 = 39$ ...

Figure 17. Task using position value system

The example in Figure 17 requires insight into our position value system: $n + 9 + n \times 9 = 10n + 9$.

We encounter another, more concrete type of pattern when representing numbers by configurations of dots. Well-known shapes, that were studied by Pythagoras and his followers, are square numbers, oblong numbers and triangular numbers.

In this way, the sequence $2 (= 1 \times 2)$, $6 (= 2 \times 3)$, $12 (= 3 \times 4)$, $20 (= 4 \times 5)$, etc. is represented by

oblong numbers

The nth oblong number can be described as $n(n+1)$ or as $n^2 + n$. Such dot patterns lead to formulas, and can be practiced interactively using the applets of Wisweb from the series 'Spotting number problems' (Kindt, 2003).

We find yet another type of pattern in the first volume of *Pythagoras,* the Dutch journal for teenagers.

In the sum $3 + 7 + 10 + 17 + 27 + 44 = 108$, the first two numbers (3 and 7) are chosen arbitrarily, and the others are derived according to a rule which you can easily find.

In this way, create other sums of six numbers, where the first two are chosen arbitrarily. It will turn out that the number following the equal sign is always related in the same way to one of the six numbers in front of the equal sign. What is this relationship? Explain.

After reviewing a number of 'Fibonacci sequences' produced by the students, it becomes apparent that the sum is always equal to four times the fifth number. In principle, this explanation can be discovered by students in the seventh grade. Take the initial numbers a and b. The following numbers in the sequence are therefore $a + b$,

$a + 2b$, $2a + 3b$ and $3a + 4b$; the sum of the six numbers is $8a + 12b$, which is equal to 4 times $2a + 3b$.

This exercise can be made even more fun. Van de Groep (2005) goes even further, and works with Fibonacci sequences of ten numbers. In this case, the sum ($= 55a + 88b$) turns out to be 11 times the seventh number ($= 5a + 8b$).

Of course, the *Pythagoras* assignment is more of a 'thinking problem' than a simple exercise, and it is defined as such in the journal. But practice and thinking can go hand-in-hand; in fact, in our vision this should often be the case.

FRACTIONS

And if there are factions,..... yes, it is difficult, but I am looking for the common denominator. (Multatuli, *The history of Woutertje Pieterse*, 1890)

A familiar complaint from teachers in secondary education (not only today, but also in the past!) is that students cannot deal with algebraic fractions. In his book *Structure and Insight*, Van Hiele (1986) observed that it is astonishing how quickly such tricks are forgotten:

In secondary education, we encounter fractions with letters. We learn that $\frac{a}{b} + \frac{c}{d} = \frac{ad + bc}{bd}$. Even at this point, the fractions are a constant source of misery for the students.

And later on in the book:

In mathematics, you encounter a great many identities. The above was an example of a such an identity. We have always believed that this identity was important, but now we are beginning to have doubts.

Does the format $\frac{ad + bc}{bd}$ make additional calculation easier? It is worthwhile to determine what people are doing with fractions in algebra; I suspect that reduction of $\frac{a}{b} + \frac{c}{d}$ causes us to lose time in as many cases as we save time. Van Hiele therefore then argues for using the notation $a \cdot b^{-1}$ instead of $\frac{a}{b}$, even in cases where natural numbers are included in the numerator and denominator. His wish will remain unfulfilled, perhaps forever, because the fraction is permanently anchored in mathematics and daily life. Granted, the designation $3 \cdot 4^{-1}$ per litre on a bottle of wine would not affect the taste, but it would still require some getting used to. Very probably, we will continue to use numerators and denominators for a long time to come; for example, the well-known thin lens formula $\frac{1}{f} = \frac{1}{b} + \frac{1}{v}$ is unlikely to change appearance overnight. However, we can agree with Van Hiele that the reduction of the right term to $\frac{v + b}{bv}$ does not make the formula more beautiful or manageable.

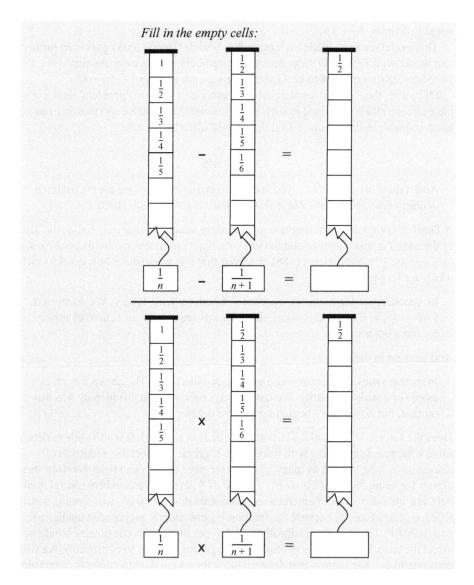

Figure 18. Calculating with number strips

Today's secondary education does pay some attention to calculating with concrete fractions, but students in grades 7–9 are rarely confronted with algebraic fractions. These first appear in other subjects such as physics and economics, in which the relationship between two quantities plays a role, and later on in calculus at the pre-academic level, where students regularly work with rational functions. It is therefore certainly advisable to work with algebraic fractions in the first classes in secondary education, although they do not have to be as complex as those in the textbooks of fifty years ago. Here as well, it would appear to us to be didactically desirable, or in fact essential, to link algebra to arithmetic. For example, this could take place by using so-called number strips (see Figure 18).

The fractions in the strips of this example will have the numerator 1, and are usually called unit fractions. The ancient Egyptians did not use any other fractions with numerators not equal to 1 except for $\frac{2}{3}$. Writing our normal fractions (< 1) as a sum of unit fractions with differing denominators is a suitable activity to brush up on and practice using concrete fractions. It is interesting to note that the Egyptians had access to tables with such partial fraction expansions (see Van der Waerden, 1961), for example for fractions with numerator 2 (and of course an odd denominator). Here are a few examples from that list:

$$\frac{2}{5} = \frac{1}{3} + \frac{1}{15}, \quad \frac{2}{7} = \frac{1}{4} + \frac{1}{28}, \quad \frac{2}{13} = \frac{1}{8} + \frac{1}{52} + \frac{1}{104}$$

The third example can be disputed, because also valid is:

$$\frac{2}{3} = \frac{1}{7} + \frac{1}{91}$$

There are systematic methods for doing this, but addressing them is going too far, certainly for young students. From the perspective of algebra, it is interesting to look at fractions with numerator 2, for which the denominator is an odd multiple of 3. For example:

$$\frac{2}{3} = \frac{1}{2} + \frac{1}{6}, \quad \frac{2}{9} = \frac{1}{6} + \frac{1}{18}, \quad \frac{2}{15} = \frac{1}{10} + \frac{1}{30}, \text{ and so on.}$$

The denominator of the second fraction in the partial fraction expansion is always three times the denominator of the first fraction and twice the original denominator. This discovery is set down in the identity:

$$\frac{2}{3n} = \frac{1}{2n} + \frac{1}{6n}.$$

which can be explained by means of partial fraction expansion:

$$\frac{2}{3n} = \frac{4}{6n} = \frac{3+1}{6n} = \frac{3}{6n} + \frac{1}{6n} = \frac{1}{2n} + \frac{1}{6n}.$$

Of course, to prove the above identity, it is just as valid to begin on the other side. The history of Egyptian mathematics therefore provides a handhold for operating with fractions or brushing up on this topic. The idea of expanding the fractions and then putting them together again gives operating with fractions a flexible quality. Essentially, the students have to be able to understand and use the distributive law

$$\frac{a+b}{c} = \frac{a}{c} + \frac{b}{c}$$

in two directions, just like the distribution rule for multiplication.

Multiplication of fractions is algebraically simpler, but conceptually more difficult than addition. During the first year of secondary education, many students appear to have forgotten the rule for multiplication, and apparently do not have a concrete orientation framework to rediscover the rule. Here, we again recommend the rectangle model to brush up on and practice the rule 'multiply the numerators and denominators', so that the model becomes the mental property of the students:

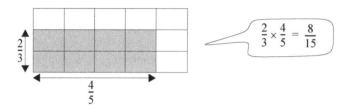

Figure 19. Rectangular model for fraction multiplication

This means making multiplication problems with pictures, and making pictures with multiplication problems. At a certain point, a rule can be formulated. When learning such formal rules by practicing them, it is once again important to combine operations, such as

$$\frac{2}{a} \times \frac{5}{b} + \frac{3}{b} \times \frac{4}{a} = \frac{10}{ab} + \frac{12}{ab} = \frac{22}{ab}$$

Here as well, many variations in presentation can be imagined, such as trees, tables, strips and patterns (Figure 20).

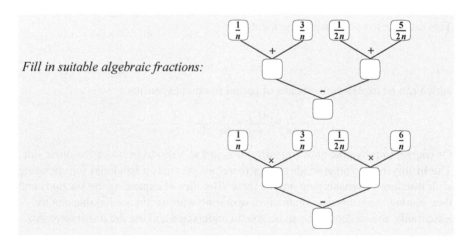

Figure 20. Trees of algebraic fractions

By making a clear connection with computing with numerical fractions, it should be possible to have young students work with algebraic fractions and practice using them.

Fill in the results.
Continue the list with two multiplications.
Here is a formula that looks complex:

$$1 - \frac{1}{n+1} = \frac{1}{1 + \frac{1}{n}}$$

$$(1 - \tfrac{1}{3}) \times (1 + \tfrac{1}{2}) = 1$$

$$(1 - \tfrac{1}{4}) \times (1 + \tfrac{1}{3}) = \ldots$$

$$(1 - \tfrac{1}{5}) \times (1 + \tfrac{1}{4}) = \ldots$$

$$(1 - \tfrac{1}{6}) \times (1 + \tfrac{1}{5}) = \ldots$$

Explain this formula. What is the connection with the list of computations?

Figure 21. Connecting algebraic and numeric fraction calculations

It is also important that the students learn to recognize the various forms in which fractions appear and be able to relate them to each other. For instance, the fact that $\tfrac{1}{2}\pi$ and $\tfrac{\pi}{2}$ are two representations of the same number should not be surprising to them; however, according to recent experiences, this is often the case with students at the pre-academic level! It is also a good idea for the students to practice tasks such as the one in Figure 22 in grades 7–9.

Fill in appropriate expressions:

$+$	$\frac{1}{5}x$	x	$\frac{2x}{-5}$
$\frac{x}{2}$			
$\frac{2}{5}x$			
$\frac{4x}{5}$			

Figure 22. Fraction addition table

COMPLETING THE SQUARE

The process of replacing a sub-expression with an auxiliary variable is important. This is a way to simplify composed expressions to more elementary or recognizable expressions[iii]. From time immemorial, it has been used to solve equations. 'From time immemorial' should be understood literally here, especially when one realizes that the Babylonians frequently used this principle around 1500 BC. They had an algorithm to solve an equation of the type $x^2 + px = q$.

This essentially amounted to taking half of p, adding the square of this value to q, finding the square root of this result and then subtracting half of this value from p. We can now formulate this process more compactly:

$$x = \sqrt{\frac{1}{4}p^2 + q} - \frac{1}{2}p.$$

This is one half of the old 'p,q formula', as it was previously taught at vocational school; at the pre-academic level, students were taught the 'abc-formula', which is in fact excessively heavy artillery, as will be shown below.

The following riddle appears on one of the many Babylonian clay tablets with completed mathematics problems:

> *I added seven times the side of my square to 11 times the area and it is $6\frac{1}{4}$. What is the side of my square?*

In short: solve for x from $11x^2 + 7x = 6\frac{1}{4}$.

The solution, converted into our algebraic language, is as follows.
First multiply both sides of the equation by 11:

$$(11x)^2 + 7 \cdot (11x) = 68\frac{3}{4}.$$

Replace $11x$ with y. Then the problem is reduced to the standard equation:

$$y^2 + 7 \cdot y = 68\frac{3}{4}.$$

with the solution:

$$y = \sqrt{(3\frac{1}{2})^2 + 68\frac{3}{4}} - 3\frac{1}{2} = 9 - 3\frac{1}{2} = 5\frac{1}{2}.$$

From $11x = 5\frac{1}{2}$ it follows that $x = \frac{1}{2}$.

It cannot be said with certainty how the Babylonians derived their algorithm for solving the equation $x^2 + px = q$. An attractive possibility is that they understood the process of completing a square by means of a geometric figure (see Figure 23), but there are other options as well.

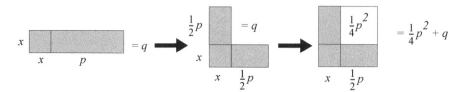

Figure 23. Geometric representation of solving procedure

The method by illustration that is sketched here is greatly appreciated by students, and exercises where they independently make sketches themselves are very useful. At a certain point, the students will take the step to an abstract approach in order to open the way to the more general case (p and/or q can be negative), and when taking square roots, the negative value must also be included. In a group that had first practiced solving such problems by making sketches in grade 9, two years later there were still students who made sketches in the margin so they could remember the algorithm for completing the square. By means of a sophisticated series of exercises with 'sketch equations', students were able to independently discover how to complete the square (Figure 24).

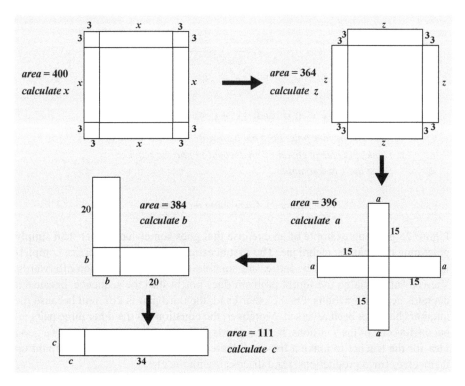

Figure 24. 'Sketch equation'

We strongly recommend completing the square, in addition to factorization, as the preferred techniques that are initially used for solving quadratic equations. Both algorithms can rely on the comprehension of the students and give them the opportunity for insightful practice.

The danger of presenting the quadratic formula at an early stage (some textbooks even expect the students to take their word for it, without any proof whatsoever!) is that the solution of quadratic equations is reduced to a simple substitution exercise in a black box.

For that matter, it is possible that students who have learned to understand and use the completing the square technique, can at some point independently discover a general formula for solving a quadratic equation, for example to design a program for the electronic calculator. It is only in a broader theoretical context, where the discriminant becomes important, that the famous quadratic formula can justifiably play an important role, although it is never truly essential.

a. *Solve by completing the square:*

$$x^2 + \tfrac{2}{3}x = \tfrac{1}{3} \qquad \text{and} \qquad x^2 + \tfrac{1}{3}x = \tfrac{2}{3}$$

Do the same with the pairs :

$$x^2 + \tfrac{2}{5}x = \tfrac{3}{5} \qquad \text{and} \qquad x^2 + \tfrac{3}{5}x = \tfrac{2}{5}$$

$$x^2 + \tfrac{2}{5}x = \tfrac{7}{5} \qquad \text{and} \qquad x^2 + \tfrac{3}{5}x = \tfrac{8}{5}$$

$$x^2 + 0.1x = 0.9 \quad \text{and} \quad x^2 + 0.9x = 0.1$$

b. *Which of the four pairs does not belong in this sequence? Why?*

c. *Think up a pair of equations that would fit into the sequence.*
   Solve these two equations.

Figure 25. Completing the square

Figure 25 gives an example of an exercise that goes somewhat further than simply practicing the solution technique. The first question is intended to practice completing the square. Questions **b.** and **c.** are suitable for a class discussion afterwards. Viewed superficially, the fourth problem does not fit into the sequence, because it contains decimal fractions. On the other hand, the third pair is different because the numbers have not been reversed. Moreover, the equations of the other three pairs all have −1 as one of the solutions, but this pair is different. With question c. it is a good idea for the teacher to make a list of all the equations that the students thought up themselves (own productions!) and discuss it with the class.

If no equations with whole coefficients emerge, the teacher could ask, for example, if the pair $x^2 + 8x = -7$ and $x^2 - 7x = 8$ would fit into the sequence.

As a follow-up to this discussion, the generalization could be addressed. Assume that the quadratic equations $x^2 + px = q$ and $x^2 + qx = p$ (with $p \neq q$) have a common solution. This common solution must therefore be equal to −1 . The reasoning is that *if there is a number that satisfies both equations, then it also satisfies the equation obtained by subtracting* $px - qx = q - p$, therefore:

$$x = \frac{q-p}{p-q} = -1 \, .$$

Substituting -1 in either of the original equations shows that $p + q = 1$.

This demands a great deal from the students because it involves a combination of reasoning and algebraic operation, but if we want them to be able to use algebra in many different situations, then these types of exercises are essential.

FORMAL SUBSTITUTION

As stated previously, formal substitution involves replacing single variables with expressions and the reverse. It is beneficial to regularly practice this technique (explicitly with auxiliary variables, with the cover-up method or with mental substitution) – where the aim is to 'convert formulas to your will' – at all levels and during all years of secondary education. It not only increases the skill in algebraic manipulation, but also trains the students in fathoming and 'peeling back' algebraic expressions with varying degrees of complication with the aim of simplifying them to a familiar, standard form.

a. Solve $\boxed{25x^2 + 20x = 5}$ with the substitution $\boxed{u = 5x}$

b. Solve $\boxed{5 + \dfrac{4}{x} = \dfrac{1}{x^2}}$ with the substitution $\boxed{v = \dfrac{1}{x}}$.

If you have completed problems a. en b. correctly, you will see that the two equations have exactly the same solutions.

c. You could have predicted this without solving the equations. Explain why.

Figure 26. Formal substitution

Figure 26 contains an example of a problem in formal substitution with quadratic equations. The ultimate aim, of course, is for students to become independently capable of solving a problem by using formal substitution. In the past, familiar exercises required solving equations such as $x^4 = 10x^2 - 9$, $2\sin^2 x - \cos x = 1$ or $2^{2x} + 2^{x+3} = 48$.

Perhaps we should start using such types of exercises again, because they undoubtedly help students to develop their algebraic skills. In calculus, formal substitution can play a clear role with the chain rule and certainly when applying this rule to integral calculus.

The traditional investigation of functions that led to drawing a graph has now been pushed far into the background due to the arrival of the graphing calculator, and justifiably so. That this does not take away from the importance of being able to reason with graphs, for example concerning asymptotes, which the graphing calculator does not do for you.

For example, take the curve $y = \dfrac{x^2 - x + 3}{x + 2}$.

Substitution of $u = x + 2$, therefore $x^2 = u^2 - 4u + 4$, helps to find the skewed asymptote:

$$y = \frac{u^2 - 4u + 4 - u + 2 + 3}{u} = \frac{u^2 - 5u + 9}{u} = u - 5 + \frac{9}{u} = x - 3 + \frac{9}{x + 2}.$$

Besides the vertical asymptote $x = -2$, the curve therefore has the skewed asymptote $y = x - 3$.

Regarding the development of algebraic skills, this method is probably preferable to the long division with remainder method, which is not really understood by many students.

In old algebra books for the first year of secondary education (7th grade) we encounter expressions for factorization such as: $x^2 y^2 - 18xy + 65$, $(x + y)^2 - z^2$, and $x^2 + 2xy + y^2 + 4x + 4y + 3$. These were actually the best bits in the algebra curriculum; they took students out of the boring automatic work by giving them 'something to think about'. People have differing opinions about such assignments, but in any case the bright students were challenged and the less talented ones were still able to follow the computation if they were given a clear explanation (for example with the cover-up method!). At every level we believe it is certainly valuable to think up questions where a formal substitution, which Freudenthal (1983) refers to as 'powerful device', is the key to the answer.

COMBINING AND ELIMINATING

A skill that is especially useful in other subjects is combining formulas to create a new formula. This usually happens by eliminating one of the variables that appears in the formulas, by means of formal substitution.

The Babylonians used a formula that expressed the area of a circle in terms of its circumference: the area of a circle is the square of the perimeter divided by 12. We are accustomed to express both the area and the perimeter of a circle in terms of the radius:

$$A = \pi r^2 \text{ and } P = 2\pi r.$$

Because the circumference of a circular object is easier to measure than the radius, it is not such a crazy idea to express the area in terms of the perimeter.

Via $r = \dfrac{P}{2\pi}$ this leads to: $A = \pi \cdot \left(\dfrac{P}{2\pi}\right)^2$ or: $A = \dfrac{P^2}{4\pi}$.

Comparing this with the Babylonian calculation rule shows that they used 3 as an approximation of π, an approximation which can also be found in the Old Testament.[iv]

Could our students also perform such an elimination? We fear this would be asking too much of many of them, even though these types of derivations are very common in subjects such as physics and economics. Figure 27 provides an example of a set of problems to use on a test, taken from Van Loon (2005).

A striking aspect is that the geometry context is reported in problem **a.**, but that the context for problems **b.** and **c.** is completely absent. This seems rather strange when you realize that the problem concerned a combination of mathematics and physics. But in any case, in this specific project the usefulness of such exercises has been ascertained.

a. *The volume of a sphere with radius r can be calculated with the formula.*

$$V_{\text{sphere}} = \frac{4}{3}\pi r^2$$

Now express the volume in terms of the diameter d of the sphere.

b. *Given the formulas:*

$$F_c = \frac{mv^2}{r} \quad and \quad v = \frac{2\pi r}{T}$$

Combine the formulas so that F_c is expressed in terms of m, r and T.

c. *Given the formulas:*

$$R = \frac{\rho \cdot l}{A} \quad en \quad A = \pi r^2$$

combine the formulas so that r is expressed in terms of r, l en R.

Figure 27. Eliminations in science contexts (Van Loon, 2005)

The booklet *Operating with standard functions* (Kindt, 1990) includes a special section about such derivations. The introductory example is the relationship between free-fall velocity and distance. From the formulas $v = gt$ and $s = \frac{1}{2}gt^2$ by eliminating t, it follows that $v = \sqrt{2gs}$. We note that reasoning beforehand using a chain of proportionalities (v is proportional to t and t is in turn proportional to the square root of s, therefore ....) can strengthen the understanding of this relationship. To create the formula, it is then only necessary to find the constant factor.

The assignment in Figure 28 is derived from the above-mentioned FI unit. Geometric contexts are probably still the best way to practice combining formulas, especially with volume, area and circumference formulas. For example, take a cylindrical tin. If r is the radius of the base and h is the height (both in cm), then the total area of the tin in cm^2 is given by: $A = 2\pi rh + 2\pi r^2$.

The volume (in l) is given by: $V = \pi r^2 h$. For litre tins, the area can simply be expressed in r. After all, from $\pi r^2 h = 1$ it follows that $A = \frac{2}{r} + 2\pi r^2$. If desired, A can also be expressed in the diameter (d) or in the circumference (p) of the tin, which leads to $A = \frac{4}{d} + \frac{1}{2}\pi d^2$ and $A = \frac{4\pi}{p} + \frac{p2}{2\pi}$, respectively.

169

By using one of these formulas, the optimal dimensions of a litre tin can be calculated, in other words, the dimensions where the area is minimal. An exact solution is found by means of differential calculus, but in practice, a numerical solution using the graphing calculator is satisfactory. This also means that the problem can be addressed as early as grades 9 or 10.

For a specific girth and 'body weight' of a quadruped, there are limitations on its 'length' due to the 'sag effect'. This idea can be represented by seeing the animal as a rod that is supported on both ends.

Someone created the following system of formulas for the particular case, where G (= body weight in g), L (= length in cm) and D (= diameter in cm) play a role.

$$(1) \quad \frac{GL^2}{D^4} = 680 \qquad (3) \quad L = a \cdot G^{1/4} \qquad (5) \quad \frac{L}{D} = c \cdot G^{-1/8}$$

$$(2) \quad LD^2 = G \qquad (4) \quad L = b \cdot G^{3/8} \qquad (6) \quad D = d \cdot L^{3/2}$$

a. *If the body weight of an animal is known, its maximum possible length can be calculated from formulas (1) and (2). Take the example of an Indian elephant weighing 5000 kg.*
   What would be the maximum possible length and diameter of such an elephant?
b. *Formulas (3) through (6) can be derived from (1) and (2).*
   Check this and then calculate the constants a, b, c and d.

Figure 28. Task from 'Operating with standard functions'

OWN PRODUCTIONS

Let us return to the fragment of text by Theo Thijssen. This not only shows that practice can be challenging, but also that the students are sometimes prepared to produce series of examples themselves. This activity, which is currently known as '*own productions*', is therefore not a recent didactical discovery. And what is possible with arithmetic, is also possible with algebra. I have borrowed an example from the method of Dutch textbook *Getal en Ruimte* ('Number and Space'):

> For a test, a class has to reduce ten expressions. Every reduced equation has the result 12ab. Think of ten problems which have 12ab as their result. Have another student check the problems.

This is a nice assignment which, unfortunately, is an exception in the corresponding book, but it is not difficult to see how other assignments could be designed in a similar way.

When practising algebraic techniques, it is actually quite obvious to have students construct assignments themselves. This can take place at every level. The example shown in Figure 29 is an 'own-production' assignment for somewhat more advanced students.

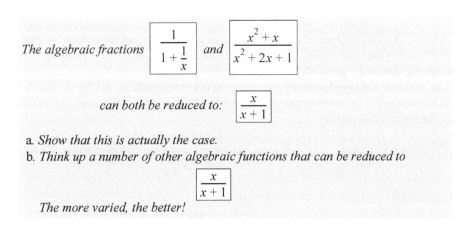

The algebraic fractions $\dfrac{1}{1+\dfrac{1}{x}}$ *and* $\dfrac{x^2+x}{x^2+2x+1}$

can both be reduced to: $\dfrac{x}{x+1}$

a. *Show that this is actually the case.*
b. *Think up a number of other algebraic functions that can be reduced to*

$$\frac{x}{x+1}$$

The more varied, the better!

Figure 29. 'Own production' assignment

At least as important as the assignment itself is its follow-up discussion. Many good variants are conceivable, such as

$$\frac{ax}{ax+a}, \quad 1-\frac{1}{x+1}, \quad \frac{x^2-x}{x^2-1}, \quad \frac{x^2+2x}{x^2+3x+2} \quad \text{and so on.}$$

which can emerge from the discussion. In addition, many incorrect suggestions will undoubtedly be made. This entire process makes collecting and analysing the discoveries of the students into an exciting and especially educational activity.

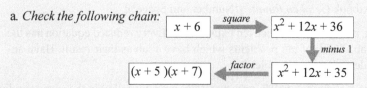

a. *Check the following chain:*

$$x + 6 \xrightarrow{\text{square}} x^2 + 12x + 36$$

minus 1

$$(x + 5)(x + 7) \xleftarrow{\text{factor}} x^2 + 12x + 35$$

b. *Perform exactly the same operation with the following sequence:*
   $x + 4,\ y + 10,\ z + 11,\ p + 1$

c. *Think up a few more examples yourself.*

d. *Can you make a general rule?*

Figure 30. A chain of algebraic operations

Another example is given in Figure 30. First of all, two types of reductions are practiced: taking the square of a binomial and factorizing a trinomial. This exercise is interesting due to the possibility it offers for the spontaneous discovery of a pattern. The students' own productions (question c) confirm this pattern, and for the smarter students there is yet another possibility to actually confirm the discovery by means of the remarkable product:

$$(x + A)^2 - 1 = (x + A + 1)(x + A - 1)$$

The other way to do this, by first working out and then factorizing, is more difficult:

$$(x + A)^2 - 1 = x^2 + 2Ax + A^2 - 1$$

$$A + 1 \qquad A - 1$$

a. *Check the sums on the board. and continue the sequence a bit further. Amazing, isn't it?*

b. *Think up a few more sums that would appear much further down in the sequence.*

c. *Can you be sure that the result will always be 2?*
   If yes, explain this with algebra.

d. *Now think of another regular sequence which also has the same result.*

$1 \times 2 - 0 \times 3 = 2$
$2 \times 3 - 1 \times 4 = 2$
$3 \times 4 - 2 \times 5 = 2$
$4 \times 5 - 3 \times 6 = 2$
$5 \times 6 - 4 \times 7 = 2$

and so on?

Figure 31. Task inspired by Sawyer (1959)

The example in Figure 31 is inspired by the work of Sawyer (1959). The explanation is given, for example, by $(n + 1) \times (n + 2) - n \times (n + 3) = 2$. But it can also be given using the rectangle model. The own production then appears in question d.

The idea of having students independently design assignments, after having practiced a technique or method themselves, cannot be applied often enough; for example, the students can design assignments for fellow students or another class that is working in parallel. It encourages the students to reflect – which is absolutely essential – on what they have learned, and will lead to greater depth of understanding. Moreover, it calls for creativity, and this gives them much satisfaction when they complete the assignment. And isn't this the basis for all learning?

ALGEBRA IN GEOMETRY

In the second section of this chapter on the importance of skills we stated that some topics in geometry offer an excellent practice terrain for algebra skills. To start with, let us address the treatment of area formulas for triangles and quadrangles. The formula for the trapezium, for example, can be written as $\frac{1}{2}h(a + b)$ or as $h \cdot \frac{a+b}{2}$ or as $\frac{1}{2}ha + \frac{1}{2}hb$. Amusingly, a suitable geometric reasoning accompanies each of these expressions (Figure 32).

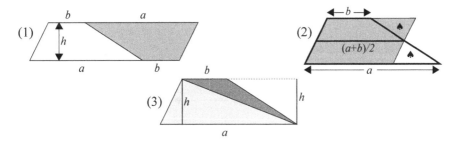

Figure 32. Geometric reasoning

In the third case, the area formula for the triangle is used, which afterwards becomes a special case of the trapezium formula (take $b = 0$). For $b = a$, the parallelogram formula returns. The students can shuttle back and forth between algebra and geometry.

Another excellent example of an interconnection between algebra and geometry is provided by the area formula for a ring that is delineated by concentric circles:

A ring is enclosed by two circles with the same centre.
One way to calculate the area of such a ring is: calculate the
average of the circumferences of the two circles, and multiply
this amount by the width of the ring.
a. Do you know another way to calculate the area of such a
*   ring?*
b. Does it give the same result in all cases as the calculation
*   rule given above?*

Figure 33. Ring task

Note that the rule $a^2 - b^2 = (a+b)(a-b)$ is useful for answering question b.

Another rich source for algebra is the Pythagorean theorem. Take the example from Figure 34, which concerns computing the height and then the area of a triangle with sides measuring 13, 14 and 15.

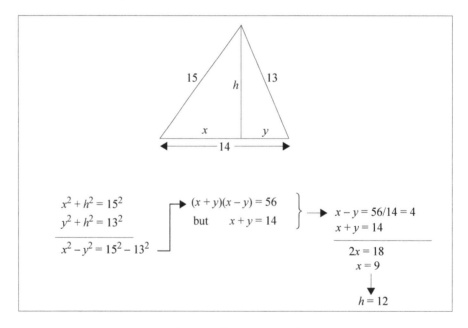

Figure 34. Pythagorean task

This is another classic example of how functional the special product $a^2 - b^2 = (a+b) \cdot (a-b)$ can be, even though it is often – unjustly – no longer acknowledged. In days gone by, this approach was an initial step towards deriving the formula of Heron, which expresses the area of a triangle in terms of the sides a, b and c and the half circumference s:

$$O = \sqrt{s(s-a)(s-b)(s-c)}.$$

This classical formula has fallen entirely into disuse. On one hand, this is understandable because it has little practical value. On the other hand, the formula is very attractive for algebra education. It leads to useful exercises such as checking the dimensions (if the sides of the triangle are each multiplied by λ the area is multiplied by λ^2), examining the special cases (what happens if $s = a$?), and special cases (for example, what happens if $a = b = c$?).

On a soccer field measuring 60 m by 100 m, the ball happens to be located at a point which is equidistant from goal A and from the two corner flags on the other side.
a. On which side of the midfield line is the ball located with respect to that goal (A)?
b. Calculate the distance from the ball to goal A.

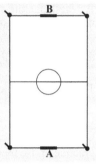

Figure 35. Soccer and Pythagoras?

Finally, Figure 35 shows another example of an exercise using the Pythagorean theorem to create an equation. The equation that must be formulated here, after working out the first degree, turns out to be

$$30^2 + (100-x)^2 = x^2,$$

which is easy to solve.

In this way, the geometry that is taught in the first years of secondary education offers plenty of possibilities for simple algebraic models. We refer here to a few more, which unfortunately no longer appear in the schoolbooks of today: various geometric representations of the arithmetic, geometric and harmonic mean, and as part of the geometry of similarity, the golden ratio.

PRODUCTIVE PRACTICE

Practice is essential to anchor skills acquired through insight. For most students, the effect of practice will improve to the extent that the exercises require more thought, elicit more independent contributions from the students and offer more possibilities for reflection. In short, the effect of practice will improve to the extent that the exercises have a more productive character. In this chapter, a number of examples of productive practice has been provided. Here are ten recommendations that have been explicitly or implicitly addressed in these examples.

1. Ask reverse questions to promote mental agility.
2. Vary the practice formats and activities as much as possible.
3. Challenge the students to reason logically (for example, by using coherent strings of problems).
4. Challenge the students to generalize (for example by means of number patterns).
5. Practice the substitution of 'formulas in formulas' (formal substitution).
6. Practice the elimination of variables in systems of formulas or equations.
7. Pay attention to the verbal reading and writing of algebra rules or formulas.
8. Challenge the students to create their 'own productions'.
9. Also practice algebra in geometry.

and more generally

10. Where possible, maintain and strengthen previously acquired computational and algebraic skills.

Of course the question is how you as a teacher or author can apply these points in practice or use them to organize a curriculum. During the first three years of secondary education, the programme is broad and the number of available lesson hours is, to put it mildly, limited. As a result, the 'pure' algebra lessons often become fragmented. However, the tendency in secondary education to differentiate according to level creates more space for teaching algebra to pre-academic students. In fact, starting in 7th grade, every week in the curriculum should contain algebra! If a non-algebra lesson does not provide an opportunity for maintaining algebra skills, then the students should be given a brief algebra assignment at least every week. In that case, supplementary material, on paper or in digital form, should be developed to accompany the various textbooks, preferably in the spirit which we have sketched out in this chapter.

The Freudenthal Institute certainly has something to offer in this area at present, but this will be greatly expanded in the near future. First of all, I refer to the algebra applets on Wisweb[v]. In addition, we offer a collection of exercises (Kindt, 2010).

At the beginning of this chapter, reference was made to 'the old days', which means roughly the first half of the 20th century. Our intention was certainly not to idealize the past, but quite the opposite. In our view, algebra at that time was often practiced in a mechanical fashion. After secondary education in the Netherlands was standardized by law, a great deal changed. The traditional deductive element disappeared from geometry, but it reappeared in algebra. Structure properties (associativity, commutativity, distributivity) acquired a more prominent place; the idea was that proper understanding of these properties was more important than doing many exercises. However, with the introduction of the current programme, the deductive element that was intended at that time disappeared almost entirely from algebra. In itself, this was an understandable change of course. But the pendulum has swung too far to the other side. Today, the question 'how should I do that?' often seems more important than 'why is that true?' In any case, this reflects the content of the textbooks and is also shown in the behaviour of the students. The core of mathematics and mathematics education is achieving true understanding of mathematics. Moreover, except for conventions, you should not have to accept anything on authority alone. This view should also resonate more and more frequently when practicing algebra.

PROPOSITIONS ABOUT ALGEBRA EDUCATION

1. During the first two years of pre-academic education, teachers must pay a great deal of attention to the *arithmetic side of algebra*, i.e. algebra in relation to arithmetic, mental arithmetic, number patterns, number theory and combinatorial counting problems

2. The *mixing* of algebra with negative numbers can be temporarily postponed ('negative numbers temporarily mothballed') due to their abstract character and the resulting complications.

3. Teachers must pay a great deal of attention to doing mathematics with regular *fractions* and *exponents*, first at the 'number level', and later on with variables.

4. It is advisable to use *historical contexts*. Babylonian, Egyptian, Greek and Arabic mathematics have a great deal to offer in the area of concrete algebra.

5. It is a good idea to memorize certain algebra rules, especially the *difference of squares rule*. These rules must be continually applied.

6. It is tempting to present algebraic rules *visually*: multiplying a sum by a sum, crossing out, cross multiplying, removing grouping symbols, etc. The danger here is that this elicits imitation behaviour, and that pupils unthinkingly transfer the methods to inappropriate situations. These are in fact nothing more than memory aids and should not play a role in the development of a skill.

7. Once pupils attain reasonable mastery over a number of techniques, algebra can – and should – be used to *make proofs*, for example of special properties of natural numbers.

8. The concept of a 'functional relation' between two quantities or variables is more abstract than many people think. In the history of mathematics, this idea appeared relatively late, and that fact alone gives pause for thought. The topic (sometimes called 'tables - graphs - formulas') is certainly very important, but is currently being emphasized *too early and too much*. It is highly questionable whether the function concept helps pupils acquire the necessary algebraic skills and insights. One disadvantage of addressing functions at an early stage is that it leads to a style of notation for which the pupils are not yet ready.

9. *Proportion tables* (didactically a rich concept!) are valuable from many perspectives. In fact, they can also be seen as naturally leading to the function concept. It is important that they are expanded at a later stage (proportional to the square/third power inverse of ...) and are also presented as a graph.

MARTIN KINDT

ACKNOWLEDGEMENT

The author thanks Ed de Moor and Chris Zaal for their contributions to this chapter.

NOTES

i   Solving equations with tiles.
ii For this, the applet 'Geometric Algebra 2D' can be very useful, see www.fi.uu.nl/wisweb/en/.
iii In early algebra this is often called the tiles method.
iv The Babylonians probably noticed that the area of the circle should be equal to half of the product of radius and perimeter. In combination with 'perimeter is about six times the radius' this immediately provides the formula.
v   See also Chapter 8 on Algebra and technology.

REFERENCES

Alders, C.J. (1953). *Algebra voor m.o. en v.h.o. deel I, 18 – 20e druk*. [Algebra for middle and higher education, part I.] Groningen: P. Noordhoff N.V.

Dormolen, J. van (1975). *Vaardigheden, 1001 redenen waarom leerlingen geen (goede) routine hebben*. [Skills, 1001 reasons why students don't have (enough) routine.] Utrecht: IOWO.

Dijksterhuis, E.J. (1934). Epistemisch wiskundeonderwijs. [Epistemic mathematics education.] *Euclides, 10*, 165-213.

Freudenthal, H. (1983). *Didactical phenomenology of mathemetical structures*. Dordrecht: D. Reidel Publishing Company.

Freudenthal, H. (1991). *Revisiting mathematics education*. Dordrecht: D. Reidel Publishing Company.

Groep, J. van de (2005). De wiskundedocent als goochelaar: snel optellen in een Fibonacci-rij. [The mathematics teacher as a magician: quick additions in a Fibonacci sequence.] *Euclides, 81*(3), 113.

Hiele, P.M. van (1986). *Structure and insight: a theory of mathematics education*. Orlando Fl: Academic Press.

Johnson, D.A., & Rising, G.R. (1967). *Guidelines for teaching mathematics*. Belmont CA: Wadsworth Company.

Kindt, M. (1990). Werken met standaardfuncties [Operating with standard functions]. Utrecht: Freudenthal Instituut.

Kindt, M. (2000). De erfenis van al-Khwarizmi [The heritage of al-Khwarizmi]. In F. Goffree, M. van Hoorn, & B. Zwaneveld (Eds.) *Honderd jaar wiskundeonderwijs* (pp. 57-69). Leusden: Nederlandse Vereniging van Wiskundeleraren

Kindt, M. (2010). *Positive algebra*. Utrecht: Freudenthal Instituut.

Kindt, M. (2003). *Algebra off course*, Utrecht: Freudenthal Instituut.

Lange, J. de, et al. (1994). *Wiskunde B vwo, rapport studiecommissie*. [Mathematics B study report.] Utrecht: Studiecommissie Wiskunde B vwo.

Loon, P. van (2005). Combi-uren wiskunde-natuurkunde. [Combined math and science lessons.] *Euclides, 80*(8), 406-410.

Moor, E., de & Schoemaker, G. (1979). *Rekenkalender, 77 problemen voor rekenachtige dagen*. [Arithmatic calendar, 77 problems for rainy days.] Utrecht: Instituut Ontwikkeling Wiskunde Onderwijs.

Sawyer, A.A. (1959). *A concrete approach to abstract algebra*. San Francisco CA: Freeman.

Sterk, H., & Perrenet, J. (2005). Kunnen (wij op) onze kinderen rekenen? [Can we count on our children?] *Euclides, 81*(2), 63-65.

Waerden, B.L. van der (1961). *Science awakening*. New York: Oxford University Press.

PAUL DRIJVERS, PETER BOON, MARTIN VAN REEUWIJK

8. ALGEBRA AND TECHNOLOGY

An algebra curriculum that serves its students well in the coming century may
look very different from an ideal curriculum from some years ago. The increased availability of computers and calculators will change what mathematics is useful as well as changing how mathematics is done. At the same time as
challenging the content of what is taught, the technological revolution is also
providing rich prospects for teaching and is offering students new paths to understanding. (Stacey & Chick, 2000, p. 216)

INTRODUCTION

It is beyond any doubt that Information and Communication Technology (ICT) plays
an increasingly important role in today's society and in the future professional practices of current students. This raises the question of whether technology might also
play a similar role in algebra education and, if so, which role that would be.

In 2008, NCTM, the National Council for Teachers of Mathematics in the United
States, formulated a position statement on the use of technology in mathematics education in general. A core paragraph in this document says:

Technology is an essential tool for learning mathematics in the 21st century,
and all schools must ensure that all their students have access to technology.
Effective teachers maximize the potential of technology to develop students'
understanding, stimulate their interest, and increase their proficiency in mathematics. When technology is used strategically, it can provide access to mathematics for all students.
(NCTM, 2008, p. 1)

NCTM acknowledges the importance of technology and recognizes its potential, for
example for enhancing students' understanding, for stimulating their interest, and for
increasing proficiency. More specific for algebra education, a Study Group of the International Commission on Mathematical Instruction, a commission within the International Mathematical Union, focuses on the effects of technology on the teaching
and learning of algebra (Stacey & Chick, 2000; Stacey, Chick & Kendal, 2004). The
quotation at the top of this page points out the challenge educators have to face while
developing contemporary technology-rich algebra education. How can the opportunities that technology offers to algebra education be exploited, without neglecting
important aspects of algebraic skills? Which roles can new technologies play in algebra education, and in which way can the teaching and learning of algebra benefit?

P. Drijvers (ed.), Secondary Algebra Education, 179–202.
© 2011 *Sense Publishers. All rights reserved.*

These are the main questions addressed in this chapter. Due to this focus on algebra education, some aspects of the integration of technology into mathematics education in general will remain unaddressed, such as the changing role of the teacher, changes in classroom arrangement and learning organization, and increasing opportunities for communication and collaborative learning in particular. For more information on these topics we refer to the recent work of Hoyles and Lagrange (2010).

AN EXAMPLE: TRIAL-AND-IMPROVE

Two students in grade 8, Annie and Michael, are working with the applet *Algebra Arrows*[i]. With the applet, they construct arrow chains, which in fact represent functions as input-output machines. The left screen in Figure 1 shows the work of this pair of students on the screen. The first task was to construct an arrow chain which gives 3, 3.2, 3.4, ... as an output table and apparently this worked out well.

The next task is to switch the order of the multiplication and the addition operations and still get the same table of output values (see Figure 1 on the right). The students start with some alternatives, such as 'plus 3 times 0.2' and 'plus 6 times 0.2'. Even if multiplying with 0.2 is correct, they change this factor into 1.2, so their chain is 'plus 3 times 1.2'. This results in an output table of 3, 4.2, 5.4, ..., which they realize is not correct. Next, the observer comes by their desk.

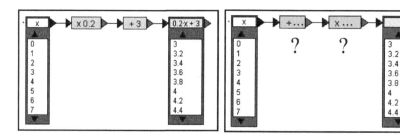

Figure 1. Student work (left) and next task (right)

Observer: Why isn't it [the factor of 1.2] correct?
Michael: Because we don't get the right numbers.
Annie: Oh, the integer numbers here ....
            (She points at the integer parts of the numbers 3, 4.2, 5.4, ... in their output table.)
            ... each time they get one more, whereas here [the integer values of the numbers in the output table that is asked for in the task] constantly 3, 3, 3, 3.

Michael seems to be looking whether the output table shows the required values, whereas Annie pays attention to the increments in the table and notices that these have become 1.2 instead of 0.2, as is required in the task. The students change the factor of multiplication back to 0.2 and try chains such as 'plus 9 times 0.2' and 'plus 18 times 0.2'. In this way, after some trials and improvements, they get the correct chain: 'plus 15 times 0.2'. Then Michael notices the relation between the 'plus 3' in the original chain and the 'plus 15' in the current one: 15 times 0.2 equals 3!

This observation is typical for the learning of algebra using technology in more than one aspect. First, the two students are skilled and clever in using the buttons of the applet and in navigating through the menus. This facilitates their problem solving behaviour, which we could call 'trial-and-improve': they try several options at high speed, hoping to get closer to the solution. Michael's first reaction to the observer's question, "because we don't get the right numbers," suggests that sometimes this approach is (too much!) like haphazardly trying to get the correct answer. At first, the students do not notice that 'plus 15 times 0.2' comes down to the same as 'times 0.2 plus 3'. Meanwhile, the work with the applet at the end leads to the reasoning which shows a growing insight in the phenomenon. After the observer's intervention, the students think about the answer they got and find an explanation for it.

DIDACTICAL FUNCTIONS OF TECHNOLOGY IN ALGEBRA EDUCATION

The question we address now is which roles new technologies can play in algebra education. Before looking for specific answers to this question for each of the strands within school algebra, we first identify the following three global didactical functions for technology in algebra education: technology as a tool for doing algebra, as an environment for practicing skills, and as an environment for developing concepts. Let us consider each of these three didactical functions in more detail.

Technology as a tool for doing algebra

The first didactical function of technology in algebra education is the function of a tool for outsourcing algebraic procedures while doing algebra. Probably the student would be able to carry out the routine procedures by hand as well, but chooses not to spend his energy on that. Just like numerical calculations can be left to the calculator, tables of numerical values can be produced using spreadsheet software such as Excel, graphs can be drawn with graphical software or on a graphing calculator, and algebraic procedures can be left to a computer algebra system (CAS). In these cases, technology acts as a tool, as an 'algebra assistant', and offers a broad range of applications, not necessarily designed for educational purpose. To play this didactical role of tool for algebra, technology should fulfil several criteria, such as mathematical soundness and correctness, as well as flexible support of conventional algebraic notations, representations and operations.

A characteristic of the use of technology as a tool for carrying out algebraic procedures is that the initiative usually remains with the students; they decide whether or not to use the technology for this purpose. A second characteristic is that this didactical function of technology is 'didactics-free,' in the sense that this type of use

PAUL DRIJVERS, PETER BOON, MARTIN VAN REEUWIJK

does not involve a specific didactic approach to or view on the teaching and learning of algebra. The advantage of using technology as a tool for doing algebra is that it relieves the student from a lot of procedural work, and therefore allows for quick investigations of several examples or situations, which can lead to exploration, reflection, and theoretical proceedings.

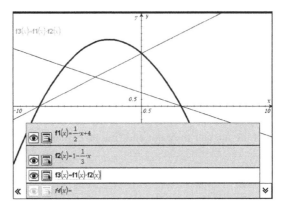

Figure 2. The task 'multiplying lines'

An example of the latter approach is the 'multiplying lines' task (Figure 2). The graphs of two linear functions and their product function are drawn. The question is how specific properties of the product graph are related to those of the 'building graphs'. Which relations exist between the zeros? What can you say about the vertex of the parabola? Which conditions do the linear functions need to fulfil in order for the parabola to touch the *x*-axis? In which cases does the vertex of the parabola coincide with the intersection point of the two lines? The technological environment – a graphing calculator in Figure 2, but it could just as easily be graphing software or Excel – takes over the drawing of the graphs and allows for exploration of the effects of changes in f_1 and f_2 on the product graph. The results of the exploration aim at inviting students to algebraic thinking.

Whether or not this works depends on the didactical setting. The danger of using technology as a generator of examples is that students stick to a superficial, phenomenological level of perception instead of entering into underlying fundamental reasoning. Through appropriate tasks and targeted questions, the teacher is in charge of focusing on this deeper thinking level.

Environment for practicing skills

A second didactical function of technology for the learning of algebra is the function of environment for practice. Technology offers several options for practicing algebraic skills. Through intelligent, diagnostic feedback, the technological environment can respond immediately to students' solutions and strategies. Randomization of task parameters allows for a huge variety of tasks, so that students can practice without straight repetition. The pace and length of the session is determined by the student himself. The technological tool is patient and consistent, and mistakes can remain invisible for peers and teacher. There is in fact no need for the teacher to correct mistakes, as this task is taken over by the tool; rather, the teacher can focus on the fundamental and conceptual difficulties that students encounter. The teacher does, however, determine the type of tasks; in that sense, the practice role of technology is often more teacher driven than is the case when ICT is used as just a tool for doing algebra. Also, a digital environment for practicing algebraic skills often implicitly contains didactical choices through the structure and sequence of algebra tasks. Therefore, the didactical function of an environment for practicing algebraic skills is not as didactics-free as the tool functionality described above. Criteria for appropriate tools for practicing algebra are good features for feedback on and registration of student work, and compatibility of problem solving strategies and procedures within the technological environment with those of paper-and-pencil algebra (Bokhove & Drijvers, 2010).

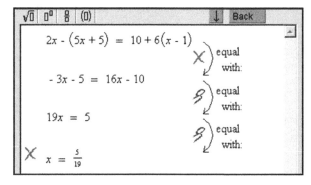

Figure 3. Practicing solving equations[i]

An example of a digital environment for solving equations is shown in Figure 3. The applet *Solving Equations* functions as an 'algebra-repetitor', which offers exercises, provides feedback, and motivates through its game-like reward structure. The applet consists of different versions or levels, that differ in the amount of support that is provided while solving the equations. At the basic level, the student just needs to indicate the operation that is needed, and the applet carries out the algebraic calculation. At the next level, the student has to carry out the algebraic operations himself, but he gets feedback on the correctness of the work. The third level is a self-assessment, which is corrected and graded by the applet. The fourth and final level is the test, which the teacher does not need to correct either.

PAUL DRIJVERS, PETER BOON, MARTIN VAN REEUWIJK

Environment for developing concepts

A third didactical functionality of technology for the learning of algebra is its use for the development of concepts and mental models. The aim is to evoke specific thinking processes and to guide the development of the students' algebraic thinking. For example, ICT may help to visualize a concept, or present it in a dynamic way, which can lead to a more versatile and deeper conceptual understanding of the mathematical object or procedure. Also, the ICT environment can function as a generator of examples, which provoke the students' curiosity and invite generalization or investigation of relationships or properties.

This didactical functionality is the most complex of the three we distinguish. First, this type of use of technology requires a careful didactical analysis of the relationship between the use of the tool with its representations and techniques on the one hand, and the mathematical thinking and skills that the students are supposed to acquire on the other. This relationship is subtle and complex: a mismatch between the two may reduce the benefit of the work with technology to zero. In addition, more than the other two, this didactical functionality of technology is guided by the teacher and also embodies didactical choices and views.

Criteria for technology that supports concept development are a perfect match between the representations and techniques in the tool environment on the one hand, and the mental images and conceptual understanding on the other. Furthermore, some construction space is needed for students to develop their thinking.

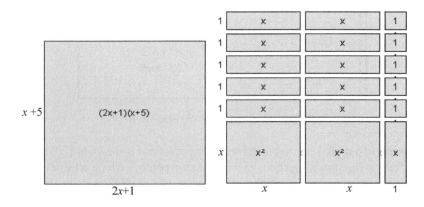

Figure 4. Multiplying two linear expressions in the applet Geometric Algebra 2D

An example of the use of technology to develop concepts is the work with the applet *Algebra Arrows*, described in Figure 1. It aims at the development of a mental image of the concept of function as an input-output machine, which transforms a number of input values into a strip of output values through a chain of operations. A second example is the applet *Geometric Algebra 2D*[i]. It represents an environment to use the

184

area of tiles as a model to think about the multiplication of two algebraic factors (Figure 4). The applet offers opportunities for splitting up, moving and merging rectangular tiles, which represent algebraic expressions. This way, the area model becomes a meaningful model to the student, one they can fall back on in future, for example with expanding.

Such a conceptual model environment allows the student to investigate many different situations. By doing so, a distance emerges between the work in the digital environment and the concrete context that forms the motive for the task. The work within the technological environment will exceed the specific context; the reasoning with the model acquires a more general and more algebraic character. This invites abstraction and the development of a mental 'algebra world'. It is in this invitation that the power of technology as an environment for concept development lies; to exploit this power remains a task for the teacher.

Didactical functions intertwined

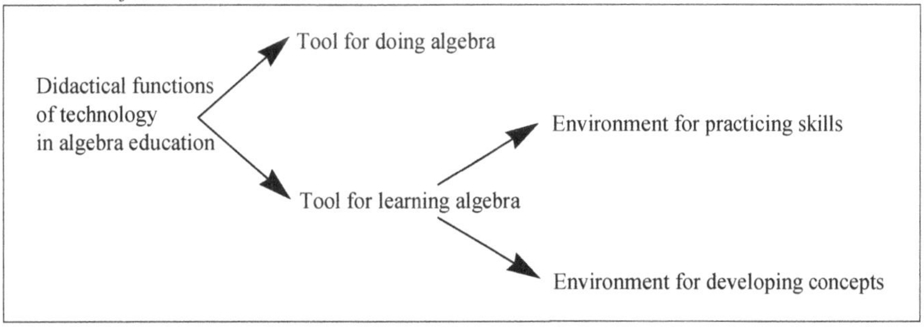

Figure 5. Schematic overview of didactical functions of technology in algebra education

Figure 5 shows a schematic overview of the three main didactical functions of technology in algebra education. It should be noted that these three functions are not properties of the technological tool, but of the way in which it is used in students' learning activities. This being said, some tools are more appropriate for specific didactical functions than others:

> Tools matter: they stand between the user and the phenomenon to be modelled, and shape activity structures. (Hoyles & Noss, 2003, p. 341)

The three didactical functions of digital tools are not mutually exclusive, but are intertwined. The insights that students develop need application in practice; practicing tasks and appropriate use of tools require conceptual understanding. As an example of the intertwinement of didactical functions, Figure 6 shows a sheaf of graphs for the set of functions $x \rightarrow x^4 + b \cdot x^2 + 1$. The didactical functionality of the technology is the tool function: the graphing, that the student could do by hand, is outsourced to the tool, because drawing a family of graphs is time consuming and not practical to do by hand. Meanwhile, through the visualization that the technology offers, and the opportunity to change for example window settings or parameter values, exploration becomes possible, and new questions arise. It seems that the curve through the vertices is a parabola, but is this really the case? How does the number of zeros depend on the value for the parameter b? This way, technology invites exploration, which leads to new insights and to the understanding of the concepts of parameter and families of functions.

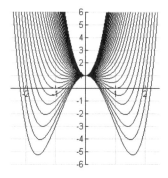

Figure 6. A sheaf of graphs: outsourcing the work to raise new questions

Nowadays, the different didactical functions of ICT for algebra education can be better exploited in educational practice than was the case in the past. Through the internet and increasing interoperability, students can continue their work at any time and in any place, and communicate with their peers and their teacher. The interactive whiteboard is a powerful means to make students engage in whole-class interactions, in which technology plays an important mediating role. Electronic learning environments such as Blackboard, Brainbox, and, more specific for mathematics, the Digital Mathematics Environment integrate many functionalities: they distribute and provide content, i.e. digital courseware, they host students' digital notebooks and portfolios, and supply virtual workspace in which collaborative work and communication are supported. The teacher can monitor the students' progress (see also Figure 14). In addition to this, he can arrange tools and, by using authoring tools, customize content and adapt it to mathematical or pedagogical goals. As a result, the teacher, in his role as designer of his course, acquires ownership of his teaching.

PATTERNS AND FORMULAS WITH TECHNOLOGY

In previous chapters of this book we distinguished three strands within algebra education: patterns and formulas, restrictions, and functions and graphs. How can the three didactical functions of technology be integrated in each of these strands? In this section, we answer this question for patterns and formulas; similar discussions of the two other strands follow in the subsequent sections.

Patterns and technology

As far as patterns are concerned, the main contribution of technology is that it can help to generate examples that invite sorting, pattern recognitions, generalization and investigation. Initially, technology functions as a tool for doing algebra. As the activities proceed, the use acquires the character of an environment for conceptual development. Figure 7 shows a first example of this, which concerns the reproduction with Excel of one of the arithmetic patterns described in Chapter 4. The regularity in the output begs for an algebraic proof. The technological environment, in this case spreadsheet software, supports the finding of similar arithmetic patterns. Research suggests, however, that young students (12-13 year old) may encounter difficulties while copying formulas in a spreadsheet (Haspekian, 2005).

A	B	C	D	E	F
n	n^2	n-1	n+1	(n-1)*(n+1)	n^2-(n-1)*(n+1)
1	1	0	2	0	1
2	4	1	3	3	1
3	9	2	4	8	1
4	16	3	5	15	1
5	25	4	6	24	1
6	36	5	7	35	1
7	49	6	8	48	1
8	64	7	9	63	1
9	81	8	10	80	1
10	100	9	11	99	1
11	121	10	12	120	1
12	144	11	13	143	1

Figure 7. Creating a pattern with Excel

An example of a higher level of pattern generation and recognition is shown in Figure 8. Computer algebra acts as a tool to factor expressions of the form $x^n - 1$ (Lagrange, 2000; Kieran & Drijvers, 2006). In itself, this is just a matter of pressing buttons. The results, however, raise several questions: in which cases does one get exactly 2 factors, and in which cases more than 2? Do we always get a factor $x + 1$ when n is even? How can you be sure of that? For $x^6 - 1$, we might have expected $(x - 1) \cdot (x^5 + x^4 + x^3 + x^2 + x + 1)$. Is the result shown on the screen equivalent with that? How does the software find its answers anyway, and how would we find the same results with paper and pencil? These and other reflective, mathematical questions enhance the development of algebraic meaning.

factor $(x^2 - 1)$	$(x-1)\cdot(x+1)$
factor $(x^3 - 1)$	$(x-1)\cdot(x^2+x+1)$
factor $(x^4 - 1)$	$(x-1)\cdot(x+1)\cdot(x^2+1)$
factor $(x^5 - 1)$	$(x-1)\cdot(x^4+x^3+x^2+x+1)$
factor $(x^6 - 1)$	$(x-1)\cdot(x+1)\cdot(x^2+x+1)\cdot(x^2-x+1)$
factor $(x^7 - 1)$	$(x-1)\cdot(x^6+x^5+x^4+x^3+x^2+x+1)$
factor $(x^8 - 1)$	$(x-1)\cdot(x+1)\cdot(x^2+1)\cdot(x^4+1)$
factor $(x^9 - 1)$	$(x-1)\cdot(x^2+x+1)\cdot(x^6+x^3+1)$

Figure 8. Factoring expressions of the form $x^n - 1$ with a computer algebra tool

This example shows that computer algebra software can invite exploration and algebraic thinking. However, the use of computer algebra does require some prior time investment, as the algebraic flexibility such environments offer has as its price a syntactic rigidity in relation to entering expressions and commands. Because of this investment, computer algebra is also used as a backbone of front-end educational technology, that is put in action to check student results on algebraic equivalence with desired results, for example. As a result, computer algebra offers better error detection and therefore student feedback.

$$\frac{d}{dx}x^2 = 2x$$
$$\frac{d}{dx}x^3 = 3x^2$$
$$\frac{d}{dx}x^4 = 4x^3$$
$$\frac{d}{dx}x^5 = 5x^4$$
$$\frac{d}{dx}x^6 = 6x^5$$
$$\frac{d}{dx}x^7 = 7x^6$$

Figure 9. A pattern of derivatives

Another example of the use of computer algebra for generating patterns is provided by Berry, Graham and Watkins (1994). The idea in the example is that students first use computer algebra to differentiate a number of functions, to investigate the pattern in the results, and finally reflect on the meaning of the differentiation (see Figure 9). This is an example of the so-called BlackBox-WhiteBox approach, in which students are first confronted with the results of working with technology, which are the motive for a subsequent investigation on what is really happening, what it means, and how one would find these results with paper and pencil. This approach is a reaction to the WhiteBox-BlackBox principle, where students carry out relevant algebraic operations by hand first, and only use ICT for outsourcing operations after skills and insights have been developed (Buchberger, 1990).

The above examples show how the didactical functions of tool for doing algebra and environment for concept development can be aligned: the algebraic power of the technology is used to generate examples that in a subsequent step are subject to algebraic reasoning.

Formulas and technology

In the second and third example of the previous section, formulas play a central role. The examples show that technology can generate formulas, and, in the case of computer algebra, transform them to other forms. It is interesting to notice that it is not always trivial to know which command leads to the form the user want to get, and, conversely, to recognize which 'story the algebraic form tells'. Figure 10, for example, shows how an algebraic function definition is rewritten by computer algebra through the commands factor and expand. An expert user, who is skilled in 'reading' formulas, recognizes the zeros and the vertical asymptote of the graph in the second form, and the equation of the other asymptote in the third form. The ability to interpret the computer algebra output requires a considerable amount of insight into the structure of algebraic expressions. That insight is part of the algebraic expertise which was labelled symbol sense in Chapter 1.

$$f(x) = \frac{4x^2 + 7x}{8x - 2} \quad \text{"Done"}$$

$$\text{factor}(f(x)) \qquad \frac{x \cdot (4 \cdot x + 7)}{2 \cdot (4 \cdot x - 1)}$$

$$\text{expand}(f(x)) \qquad \frac{1}{4x - 1} + \frac{x}{2} + 1$$

Figure 10. Rewriting a function definition

Several technological tools can help students to acquire that insight, and thus act as environment for the development of algebraic concepts. An example of this didactical functionality is the applet *AlgebraExpressions*, in which students create tree representations of algebraic expressions[i] (Figure 11). These expressions can have an increasing complexity, in which the structure of partial trees and the hierarchy of operations remain transparent. The tree representation is a model that can also back up students' paper-and-pencil work, when they encounter complex formulas.

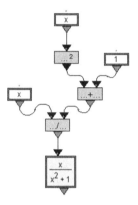

Figure 11. A tree representation of an expression made in the applet AlgebraExpressions

Entering formulas needs attention while working with formulas and expressions in technological environments. Some ICT-applications provide one-line formula entry, which means that using brackets is required. Figure 12, for example, shows how the expression

$$\frac{x}{x^2 + 1}$$

is entered in the graphing calculator TI-84 and in Excel. One can imagine a student forgetting to use brackets, and thereby accidentally entering

$$\frac{x}{x^2} + 1$$

To avoid such mistakes, a two-dimensional 'pretty print' formula editor is preferable, and is getting more and more common.

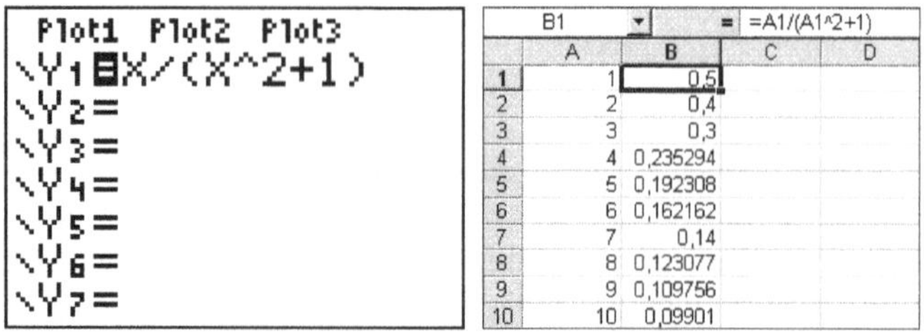

Figure 12. Entering expressions in the TI-84 and in Excel

RESTRICTIONS WITH TECHNOLOGY

For solving equations and dealing with restrictions, a range of technological tools is available, each with its own focus on mental models, practice or use. For practicing solving equations, applets can be used (see for example Figure 3). Figure 13 shows a variation of this applet, as well as how a student solves a similar equation with paper and pencil. The student's writing clearly reveals the transfer of strategy and notation from the applet environment to paper-and-pencil.

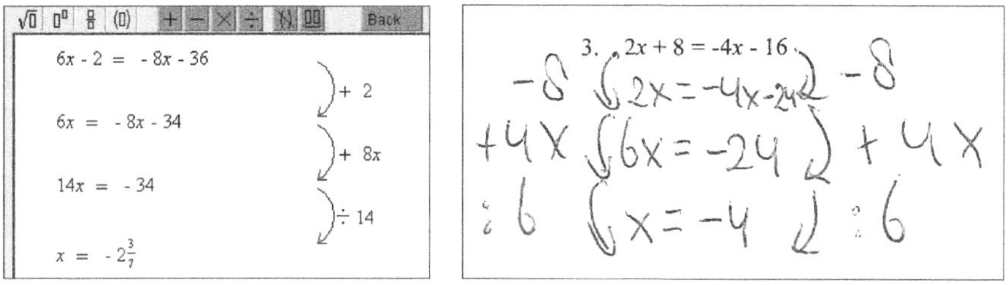

Figure 13. Solving equations: strategy transfer from technology to paper and pencil

There is a danger that work with technology has a fleeting character for the student. Screens appear, screens disappear and not much tangible remains after the session. To avoid this, student results can be saved in an individual digital workspace. This allows students to review and revise their work and in this way create their personal digital notebook; for the teacher, this type of registration offers means to monitor student progress, and to correct and eventually grade work. Figure 14 shows an example of the features of such a system for the teacher, in this case the Digital Mathematics Environment[ii]. In such systems, teachers can easily check the students' homework and, while preparing the next lesson, identify any difficulties they need to give more attention to.

The graphing calculator can be used as a tool for just solving equations graphically or numerically. One method consists of intersecting two graphs, corresponding to the left hand side and the right hand side of the equation, respectively. An advantage of this approach is that students develop a mental image of solving an equation as finding intersection points, which is an appropriate image for equations in one single variable. An alternative approach for solving equations with a graphing calculator is to use the solve module.

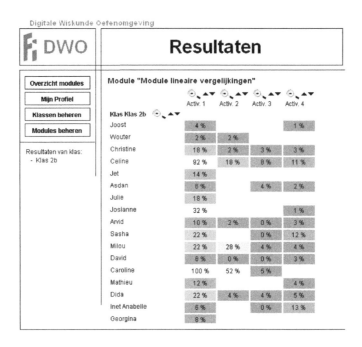

Figure 14. Screen shot of the Digital Mathematics Environment for student registration

If exact or symbolic solutions are required, a computer algebra tool is needed. Solving an equation with such CAS tools, which are available for both desktops and handheld devices, seems straightforward and easy. For novice users of this type of technological tool, however, this is not trivial, because the solve technique highlights aspects of solving equations that often remain underexposed in work with paper and pencil (Drijvers & Gravemeijer, 2004). For example, students often are unaware of the differences between algebraic expressions and equations, which leads to trying to solve for example $x^2 + b \cdot x + 1$ instead of $x^2 + b \cdot x + 1 = 0$. Also, in cases of equations with more than one variable, students often do not realize that an equation is always solved *with respect to an unknown*, and we can not expect the technology to know which variable plays that role in the equation at stake. The unknown, therefore, must be specified, something which often remains implicit while solving with paper and pencil. If the solution of a parametric equation turns out to be an expression instead of a numerical value, students may feel that 'nothing is really solved', as their interpretation of a solution is restricted to numerical outcomes. As a final issue while solving equations with a computer algebra tool, the upper part of Figure 15 shows that the solution of the general quadratic equation in some cases is represented differently from the form in which it usually appears in text books. The solution of the second equation, $x^2 + b \cdot x + 1 = 0$, is not copied correctly by one of the students in her notebook (Figure 15 bottom part).

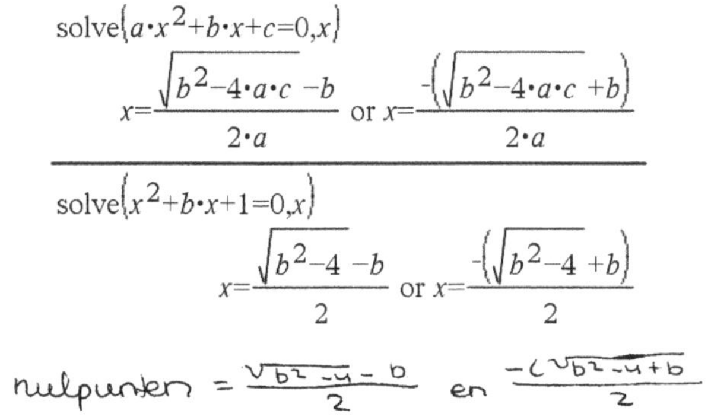

$$\text{solve}\left(a \cdot x^2 + b \cdot x + c = 0, x\right)$$
$$x = \frac{\sqrt{b^2 - 4 \cdot a \cdot c} - b}{2 \cdot a} \text{ or } x = \frac{-\left(\sqrt{b^2 - 4 \cdot a \cdot c} + b\right)}{2 \cdot a}$$
$$\text{solve}\left(x^2 + b \cdot x + 1 = 0, x\right)$$
$$x = \frac{\sqrt{b^2 - 4} - b}{2} \text{ or } x = \frac{-\left(\sqrt{b^2 - 4} + b\right)}{2}$$

$$\text{nulpunten} = \frac{\sqrt{b^2 - 4} - b}{2} \text{ en } \frac{-(\sqrt{b^2 - 4} + b}{2}$$

Figure 15. Difficult representations in computer algebra software

Solving an equation algebraically using computer algebra requires intertwined technical and conceptual insight. This is expressed graphically in Figure 16, taken from Drijvers & Gravemeijer, 2004. In general, the execution of a problem solving procedure in a computer algebra environment highlights different insights than the paper-and-pencil method: there is a certain distance to the executive work, but the work must be formulated at a more abstract level. One has to 'make the work be done' instead of doing it oneself. This requires a much deeper awareness of underlying conceptual aspects.

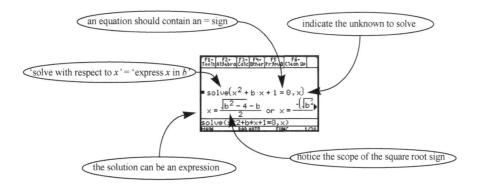

Figure 16. Conceptual and technical aspects of solving equations with CAS

FUNCTIONS AND GRAPHS WITH TECHNOLOGY

The concept of function and its representations

In this section we address the part technology can play in the teaching and learning of functions and graphs. In which ways can technology support the acquisition of the function concept?

The introductory example of this chapter concerns the applet *Algebra Arrows* (see Figure 1). This applet provides options for building arrow chains of operations, an activity which is intended to support students' concept image of functions as input-output machines (see also Chapter 6). It emerged that students also used the arrow chains as representations of functions on paper (Figure 17).

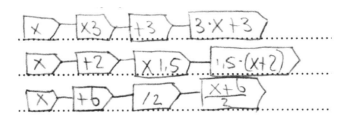

Figure 17. Transfer of the arrow chain notation to paper-and-pencil work

The same applet can be used to evoke the concept image of a function as a mathematical object with different, interrelated representations (Figure 18). In this case, the input is variable, and this variation causes the output to vary as well. With the function as input-output machine as a point of departure, the different function representations appear in one window: the arrow chain, the table, the graph and the formula (Doorman et al., in press; Drijvers et al., 2007). These representations are connected to each other. For instance, when scrolling through the values of x in the input table, the output value in the other table changes accordingly, as well as the point in the graph. This allows students to experience the different representations as different views on the same mathematical object. This way, thee applet provides an environment that supports the development of an integrated function concept. As such, it is not unique; many technological environments offer means to view different function representations simultaneously, and to study the effects of changes in one representation to the others. Technology has a lot to offer here.

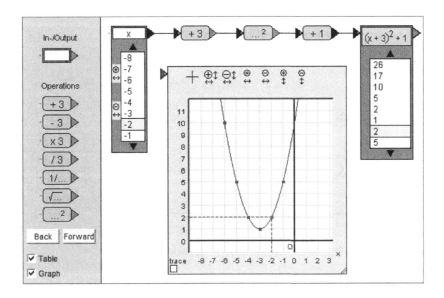

Figure 18. Function with different representations in the applet Algebra Arrows[i]

Graphs as particular function representations

With formulas, graphs can be seen as the most important function representations. ICT tools such as graphing calculators, graphical software and spreadsheet software can draw graphs quickly and accurately. By changing the window settings, students can easily get different views on a graph and zoom in on relevant details. By tracing a graph, students can investigate the co-variation of dependent and independent variable (Figure 19, left screen). The independent variable is no longer a placeholder or a generalized number, but a changing quantity which runs through the horizontal axis, causing the dependent variable to change on the vertical axis.

Probably the most powerful image of a variable as a changing quantity is generated through a slider bar, as available in Excel and many other function graphing tools. By dragging the pointer along the slider bar, the student can dynamically vary the value of a variable, for instance a parameter, in a seemingly continuous way. The right screen of Figure 19 provides an example, which is unfortunately static on paper.

In short, there are many technological tools that generate tables and graphs. Students can use them to explore change and to experience the dynamic character of a variable. These ICT-applications are considered meaningful, as they enrich the students' concept image of function. Whereas in the past, graphs used to be the end point of a laborious algebraic function investigation, now they form accessible starting points for further exploration (Kindt, 1992ab). In this way, the use of technology gradually affects the content and pedagogy of algebra education.

195

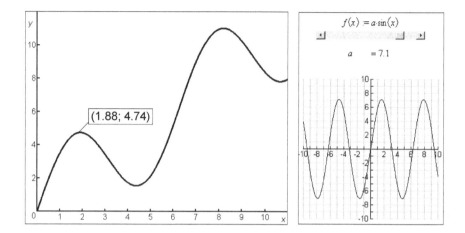

Figure 19. Tracing a graph and using a slider bar

Even if technology can be very useful for graphing functions, we need to be aware of the difference between the graph as a set of pixels that students see on a screen, and the mathematical object of a graph, which in fact comes down to the function definition as a set of ordered pairs. Particularly when screen resolution is low, as is the case on graphing calculators, the difference can be striking and students are not always able to bridge the gap between the two.

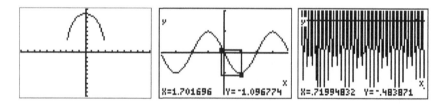

Figure 20. Misleading graphs on the screen of a graphing calculator

As an example, Figure 20 shows two misleading graphs. The left one is the graph of $x \rightarrow 3\sqrt{9 - x^2}$ on the domain [-10, 10]. The half circle that the graph in fact is, does not touch the x-axis on the screen of the – first generation! – graphing calculator. The graph in the middle is the graph of $x \rightarrow \sin(95 \cdot x)$ on the interval [-2π, 2π]. However, zooming in on the box shown in the middle screen provides the graph in the right screen. Apparently, the graph in the middle screen is too smooth and hides much of the function's variation! Student will have to learn to deal with graphical limitations such as the ones shown here. Classroom discussions are a way to make explicit the differences between discrete graphs consisting of approximated screen pixels, and smooth, continuous graphs as they exist in mathematical theory. Another teaching strategy is to exploit technology's limitations by challenging students to create misleading graphs on their screens. This somewhat surprising task may fascinate students and can invite deeper understanding of graphs.

The above example shows that the graphing options of technological tools can be used to work on unusual tasks. Another example of this is shown in Figure 6. In line with this is the example in Figure 21. The task is to find an equation of the curve that 'touches' each of the line segments of this pattern, or, as an easier variant, to show that the graph of the function $f(x) = x + 10 - 2\sqrt{10x}$ has this property.

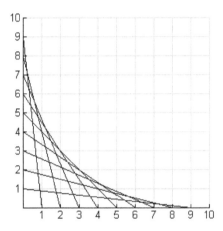

Figure 21. A sheaf of segments motivating algebraic questions

To summarize this section, we conclude that technology offers opportunities to work with formulas, to draw graphs and tables, and to combine and integrate different function representations. The technology plays the didactical roles of tool to carry out the work, and of environment for concept development.

CONCLUSION AND REFLECTION

Conclusion

The central question in this chapter is which roles new technologies can play in algebra education, and how the teaching and learning of algebra can benefit from these roles. In answer to the first part of this question, three didactical functions of technology in algebra education are distinguished: the function of tool for carrying out the algebraic work, the function of environment for practicing skills, and the function of environment for concept development. These three didactical functions, which differ in their degree of guidance by the teacher, are not mutually exclusive and may merge. However, each function does put specific demands on the technology. For the tool functionality, it is important that conventional mathematical notations can be used, that a standard repertoire of algebraic procedures is available and that it is carried out correctly. For the functionality of environment for practice, it is important that the techniques supported by the technology match with the paper-and-pencil strategies that students need to master. Furthermore, adequate feedback is an important feature. For technology as an environment for developing concepts, a requirement is that the activities, techniques and representations in this environment will indeed evoke the concept images and insights as intended. Even if these criteria may sound trivial, it is not always easy in practice to foresee the subtleties of the use of technology in each of the three roles in detail while preparing a lesson. This brings us to the second part of the question: how can the teaching and learning of algebra benefit optimally from these roles?

For each of the three algebra strands, patterns and formulas, restrictions, and functions and graphs, the chapter provides examples of meaningful ICT applications, which aim at capitalizing on the opportunities technology offers for algebra education. These opportunities can be labelled as variation and dynamics (e.g. see Figure 19), as generation of examples that invite pattern recognitions and generalization (e.g. see Figure 8 and Figure 9), as visualization (e.g. see Figure 1 and Figure 11) and finally also concern exploration and investigation (e.g. see Figure 2). This set of opportunities, exemplified in these concrete tasks, forms the answer to the question of how to use technology in algebra education. These opportunities have in common that they can help in changing the student from a passive 'consumer' of algebra into an active investigator, which may improve students' motivation as well as the efficiency of their learning.

Reflection

In this reflection we first focus on the *role of the teacher*. In spite of the positive description of the opportunities technology offers for algebra education, ICT is not a panacea that will make all old didactical difficulties of algebra education disappear. Exploiting the opportunities identified above requires a profound didactical consideration and preparation of the way in which technology plays a role in the learning process of the algebra topic under consideration, and how this is made concrete in the mathematics lesson. Research suggests that this so crucial didactical consideration and preparation is not an easy job for the teacher (Drijvers & Trouche, 2008; Drijvers et al., in press; Lagrange & Ozdemir Erdogan, 2009; Ruthven, Deaney, & Hennessy, 2009). Even if the feedback functionality of an ICT environment, for example, can relieve the teacher from providing feedback, other aspects of teacher-student interaction cannot be taken over by the technology. There remains much to do for the teacher: raising reflective questions, summarizing, enhancing convergence by means of whole-class discussions, sketching lines of thought, inviting exploration of and reasoning about the results found through the use of technology, relating the work with technology and the work with paper and pencil, monitoring student achievements, diagnosing difficulties students encounter in working with technology, etcetera. All these issues require thoughtful attention, and may require the development of new teaching techniques and didactical skills. For technological tools that will be used for a longer period, such as for example Excel or graphing calculators, the teacher may want to orchestrate the development of shared machine skills, so that a set of standard techniques emerges in the class. Also, the teacher may need to take care of the changing didactical contract. For example, students need to develop a critical attitude towards the limited power of technology in mathematical proofs and will need some guidelines on the paper-and-pencil skills they are supposed to master. Responding to all the needs and questions the use of technology brings to the fore, the teacher may extend and adapt the didactic repertoire of teaching techniques en orchestrations used in teaching.

A prerequisite for this process to happen, of course, is a good infrastructure. This comes down to good and accessible ICT facilities, adequate technical support, the possibility to access work from home as well as at school, and the availability of appropriate means for communication with students and evaluation of their work. Technological developments such as wireless networks, netbooks, handheld computers and interactive whiteboards contribute to such an infrastructure.

As a second reflection, we want to address an important issue in the discussion on the role of ICT in mathematics education in general, and algebra education in particular: the tension that is often assumed to exist between the use of technology for algebra and *the acquisition of procedural algebraic skills with paper and pencil*. Do students learn how to carry out algebraic work with paper and pencil, if they can outsource all the work to a technological device? What is the relationship between the use of technology for algebra and paper-and-pencil basic skills? As a first remark, we claim that the use of ICT can contribute to the development of algebraic insight and the mastery of algebraic skills, as they play a role in paper-and-pencil work. Several studies (e.g. Heid, 1988) suggest that techniques carried out in a technological environment prepare for the algebraic by-hand skills. A prerequisite for this transfer to take place is that the techniques used with the technology are to a certain extent similar to the paper and pencil ones, and that students are able to reconcile the results of their paper and pencil work with the output technology provides (Kieran & Drijvers, 2006). In addition to this, the use of technology can complement the work with paper and pencil. The example shown in Figure 16 suggests that solving an equation in a computer algebra environment stresses other aspects than solving by hand, such as the notion that one of the variables plays the role of the unknown. Similarly, solving an equation graphically with a graphing calculator with an intersect technique highlights the idea that solving an equation can be considered as finding an intersection point of graphs. As applying ICT-techniques stresses different aspects compared to the paper-and-pencil work, it can complement the traditional methods.

Meanwhile, algebraic work with technology often has a different character in comparison to work with paper and pencil, as the student takes on more the position of a supervisor than that of labourer. Because one cannot be a good supervisor without experience as labourer, some paper-and-pencil skill remains indispensable. Paper-and-pencil skills need to be acquired, practiced and maintained in order to remain operational. If the use of technology means that skills are not maintained, it can only be expected that mastery decreases. Our concern, therefore, is to find a balanced combination of algebra 'with the mind, on paper and on a screen'. Even if we do acknowledge the additional value of technology in mathematics education, it will not render paper and pencil redundant, but rather support and complement it.

As a final reflection, let us briefly consider the *future of technology in algebra education*. The development of ICT tools, which mainly takes place outside the educational community, is expected to continue at a high pace. Think of mobile technology, netbooks and handheld computers, of serious gaming. Learning can happen any time, any place, on interoperable platforms; communication facilities guarantee that the learning process does not need to be a solitary one. Therefore, connectivity in more than one sense is a key idea for future developments (Drijvers, Kieran & Mariotti, 2010). The opportunities for the teacher to monitor, support and evaluate student work will further increase. Digital portfolios are ways to avoid the fleeting character that sometimes characterises the use of technology. Assessment can take place digitally as well, and can be flexible in time and in content. Teacher and students communicate through the digital learning environment and during digital meeting hours. These developments have pedagogical consequences. We already mentioned the need to find an equilibrium between paper-and-pencil skills and the skills that a technological environment requires to become a meaningful algebra tool in the hands of a student. The exact position of this equilibrium depends on the goals of algebra education, which are subject to reconsideration due to the current technological developments. As a tentative outcome, one may expect a shift towards processes such as mathematizing and modelling, at the cost of basic procedural skills. The ability to translate a problem situation into algebraic terms and into machine techniques, for example, is likely to become more important than it already is, as is the case for the ability to relate graphical and algebraic properties. Flexible problem solving behaviour is required, as the affordances and constraints of the technology will appeal to creative and inventive problem solving behaviour. Assessment of these types of higher order skills is not easy, but it seems logical that technology will play a role there as well. Meanwhile, assessment will also include paper-and-pencil tests for basic algebraic skills.

Conclusive for the success of the use of technology in algebra education will be the way in which teachers and the mathematics educational community as a whole manage to integrate the new media into teaching in a natural and meaningful way. To make the somewhat optimistic scenario sketched above come true, it is crucial that teachers' professional expertise concerning the use of technology in mathematics education will be further developed and that the design of good practice teaching examples and courses for professional development will be facilitated.

NOTES

i   Available at http://www.fi.uu.nl/wisweb/en/
ii Available at http://www.fi.uu.nl/dwo/en/

REFERENCES

Berry J., Graham, E., & Watkins, A. (1994). Integrating the Derive program into the teaching of mathematics. *The international Derive journal, 1*(1), 83-96.

Bokhove, C., & Drijvers, P. (2010. Assessing assessment tools for algebra: design and application of an instrument for evaluating tools for digital assessment of algebraic skills. *International journal of computers for mathematical learning.* Online First.

Buchberger, B. (1990). Should students learn integration rules? *Sigsam bulletin, 24*(1), 10-17.

Doorman, M., Boon, P., Drijvers, P., Van Gisbergen, S., Gravemeijer, K., Reed, H., & Drijvers, P. (submitted). Tool use and conceptual development: an example of a form-function-shift.

Drijvers, P., Doorman, M., Boon, P., Van Gisbergen, S., & Gravemeijer, K. (2007). Tool use in a technology-rich learning arrangement for the concept of function. In D. Pitta-Pantazi & G. Philippou (Eds.), *Proceedings of the V Congress of the European society for research in mathematics education CERME5* (pp. 1389-1398). Larnaca, Cyprus: University of Cyprus.

Drijvers, P., Doorman, M., Boon, P., Reed, H., & Gravemeijer, K. (in press). The teacher and the tool; instrumental orchestrations in the technology-rich mathematics classroom. *Educational studies in mathematics.*

Drijvers, P., & Gravemeijer, K.P.E. (2004). Computer algebra as an instrument: examples of algebraic schemes. In D. Guin, K. Ruthven, & L. Trouche (Eds.), *The didactical challenge of symbolic calculators: turning a computational device into a mathematical instrument* (pp. 163-196). Dordrecht, the Netherlands: Kluwer Academic Publishers.

Drijvers, P., Kieran, C., & Mariotti, M.A. (2010). Integrating technology into mathematics education: theoretical perspectives. In C. Hoyles & J.-B. Lagrange (Eds.), *Mathematics education and technology - rethinking the terrain* (pp. 89-132). New York/Berlin: Springer.

Drijvers, P., & Trouche, L. (2008). From artefacts to instruments: a theoretical framework behind the orchestra metaphor. In G.W. Blume & M.K. Heid (Eds.), *Research on technology and the teaching and learning of mathematics: vol. 2. cases and perspectives* (pp. 363-392). Charlotte, NC: Information Age.

Haspekian, M. (2005). An "instrumental approach" to study the integration of a computer tool into mathematics teaching: the case of spreadsheets. *International journal of computers for mathematical learning, 10*(2), 109–141.

Heid, M.K. (1988). Resequencing skills and concepts in applied calculus using the computer as a tool. *Journal for research in mathematics education, 19*, 3-25.

Hoyles, C. & Lagrange, J.-B. (Eds.), *Mathematics education and technology - rethinking the terrain.* New York/Berlin: Springer.

Hoyles, C., & Noss, R. (2003). What can digital technologies take from and bring to research in mathematics education? In A.J. Bishop, M.A. Clements, C. Keitel, J. Kilpatrick. & F.K.S. Leung (Eds.), *Second international handbook of mathematics education* (pp. 323-349). Dordrecht, Netherlands: Kluwer Academic Publishers.

Kieran, C., & Drijvers, P. (2006). The co-emergence of machine techniques, paper-and-pencil techniques, and theoretical reflection: a study of CAS use in secondary school algebra. *International journal of computers for mathematical learning, 11*(2), 205-263.

Kindt, M. (1992a). Functieonderzoek begint met de grafiek I. [Function investigation start with the graph I.] *Euclides, 67*(7), 200-204.

Kindt, M. (1992b). Functieonderzoek begint met de grafiek II. [Function investigation start with the graph II.] *Euclides, 67*(8), 227-230.

PAUL DRIJVERS, PETER BOON, MARTIN VAN REEUWIJK

Lagrange, J.-B. (2000). L'intégration d'instruments informatiques dans l'enseignement: une approche par les techniques. [The integration of digital tools in education: an approach through techniques.] *Educational studies in mathematics, 43*(1), 1-30.

Lagrange, J.-B., & Ozdemir Erdogan, E. (2009). Teachers' emergent goals in spreadsheet-based lessons: analyzing the complexity of technology integration. *Educational studies in mathematics, 71*(1), 65-84.

NCTM (2008). *The role of technology in the teaching and learning of mathematics. a position of the national council of teachers of mathematics.* Retrieved on August, 5th, 2009, from
http://www.nctm.org/uploadedFiles/About_NCTM/Position_Statements/Technology%20final.pdf

Ruthven, K., Deaney, R., & Hennessy, S. (2009). Using graphing software to teach about algebraic forms: A study of technology-supported practice in secondary-school mathematics. *Educational studies in mathematics, 71*(3), 279-297.

Stacey, K., & Chick, H. (2000). Discussion document for the twelfth ICMI study: The future of the teaching and learning of algebra. *Educational studies in mathematics, 42*(2), 215-224.

Stacey, K., Chick, H., & Kendal, M. (2004). *The future of the teaching and learning of algebra: the twelfth ICMI study.* New York / Berlin: Springer.

HENK VAN DER KOOIJ, AAD GODDIJN

9. ALGEBRA IN SCIENCE AND ENGINEERING

Traditionally, and philosophically, mathematics has been thought of as a science of ideal objects – numbers, quantities, and shapes – that are precisely defined and thus amenable to logically precise relations known as theorems. In practice, mathematics presents a more rough-and-ready image: it is about solving problems in the real world that involve measured quantities that are never perfectly precise. (Steen, 2003, p. 59)

INTRODUCTION

Preparation for future work is one of the goals of mathematics education. For that reason it makes sense to have a look at how mathematics is used in workplace settings. From international research (e.g. Bakker et al., 2008; Steen, 2001; Hoyles et al., 2002) it is well-known that the way in which mathematics is used at the workplace is quite different from the way it is learned in school. Some important general aspects of mathematics in a professional context are: reading and interpreting tables, charts and graphs, use of IT (e.g., spreadsheets), dealing with numbers, often not precise and with units of measurement, proportional reasoning, representing and analyzing data, and multi-step problem solving. Strangely enough, most of these aspects are not found in mathematics curricula in secondary education. Where mathematics learned in school is embedded in a well-defined formal structure, the mathematics used in the workplace is embedded in a professional context. Practitioners at work do use situated abstraction in which local mathematical models and ideas are used that are only partly valid in a different context because they are connected to anchors within the context of the problem itself (Noss & Hoyles, 1996; Hoyles, Noss, Kent, & Bakker, 2010; Van der Kooij, 2001).

If we look more closely at how algebra is used in natural sciences and engineering, then it turns out that there are differences in the approach to important concepts such as variable, in the nature of the formulas used and even in the approach to 'regular' numbers. Algebra is present in vocational courses in secondary and higher vocational education and in all science subjects throughout secondary school, especially in science.

In this chapter, we argue in favour of anticipating how algebra will be used outside the mathematics classroom. This may narrow the gap between mathematics and engineering, and more appropriately emphasize the applicability and usability of algebra. Moreover, we can perhaps learn something from the approaches in STEM

P. Drijvers (ed.), Secondary Algebra Education, 203–226.

HENK VAN DER KOOIJ, AAD GODDIJN

(Science, Technology, Engineering and Mathematics) that might also be useful in the mathematics classroom.

ORIENTATION AND DEFINITION OF TERMS

How is algebra used in science and engineering? To answer this question, as part of the TWIN project[i], engineering textbooks were analysed and engineering teachers were interviewed in relation to the algebraic/mathematical concepts and skills that are important in vocational courses (Van der Kooij (Ed.), Goris & Temme, 2003). As part of the SONaTe project[ii], a similar approach was taken for the science subjects in grades 10-12 of pre-university education. Both surveys reached the conclusion that in mathematics teaching, little or no attention is paid to a number of important algebraic concepts in science. Below, we refer to a number of these concepts, and illustrate them by a brief explanation. In the remainder of this chapter, these aspects will be addressed in more detail, based on examples in which the themes emerge in an integrated way.

Variables

In science and engineering, variables consistently have a meaningful name that links a specific situation: pressure, temperature, cutting rate or density. In mathematics as taught in school, variables have standardized names: x, y and z for unknowns, a, b and c for coefficients, and k, m and n for natural numbers. They take various roles, such as unknown, parameter or slope.

Quantities

Length, area and volume are geometric quantities. Mathematics, as taught in school and otherwise, also uses the quantity 'angle', but this is pretty much the end of the story, and beyond this there are only the pure numbers. Engineering has physical quantities such as time, mass, length and temperature, and can use these quantities to construct new, derived quantities: velocity, density or specific heat. The nature of the physical quantity is called the dimension, which is a word that already has a more extensive meaning than 'the number of independent spatial directions'.

Proportionality as a key concept

In mathematics education in grades 7-9 of secondary school, the linear function $f(x) = mx + b$ takes a prominent place. In the science subjects and engineering, a comparable central theme is the question about the proportionality of two quantities, such as weight and volume, or voltage and resistance. In this regard, we should not think about a linear function with $b = 0$, but about the relationship between the varia-bles. The concept of proportionality is also used in situations where one variable is proportional to the square or to the inverse of another variable. This multifaceted use of proportionality is important, and is still insufficiently addressed in algebra education.

The nature of the formulas used

Formulas in science applications often concern situations where the relationship between more than two variables is described. Multiple proportionalities are frequently combined; the variables are not neutral because they represent physical quantities with a specific nature. Such formulas therefore require a different algebraic approach than a purely mathematical one.

Numbers, units of measurement and imprecise values

In science applications, a number can be the value of a quantity or a 'pure' number such as π. However, a number represents the value of a variable. This assumes the use of a unit of measurement, for example the unit meter; the number actually indicates the ratio with that unit. Different quantities, different units. In applications, numbers often originate from measurements. This inevitably means inexactness instead of exactness. But it is possible to deal with inexactness in an exact way. This is an aspect of algebra that makes sense in the world of applications, but is poorly illuminated in mathematics education.

Many kinds of graphs

The way in which relationships between variables in science or engineering are respresented in graphs are more diverse than one would suspect from the use of mathematical coordinate systems. The nature of the applications leads to many variations and types of scales, and sometimes to complex representations. In engineering, graphs are compact and clearly presented data sets, with very specific forms of use, which go far beyond dealing with the classical mathematical graph.

SPECIAL GRAPHS FOR BICYCLES AND LATHES

Figure 1 shows two sets of graphs, which in engineering are generally called nomograms. The set on the left concerns a bicycle and represents the relationship between the variables *pedalling rate* (in rotations or pedal strokes per minute), *gear ratio* (number of meters travelled per rotation) and *velocity* (in km per hour). The graph on the right shows the relationship between *number of revolutions* (revolutions per minute), *turning diameter* (in mm) and *cutting speed* (in m per minute) of a chisel on a lathe. These graphs are similar in several respects. There are three variables, of which one (*pedalling rate, number of revolutions*) plays the role of the parameter in the sheaf of lines.

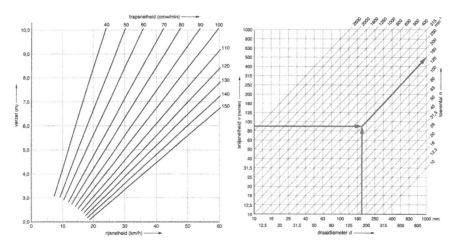

Figure 1. Two nomograms that show proportionality (Van der Kooij et al., 2003)

The other two variables have equivalent roles; so these are not just graphs with an input variable on the horizontal axis and an output variable on the vertical axis.

Both graphs have axis scales that are chosen specifically according to the nature of the situation to which they are applied. The chosen units are always shown on the graph; with the bicycle, the velocity is expressed in km per hour and the gear ratio is expressed in meters. For bicycles, the usual velocities are 5 to 60 km/h, and the usable range of gear ratios is 2-10 meters. This is not a very wide range; we can therefore read the linear scale with relative precision on both the low side and the high side.

This is different with the lathe. The ratios between the extremes on both scales are 1 to 100. Nevertheless, on the velocity scale we can easily see the difference between 10 and 12.5 m/min on the low side and between 800 and 1000 on the high side. This has been accomplished by showing the equivalent proportions 10 to 12.5 and 800 to 1000 with equal length scaling, while ignoring the absolute magnitudes. Both scales on the cutting speed nomogram are logarithmic.

There are proportionalities in both situations. For the cyclist:
   velocity (in km/h) = c_1 × rotational speed (in RPM) × gear ratio (in m)
For the lathe:
cutting speed (in m/min) = c_2 × number of revolutions (in RPM) × diameter (in m)
   With the bicycle, we therefore see straight lines with various slopes that pass through the origin (0, 0) of the graph (even though the origin cannot be seen). With the lathe, all lines are parallel; this is because at every rotational speed, a fixed proportion on the rotating diameter scale has a fixed proportion on the cutting speed scale.

   Students in vocational education must be able to read and interpret such graphs; if algebra education can support them in doing so, this is beneficial. However, the above graphs obviously describe the use of logarithms completely differently from the logarithm as the inverse of the exponential function.

PROPORTIONALITIES AND FORMULAS

An elegant and purely mathematical use of the concept proportionality can be found in the following, somewhat archaic algebraic proposition:

The areas of two circles are proportional to the squares of their radii.

The proportionality of the areas is one of the same type of quantities, the one of the radii as well. This is a meaningful proposition which does not include π. The relationship can also be formulated in this style:

The area of a circle is proportional to the square of its radius.

This is a more dynamic definition; there is a very strong suggestion that the area will become four times as large if the radius is doubled. The corresponding formula $A = \pi r^2$ makes the proportionality constant visible and is suitable for use in numerical algebra. In modern applications, this second style is therefore used more frequently; the relationship is formulated as a proportionality.

We have selected the following formulas from the current science examination syllabus for pre-university education in the Netherlands:

$$P = \frac{F}{A} \qquad F_z = G \cdot \frac{m_1 \cdot m_2}{r^2} \qquad F_{mpz} = \frac{mv^2}{r}$$

$$R = \rho\frac{l}{A} \qquad \eta = \frac{P_{useful}}{P_{in}} \cdot 100\%$$

It is immediately obvious that proportionalities are involved here. Consider the formula for gravitational attraction between two bodies F_z. If we think about a planet revolving around the sun, then we see that F_z is inversely proportional to r^2, the square of the distance between the bodies. If we think about weights falling to earth, then r is virtually constant and the formula shows that F_z is proportional to the mass of the falling weight. In the formula, G is the gravitational constant, not to be confused with the gravitational field strength $g \approx 9.81$ m/s^2.

In science and engineering courses, it is important that students are capable of verbalizing such proportionalities, converting the verbalizations to formulas, and describing and recognizing the behaviour of the corresponding graphs. The fact that little explicit attention is paid to proportionality in mathematics education is a missed opportunity. Proportionality is one of the most frequently occurring algebraic phenomena in science and engineering, and it is not difficult to link interesting mathematics to this topic. The booklet *Evenredigheden en machten* (Proportionalities and powers) was compiled in the SONaTe project based on the materials that were developed in the Profi-project for the fourth year of pre-university education (Goddijn, Reuter & Kindt, 1998; Van der Kooij, 2004). A number of ideas in this chapter originated from this booklet.

The nature of proportionality formulas

Formulas and equations as they appear in science and engineering usually concern situations in which more than two variables are involved. If the variables are mutually proportional, then there are usually products or quotients in the formula, only rarely sums or differences. For example, in a circuit where a current I flows through a resistance R, a voltage difference V occurs across the resistance. If I is constant, then V and R are proportional; if R is constant, then V and I are proportional. Consequently, the relationship must be both $V = c_1 \times R$ and $V = c_2 \times I$. The voltage must therefore be a constant times the product of R and I; in that case, the constant is chosen as the neutral '1', which defines the nature and the unit of resistance (more about this later). Ohm's law states: $V = I \times R$.

For these reasons, the formulas that indicate proportionalities between variables almost always consist of products and quotients of powers. The addition of formulas and variables is restricted: only similar types of quantities can be added. In applied formulas, addition and subtraction can often be interpreted as shifts in space or time, as with the harmonic motion

$$U = U_{max} \times \sin(\omega t)$$

where a time interval t_0 precedes the motion

$$V = U_{max} \times \sin(\omega(t - t_0)).$$

Addition and subtraction can also indicate that a formula concerns the difference between two levels, such as the Balmer formula, which shows the wavelength of a photon that is emitted when an electron in a hydrogen atom jumps from quantum level 2 to quantum level n; the formula describes the energy difference:

$$\frac{1}{\lambda} = R_\infty \cdot \left(\frac{1}{4} - \frac{1}{n^2} \right)$$

We also encounter many trigonometric functions and exponential functions in the world of applications. Remember that trigonometric functions have their background in the proportions of lengths. The function value is therefore not a quantity that is apparent in nature, but a pure number. The fact that the sine function has kept the role of a neutral number can be seen in the formula $U = U_{max} \times \sin(\omega t)$. The displacement is shown in proportion to the maximum displacement U_{max}, a chosen unit of length. Such considerations also apply to exponential functions, which indicate neutral factors as well. There will be more about quantities and their dimensions later on.

Global reasoning with proportions

Another example of more than two variables appearing in formulas in science concerns rectangular beam deflection. The deflection (bending) depends on the three measures of the beam, the load, the quality of the material, and even on gravity, which is different on the moon, for example. Some of these variables, such as the characteristics of the material and gravity, can be considered to be parameters, but then we still have five variables left: deflection, load and the three measures. Assume that the beam is attached at both ends, (as with a bookshelf) and is loaded with a total load of Q (kg). The special algebraic possibilities of proportional formulas can be shown clearly with the formula for deflection f (in mm):

$$f = \frac{5 \cdot Q \cdot l^3}{32 \cdot E \cdot w \cdot h^3} \cdot 9,81$$

E is the modulus of elasticity, a quality characteristic of the material used (N/mm^2), w, l and h are the width, length and height of the beam (in mm). What effect does a change in each of the quantities have on the deflection? It is clear that doubling the value of h has a more beneficial effect than doubling the value of w: the deflection then becomes eight times smaller. Floor and ceiling beams have a rectangular cross-section. We therefore always place the beam on the narrow side, in order to benefit as much as possible from the cube of h! In addition, an increase in E has a positive effect on deflection: the bigger the value of E, the stiffer the beam is, and therefore the deflection becomes less. Such global reasoning with proportionalities is very functional in applications, and therefore also deserves a place in algebra education.

Algebraic reasoning in such examples is supported by practical experience. This turns out to be an important factor in vocational education. As long as the manipulation of and reasoning with algebraic expressions and formulas is linked directly to matters that can be imagined in practice, students can deal with it effectively. For meaningful algebra teaching, this link is especially important in (pre-)vocational secondary education. In engineering, students are frequently confronted with similar formulas: seemingly complex relationships, specifically involving proportionalities. One objective of algebra education can be to learn to see through such complexity.

Proportionality in words, formulas, tables and graphs

As is frequently the case in algebra, with proportionality it is also important for students to be able to transform a verbal description into a formula, table or graph. In a dictionary, proportionality is defined as follows:

> If one quantity is multiplied by a certain number, the other quantity becomes that same number of times larger.

HENK VAN DER KOOIJ, AAD GODDIJN

In practice, the value of one variable, such as P, is usually given, and the task is to find the corresponding value of the other variable, such as Q, so we use the characteristic:
– P and Q are proportional if their quotient is constant, so $\frac{P}{Q} = c$,
  or the equivalent:
– P and Q are proportional if $P = c \times Q$

The dictionary could define 'inversely proportional' as:

> If one quantity is multiplied with a certain number, the other quantity becomes that same number of times smaller.

Inverse proportionality therefore has the following characteristics:
– P and Q are inversely proportional if their product is constant, so $P \times Q = c$.
– P and Q are inversely proportional if $P = c \times \frac{1}{Q}$.

With these characteristics, the proportionality – or inverse proportionality – of the quantities P and Q can be investigated based on a double table with values such as measurement data: if the quotient or product of P and Q is constant (approximately), this suggest proportionality or inverse proportionality. An alternative is to determine whether any multiplication factor in one column correlates with the same factor in the other column: if P jumps from 2 to 6, does Q jump from 15 to 45 (with proportionality) or to 5 (with inverse proportionality)? This agrees with the definition in the dictionary. Aa an example, Table 1 shows a directly proportional and an inversely proportional relationship, taken from the Dutch TWIN textbook series. The numbers at the top of the columns represent the number of teeth on the front sprocket of a bicycle with multiple speeds. Next to the rows is the number of teeth on the rear sprocket. The cells contain the gear ratio, expressed in meter per revolution. In this example, practice also supports algebraic reasoning: a rear sprocket with half the number of teeth doubles the gear ratio, while reducing the number of teeth on the front sprocket by half reduces the gear ratio by half.

Aantal tandjes van het voorblad (t_v)															
26	28	30	32	34	36	38	40	42	44	46	48	50	52	54	56
t_a															
12	467	502	538	574	610	646	682	718	754	790	826	861	897	933	969	1005
14	400	431	461	492	523	554	585	615	646	677	699	739	769	800	830	861
16	350	376	403	431	458	484	511	538	565	593	619	646	673	700	727	754
18	311	335	359	383	407	431	455	479	502	526	550	574	598	622	646	670
20	280	301	323	345	366	388	409	431	452	474	495	517	538	560	581	603
22	254	274	294	313	333	353	372	392	411	431	451	470	490	509	528	548
24	233	251	269	287	305	323	333	359	377	395	413	431	449	467	484	502
26	215	231	249	265	282	298	315	331	348	365	381	398	414	431	447	463
28	199	215	230	246	262	277	292	308	323	338	354	369	384	400	415	431

tabel 2.1 Verzet, afgerond op hele centimeters

Table 1. Directly and inversely proportional (Van der Kooij et al., 2003)

210

In many applications, the proportionality constant c in the formula has the character of a 'quality indicator'. For example, Table 2 shows the so-called finesse F or glide ratio for various gliding objects. This finesse represents the horizontal distance that can be travelled for each meter of lost altitude (engines off, wings still). The formula $g = F \times d$, where g is the horizontal gliding distance and d is the vertical drop, both expressed in m, applies to all gliding objects. F can therefore be considered as an indicator of the gliding capacity of the object: the larger the value of F, the further the object can glide.

gliding object	F
glider	40
albatross	20
Boeing 747	14
swift	10
vulture	11
cabbage butterfly	4
flying squirrel	2.5
grasshopper	1.5

Table 2. The finesse of various gliding objects (Tennekes, 1992)

Figure 2 shows on the left the graphs of the albatross (A), vulture (B) and flying squirrel (C) on a coordinate system with a standard axis layout. According to the model, for these three gliding objects, and for all the others, the following applies: if altitude loss doubles, then the horizontal gliding distance also doubles. This is shown clearly in the illustration: all three graphs are straight lines through the origin, but with different slopes.

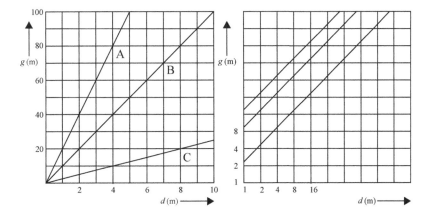

Figure 2. Gliding distance as a function of altitude loss for various gliding objects

The right graph of Figure 2 has logarithmic scales on the axis. Because of the direct proportionality, the graphs have a 45-degree angle with the horizontal axis. With proportionality of powers, as we will see below, this is different. In such a graph, proportionality to a square is shown as: one horizontal step results in a vertical step that is twice as big. A good example where this principle can be used is the measured relationship between leg length l and body mass m of a number of cockroaches; the corresponding graph is shown in Figure 3.

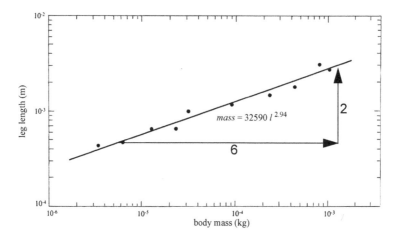

Figure 3. Leg length as a function of mass (McMohan & Tyler Bonner, 1983)

The given formula $mass = 32590 \cdot l^{2.94}$ is the result of regression analysis. The arrows on the graph indicate that a formula with an exponent 3 fits reasonably well. Based on theoretical considerations, this could be expected: leg length is a unit of length, and mass is proportional to volume, so mass is proportional to the unit of length to the power 3.

Proportionality of powers

Proportionality between powers of quantities deserves special attention. This type of proportionality is very common in science and engineering. The well-known third law of Kepler, in the classical form

the square of the orbital period of a planet is directly proportional to the cube of the orbital radius[iii]

can be converted to

$$T^2 = c \cdot R^3$$

If we multiply T by 1000, then R should increase by a factor 100. Three factors 10 for T, two factors 10 for R. This applies in the same way to factors other than 10. Multiplying T by 8 ($= 2^3$) corresponds with R multiplied by 4 ($= 2^2$).

In principle, this is the algebraic essence of general reasoning about proportionality of powers. With the previously used graph paper, on which constant proportions can be seen on the scales, that should produce a special result. We can see this in data of the four moons of Jupiter that can be observed with a simple telescope. By making periodic observations, one can determine the orbital periods. Galileo did this in 1610; the results are shown in Table 3.

moon	orbital period T (in days)	distance R to Jupiter (in 10^3 km)
Io	1.76	422
Europa	3.55	671
Ganymede	7.15	1070
Calypso	19.69	1882

Table 3. Orbital periods and distances of four of Jupiter's moons

Figure 4 shows the graph on a logarithmic scale. On paper, the ten steps must be of equal size horizontally and vertically, but we can adapt the necessary part of the scale to the data. The slope of the line is $\frac{3}{2}$, as expected. The graph can be expanded to include the 28 moons that are currently known.

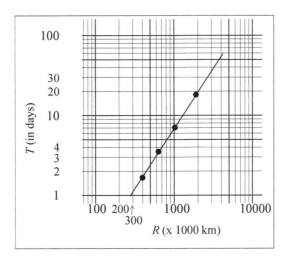

Figure 4. Graph on a logarithmic scale

Generally speaking, proportionality of powers means that the relationship has the following algebraic form:

$$y = c \cdot x^b$$

In this equation c is the proportionality constant, and the exponent b is a real number, which can be fractional or negative. The above approach is a good way to investigate proportionality relationships between powers of variables. The slope of the line indicates the ratio between the powers; changes in the constant c cause the line to shift. 'y is proportional to x^b' can also be described as 'x is proportional to $y^{1/b}$', as is illustrated in the following scheme:

$$x \overset{\wedge b}{\to} x^b \overset{\times c}{\to} c \cdot x^b (= y) \quad \text{and} \quad y \overset{\times (1/c)}{\to} \frac{1}{c} \cdot y \overset{\wedge b}{\to} \left(\frac{1}{c} \cdot y\right)^{\frac{1}{b}} (= x)$$

Such algebraic skills are useful in science and engineering.

There is another way to illustrate proportionality of powers on a graph. In the example of F_{mpz} which is proportional to v^2, we can use v^2 for the scale on the horizontal axis instead of v. The graph then becomes a straight line. Dutch science books in pre-university education call this coordinate transformation. Perhaps it is clearer to call this substitution: v^2 is replaced by the variable u. The equation $F_{mpz} = c \times y^2$ then changes into $F_{mpz} = c \times u$, and the graph becomes a straight line (see Figure 5).

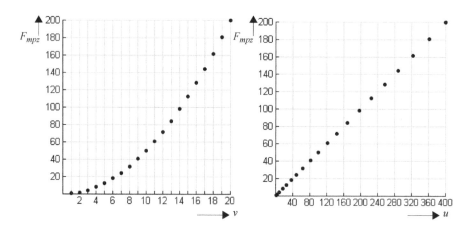

Figure 5. Change of scale on the horizontal axis to illustrate proportionality

When an algebraic model on a theoretical basis is available, proportionality is apparent in the formula, and a graph like the one above can be made. If such a model is not available, but measurement data are, we cannot use this method because the choice of the coordinates transformation depends on the model. In this case, the scale division that is based on the principle that equal length differences correspond to equal proportions is helpful. For every power function $y = c \cdot x^b$, a straight line will appear, and the exponent can be determined from the slope of this straight line.

Proportionality and density

Two equations from the selection of science formulas deserve specific attention:

$$p = \frac{F}{A} \text{ and } \eta = \frac{P_{useful}}{P_{in}} \cdot 100\%$$

Although they are very different, they have something in common: they are essentially scalings with respect to a total. Pressure P is the force per unit of surface area and efficiency η is the best achievable effect *relative* to the maximum effect. Such relative measures are common; consider mass density, population density, relative humidity... in fact, density involves proportionality, where the proportionality constant is the inverse of the total. This becomes visible after rewriting the formula:

$$P = \frac{1}{A} \cdot F \text{ and } \eta = \frac{1}{P_{in}} \cdot P_{useful} \cdot 100\% \, .$$

As a result, a relative unit is created, which allows two or more different situations to be compared. With densities, direct and inverse proportionality are packaged very naturally into a single formula: an increase in the population leads to an increase in population density; annexation of new territory leads to a lower population density.

In summary, many algebraic relationships that occur in science and engineering are essentially proportionalities. In algebra, proportionality deserves more attention.

QUANTITY, DIMENSION AND UNIT

Traditional geometry, and the algebra that is closely related to it, only deals with a few quantities: the spatial quantities of length, area and volume, and angle components. In terms of both the number of different quantities and how they are treated, science made us progress further. This is why we are first looking slightly deeper into the concept of quantity and related matters.

Measuring quantities

A quantity is a physical concept that is measurable, such as distance, time, temperature, mass, velocity, current, force, hardness and colour. Even this brief list shows how complex the world of quantities is, because the above concepts are measured in very different ways. Some of them (such as velocity) appear to be a combination of two others (time and distance in this case). Moreover, there are obvious questions about standard quantities, and last but not least, precision.

Quantities can be measured in many different ways. For example, before crowning a tooth, a dentist has to precisely measure the colour of the adjacent teeth. For this purpose he uses a sample card with many subtle shades of white. In this case, measuring is essentially comparing. The values to be measured do not appear in a single linear sequence. This is different when measuring wind speed with the Beaufort scale, a somewhat outdated method where you compare the wind with a force three wind, which causes a flag to start moving. Or you compare it with a force 9 wind, a storm wind, which may damage chimneys or tear off roof tiles, and causes light damage to forests. There is a standard scale which ranges from 0 (wind still) to 13 (hurricane force). Our concept of temperature is determined by two calibration points: absolute zero, the lowest possible temperature, and the triple point of water. This is the temperature at which water, ice, and water vapour can coexist in a stable equilibrium. This temperature is defined as 273.16 Kelvin.[iv]

Compared to the above, measurement scales for length and time appear to be simple: you can measure length and time by comparison with an agreed scale unit of length or time, by repeating measurements, and possibly by refining the unit. Scales that are created in this way clearly have a strong connection with the world of numbers: you can add such measurements (if they are the same type); the numerical value that corresponds with the sum is the sum of the numerical values of the parts. Such units are suitable for proportions and for computation, although there are a few snakes in the grass. With velocity, it appears that we are measuring with two different measures – distance travelled and elapsed time – which are divided by each other. That is the customary representation; before we look deeper into such composite quantities, we will provide some information about standard units.

Units

In 1960 the SI (*Système International*) was implemented as a standard system for scientific units. It provides an overview of units that can be used in science and engineering. The SI defines seven basic units, those for length, mass, time, electric current, temperature, amount of substance and luminous intensity.

For example, take the units for length. The prevailing unit of length is the meter; this was redefined in 1983 as the distance that light travels, in a vacuum, in exactly 1/299792458th of a second. The second has been defined as a natural phenomenon that can be theoretically counted, and is therefore also exact: the duration of 9 192 631 770 periods of the radiation corresponding to the transition between the two hyperfine levels of the ground state of the caesium 133 atom. This definition refers to a caesium atom at rest at absolute zero.

Another example is the unit of mass. The unit of mass is still defined in the old-fashioned way: a cylinder of platinum-iridium located in Sèvres, Paris is used for the international prototype of the *kilogram* (the kilogram is therefore the basic unit, not the *gram*!).

From the basic units, other units are derived such as the centimeter and the light-year for length, and composed units such as velocity, based on meters per second.

The SI has also standardized the series of prefixes, of which kilo and deci are perhaps the most familiar, a series that ranges from *yocto* for 10^{-24}, to *yotta* for 10^{24}. From this we can also see that the metric system was clearly a predecessor of the SI. In the years following the French Revolution (1795), the metric system initially intended to completely decimalize all units, including a different division of the calendar and the angle[v]. For that matter, Napoleon appears to have been an opponent of the metric system; King Willem I implemented the system in the Netherlands in 1816. The USA is still out of step with inches and miles.

Making quantities and calculating with quantities

For your security, this bicycle parking facility is under 24-hour video surveillance.

There is something annoying about this notice at the automated bicycle parking facility at the train station. We assume that 24 hours per day is meant. But even this is rather strange, isn't that the same as '60 seconds per minute'? In fact you could say this, but 24 hours per day somehow sounds much more secure. Obviously, day-to-day language and the language of science and engineering have their own standards. We are familiar with velocity in terms of kilometers per hour, but when we drive a car we often say: I am doing 80. We can convert to SI units as follows: 80 kilometers per hour is 80000 meter per 3600 seconds. This is 80000/36000 meter per 1 second, which is 22.22 meter per second, or 5 seconds between each hectometer marker. The operations used in combining and converting are division and multiplication, that much is clear. If we express a quantity in terms of a unit, then we use a number to illustrate this relationship: the numerical value. We can illustrate the relationship between the numerical value, quantity and unit as follows:

quantity = numerical value · unit

By doing so, we indicate that we are aware of the underlying proportional structure of the system of linear measurement, but that we still want to work algebraically with numbers and use multiplication. The relationship is usable because it is so consistent. For example, take the concept of the area of a rectangle.

quantity of area = numerical value of area · unit of area

However, we also determine the area by using the formula *area = length · width*. This formula gives us the following:

(numerical value of length · unit of length) · (numerical value of width · unit of width)

and from this, of course, we can make:

(numerical value of length · numerical value of width) · (unit of length · unit of width).

We are very familiar with the component (*numerical value of length · numerical value of width*), which belongs to the world of numbers, and we have

numerical value of area = numerical value of length · numerical value of width.

However, in the second component we must have:

unit of area = unit of length · unit of width

If we use the meter m for the two linear measurement units, than the unit of area, as a consequence of the multiplication structure, is m^2. To this rather abstract analysis, we can add the conversion rules for the same types of units as in 1 inch = 25.4 · mm or 1 foot = 12 · inch; this is not especially problematic. However, this analysis as a whole shows that it is certainly possible to provide mathematical support or description to the physical phenomenon of quantity[vi], and that the frequently criticized formulation 'distance divided by time' can in fact be justified.

Dimension

We measure velocity in terms of distance travelled per unit of time, or length divided by time, but a physicist states this somewhat differently: the dimension of velocity is LT^{-1}, or L/T. L stands for length, T stands for time and the algebraic structure of the formula illustrates the relationship: length divided by time, or per time. Every quantity in science has such a dimension. For example, take the quantities of distance, width, height, distance travelled, braking distance and string length. These are all representatives of the dimension length. It does not matter whether we measure in units of kilometers or millimeters, the dimension of braking distance is length. A dimension of a quantity is generally indicated with square brackets around that quantity. If we abbreviate length with L and time with T, you could write the dimensions as:

[*distance travelled*]=[*distance*]=[*width*]=[*height*]= L.   [*area*]= L^2 and [*velocity*] = LT^{-1}

All quantities of area have the dimension L^2; this requires no further explanation. We measure the frequency of a periodic phenomenon in Hertz, meaning number of cycles per second. The dimension of frequency is therefore T^{-1} or $1/T$. The numerical values that we used above are dimensionless.

Dimensional analysis

Force is mass times acceleration, and therefore has the dimension $M \cdot L \cdot T^{-2}$. Work is force times distance, power is work per unit of time. For power we therefore find the dimension $L^2 \cdot T^{-3} \cdot M$. We have now become involved in dimensional analysis, which is essentially the bookkeeping that keeps track of the type and nature of the units. In a formula that describes a relationship between quantities, the dimensions must obviously be correct. This is something that a physicist automatically pays attention to. For example, take the formula for the period of a pendulum:

$$T = 2\pi \sqrt{\frac{l}{g}}$$

Here, the variables are quantities with a specific meaning: the period of the pendulum T with unit s, the length of the pendulum l with unit m and the acceleration of gravity g with unit m/s^2. In this case the dimensional analysis involves an interesting exercise in fairly basic algebra. Because $[T] = T$, $[l]= L$ and $[g]= L/T^2$ and because 2π is a dimensionless number, the dimensions in the formula are indeed correct:

$$[l/g] = L/(L/T^2) = T^2 \text{ so } \left[\sqrt{\frac{l}{g}}\right] = T = [T]$$

A good illustration of the dimensions of composite quantities expressed in length, time and mass is shown in Figure 6. Here, the dimensions $L^xT^yM^z$ are all shown as points (x, y, z) in space. This illustration is from an elegant science-philosophy essay, *On thinking in terms of co-ordinates* by Stefan Themerson. However, Themerson still gives the Ampere the dimension that the quantity had in the m-s-kg system; This is no longer correct in the SI system, where the Ampere has been redefined as a distinct basic unit.

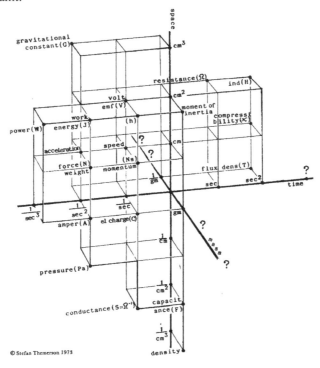

Figure 6. Dimensions of composite quantities (Themerson, 1974)

219

Formulas and dimensions

The following example contains two different but equivalent formulas; a dimensional analysis shows that 'regular' algebra disregards some important matters (Van der Kooij, 2000). This involves the problem of two cyclists who take the same route and travel at the same velocity, but leave fifteen seconds apart. If the cycling velocity is 4 m/s and the first cyclist (A) leaves at time $t = 0$, then the two formulas for the distance travelled s for the two cyclists are $s = 4t$ (for A) and $s = 4(t - 15)$ for B.

The dimensional analysis shows the dimensions are correct: $[s] = L$ and $[4t]$ has dimension $(L/T) \times T = L$. An analysis of the second formula results in the same conclusion because $t - 15$ has dimension T. Nevertheless, something special is happening here! In pure algebraic terms, $s = 4(t - 15)$ is the same as $s = 4t - 60$, but the dimension test now provides an insight that dimensionless algebra hides. When rewriting $4(t - 15)$ to $4t - 60$, it turns out that the original number 15 (with dimension L/T), which has been transformed into the number 60, must also have the dimension L and unit m. This is not apparent during the multiplication of 4×15, where numbers simply produce numbers. The second formula therefore does not describe a second cyclist who leaves 15 seconds later from the same starting position. Instead, it describes a cyclist who starts at the same time as A, but from a position 60 m behind A. This additional dimensional analysis is truly an enrichment of the 'regular' algebra used in the problem. Consequently, there are two different graphs corresponding to two different problem situations. However, the two problems are algebraically equivalent if you disregard the dimensions of the numbers and variables (Figure 7).

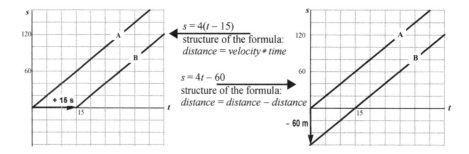

Figure 7. Two ways to look at equivalent formulas

Dimensional analysis can also clarify problems involving exponential growth or decline, which are frequently used during grades 10-12 of pre-university education, to acquire a better grasp of the variables and parameters that play a part.

Variables with roles and dimensions

We have seen that variables in the algebraic formulas and functions used in science and engineering have a different character than in mathematics, because they represent quantities with dimensions and a unit. There is yet another difference that we want to emphasize here. A variable in a science or engineering formula has a specific role in the applied situation. More than in pure mathematics problems, this role is often expressed as a traditional abbreviation of a variable name, such as s for distance travelled, V for voltage, t for time, ω for angular velocity, F for force, and so on. This not only clarifies the connection with the application, but also ensures that the dimensional and unit structure of the formula remains visible. For example, take the following two formulas, the first representing a rational function and next the formula for the period of a pendulum:

$$f(x) = \frac{x-1}{x^2+3} \text{ and } T = 2\pi\sqrt{\frac{l}{g}}$$

In the pendulum period formula, the variables have functional names, dimensions and units: pendulum period T with unit s, pendulum length l with unit m and acceleration of gravity g with unit m/s^2. Actually, there is a connection between T and l: if we know l, then we also know T, and the reverse. In the formula, the constant (but not dimensionless!) quantity g is preferable to the number 9.81, as it shows more explicitly that the dimensions are correct. In the rational formula, the variables are not linked to a specific meaning, and there is no problem in replacing x with u. This has no effect at all on its functioning as an algebraic object. The x in the formula is not a variable that refers to something outside the definition, but is only a symbol to briefly notate the structure of an algebraic relationship. In other words, the x is a 'dummy' variable, just like the k in the following summation formula and the t in the adjacent integral formula. Both the sum and the integral are constants!

$$\sum_{k=1}^{\infty} \frac{1}{k^2} \qquad \int_{1}^{\infty} \frac{dt}{1+t^2}$$

The fact that variables in formulas from science and engineering represent quantities with dimensions and units is an important difference with the way variables often function in algebra. It is important to be aware of this difference.

WORKING WITH INACCURATE NUMBERS

The numerical values that are used in science and engineering are often values of measured quantities and therefore are intrinsically imprecise. Dealing with this issue correctly is a specialism in itself, which is called error analysis.

When entering values into a formula such as $V_0\sin(\omega t)$, there are still other issues; the time t will not be known exactly, ω is possibly expressed as radians per sec-

HENK VAN DER KOOIJ, AAD GODDIJN

ond and will be based on the number of decimals of π that are used, the sine of the calculator is an approximation, and the multiplication with the value of V_0 will be imprecise: a limited number of decimals is given. The result is an approximation.

There are always inaccuracies in manufacturing processes, which can be disastrous in some cases. For example, consider manufacturing a cylinder-shaped bar 10 mm in diameter which must fit into a hole 10 mm in diameter; this is a risky endeavour. If we require the cylinder diameter to be manufactured with a negative tolerance of 0.01 mm and the hole has the same positive tolerance, then success is more likely. However, a two-sided tolerance can be problematic. Correct indications of errors and guaranteed tolerances are important. For the above reasons alone, it is clear that there is more involved in using numbers in science and engineering than the mathematical approach would initially lead one to suspect.

Error analysis

In mathematics education, working with inaccurate values should be given more attention. A concept such as tolerance (allowable deviation above and below a given measurement in absolute numbers or as percentages) is desirable in many situations. Algebra is very suitable for describing the effects of errors, i.e. deviations in numerical values.

For example, place two boards end-to-end; each board is 200 cm long, with a tolerance of 0.5 cm. This results in a total length of 400 cm, with a maximum deviation of 1 cm. When you compare the difference of two units of length, you must also take account of the sum of the deviations. After all, the extremes of tolerance with $a \pm \Delta a$ and $b \pm \Delta b$ are shown by the sum of a and b by $\pm(\Delta a + \Delta b)$ and in the difference by $\Delta a - (-\Delta b)$ and $-\Delta a - (\Delta b)$. The simple rule with sums and differences is therefore:

For the sum and the difference, the absolute error is equivalent to the sum of the absolute errors.

It becomes more difficult with the product and quotient of two quantities a and b
$$(a + \Delta a)(b + \Delta b) = ab + a\Delta b + b\Delta a + \Delta a \cdot \Delta b$$
so $\Delta(ab) = (a + \Delta a)(b + \Delta b) - ab = a\Delta b + b\Delta a + \Delta a \cdot \Delta b$
With relatively small deviations, the higher order term can be neglected:
$$\Delta(ab) = (a + \Delta a)(b + \Delta b) - ab \approx a\Delta b + b\Delta a$$
With a quotient, it becomes even worse. In that case, you obtain the largest deviation by dividing the largest possible numerator by the smallest possible denominator.
$$\Delta\left(\frac{a}{b}\right) = \frac{a + \Delta a}{b - \Delta b} - \frac{a}{b} = \frac{b\Delta a + a\Delta b}{b(b-\Delta b)} \approx \frac{b\Delta a + a\Delta b}{b^2}$$
These expressions lead to complicated formulations for the deviations in the product or quotient. However, if you are looking for the relative error instead of the absolute error, then the rules are still rather simple:

$$\frac{\Delta(ab)}{ab} = \frac{a\Delta b + b\Delta a}{ab} = \frac{\Delta a}{a} + \frac{\Delta b}{b}$$

and

$$\frac{\Delta\left(\dfrac{a}{b}\right)}{\dfrac{a}{b}} = \Delta\left(\frac{a}{b}\right) \cdot \frac{b}{a} = \frac{b\Delta a + a\Delta b}{b^2} \cdot \frac{b}{a} = \frac{b\Delta a + a\Delta b}{ab} = \frac{\Delta a}{a} + \frac{\Delta b}{b}$$

The surprising result of using algebra is the simple rule for product and quotient:

> For product and quotient, the relative error is equivalent to the sum of the relative errors.

At this point we should perhaps issue a warning: the relative error of $a - b$ does not behave so predictably and can become unexpectedly large!

In physics, the coefficient of linear thermal expansion α is a property of materials that indicates the factor with which the material increases in length (relative to the initial length) for each degree of temperature rise.

$$\alpha = \frac{\Delta l}{l}$$

The surface expansion and the cubic expansion have expansion coefficients 2α and 3α, respectively. These are direct applications of the above rule for the product. In algebraic terms, this means that in the solution of the expressions $(l + \Delta l)^2 - l^2$ and $(l + \Delta l)^3 - l^3$, higher powers of the relative error are disregarded. Solved for the volume coefficient

$$\gamma = \frac{(l + \Delta l)^3 - l^3}{l^3} = \frac{3l^2\Delta l + 3l(\Delta l)^2 + (\Delta l)^3}{l^3} = 3\left(\frac{\Delta l}{l}\right) + 3\left(\frac{\Delta l}{l}\right)^2 + \left(\frac{\Delta l}{l}\right)^3$$

This example shows that error analysis, which is extremely relevant to science and engineering, can lead to interesting, albeit rather complex, algebra.

ALGEBRA TUNED TO SCIENCE AND ENGINEERING

One of the early findings of the Dutch SONaTe project was that the teachers of the science subjects do cooperate (even if this just involves using the same lab), but that mathematics operates entirely separate from the other subjects. The need for more cooperation between the subjects in the pre-university profiles in secondary education has led to a search for common ground between mathematics and science. Through the development of two text booklets (*Proportions & powers* for mathematics and *Investigating relationships* for science) the gap between the subjects has become somewhat smaller. During this process it turned out that the different disciplines could benefit from each other by using shared notation and concepts. In the actual lessons given at the participating schools, the attention in mathematics for proportions strengthened the understanding of experimental research involving proportions in the science lessons. But the students also thought the treatment of the same phenomenon in maths or science corresponded specifically to one discipline or the other. This is comparable with the observations that during mathematics lessons, students have difficulty tackling a geometric problem with algebraic techniques, and the reverse. In such a case, reminders such as "But you also did that in science" appear to be essential to encourage this recognition. Perhaps it would help to teach in a team context: the science and mathematics teacher could work as a team to teach the areas where both disciplines share common ground. During these lessons the teachers could also explicitly address the different ways in which the two subjects deal with relations. Whether tuning and aligning with other subjects is voluntary or mandatory, it remains a praiseworthy pursuit.

In this chapter, several topics are identified where this supporting role of mathematics can be very successful. The emphasis was primarily on the deficiencies in current mathematics programmes: lack of attention for proportionalities and disregard for dimensions and units and for working with non-exact numbers.

In all application areas for mathematics, quantities play an important role. For this reason alone, they should not be ignored in mathematics education. The fact that algebra in formal terms does not have anything to do with situation-linked meanings of variables is an inadequate counterargument. Some algebraically correct methods lose their value when applied outside mathematics. But including such meanings also makes algebra accessible for large groups of students. During the TWIN project it turned out that students in secondary vocational education (grades 9-11), who had practiced algebra based on quantities and became rather skilled at this, lost many of these skills in the upper grades because a more formal system of algebra was offered with an eye to higher vocational education. The consideration of dimensions and units, besides offering a critical perspective on formulas and the meaning of parameters and numbers, also provides some elementary algebraic activity as part of dimensional analysis.

Attention for working with imprecise numbers appears to be useful, due to their use in science and engineering. But also within mathematics education itself, there is good reason to pay attention to this. Graphing calculators (and computers as well) show points on a graph as pixels with larger or smaller dimensions. This is why the Trace option on a graphing calculator may provides strange coordinate values: the chosen range for x is simply divided by the number of pixels in the horizontal direction, and this defines the step size of Trace (see Chapter 8). Similarly, differential equations in simulation software are calculated with the discrete steps of the Euler method or its more advanced variants. However, these are still numerical methods, which provide only approximations of the real, theoretically continuous models. As a result, you automatically introduce inaccuracies with respect to the theoretical model, which is based on a continuous scale. Therefore, giving some attention to numerical methods in mathematics education appears to be a step, also in view of the increasing availability of computer software.

Let us finish by providing some examples of English language student materials showing the link between mathematics and science/technology. For the TechMap project[vii] three modules were developed for use in High School: *Circular Motion, Clocks, Insulation and Sound*. All three connect mathematical topics to Technology and Science (Van der Kooij & Goris, 2005 abcd). For a small-scale pilot project in a Community College in Colorado, a chapter of the College Algebra course was replaced by a module on exponential and logarithmic functions, in which scientific contexts are used to develop the notion of exponential growth and a common-sense introduction of logarithms (Van der Kooij, 2006).

NOTES

i   The TWIN project (Technology, Mathematics, ICT, science ran from 1996 until 2000. It developed a modified mathematics curriculum for secondary vocational education, so that it supports engineering in the technology sector. See Van der Kooij (Ed.), Goris & Temme (2003).

ii The SONaTe project (Interconnected Education in Science and Technology) has as its goal taking stock of how the four science subjects can be better integrated in secondary education which prepares for univerity studies in science and mathematics.

iii Assuming circular trajectories. For ellipses the proportionality is with the third power of the long axis of the ellipse. See http://solarviews.com/eng/jupiter.htm#moons

iv Obviously, such a definition is complex and has a lot more background than can be gone into here. Wikipedia can be a starting point for finding more information, in this case: *http://en.wikipedia.org/wiki/Triple_point*

v   The right angle was defined as 100 degrees; the system is still used in surveying.

vi Chapter 2 shows that the French mathematician Viète already made advances in this direction in the 16th century. Also see Van Dormolen (1971) and Griesel (1969).

vii The TechMap project had as its goal connecting mathematics and various vocational fields. The NSF-funded project was directed by Sol Garfunkel, COMAP. See http://www.comap.com/highschool/projects/techmap/

REFERENCES

Bakker, A., Kent, P., Derry, J., Noss, R., & Hoyles, C. (2008). Statistical inference at work: The case of statistical process control. *Statistics Education Research Journal, 7*(2), 130-145.

Dormolen, J. (1971). Grootheden. [Quantities]. *Euclides, 46,* 363-368.

Goddijn, A., Reuter, W., & Kindt, M. (1998). *Evenredigheden en machten.* [Proportionalities and powers]. Utrecht: Freudenthal Instituut.

Griesel, H. (1969). Algebra und Analysis der Grössensysteme. *Mathematisch-Physicalische Semesterberichte*, Band XVI.

Hoyles, C., Noss, R., Kent, P. & Bakker, A. (2010). *Techno-mathematical literacies.* London: Routledge.

Hoyles, C., Wolf, A., Molyneux-Hodgson, S., & Kent, P. (2002). *Mathematical skills in the workplace: Final report to the Science, Technology and Mathematics Council.* London: CSTM.

Kooij, H. van der (2000). Dimensievolle algebra. [Dimension-full algebra.] *Nieuwe Wiskrant, Tijdschrift voor Nederlands Wiskundeonderwijs*, 20(2), 33-38.

Kooij, H. van der (2001). Modelling and algebra: how 'pure' shall we be? In J.F. Matos, W. Blum (Eds.), *Modelling and mathematics education. The 9th international conference on the teaching of mathematical modeling and applications: applications in science and technology* (pp. 171-184). Chichester, England: Horwood Publishing.

Kooij, H. van der (2006). *Exponents and logarithms.* Utrecht: Freudenthal Institute.

Kooij, H. van der, & Goris, T. (2005a). *Clocks*. Lexington, COMAP, http://www.comap.com/highschool/projects/techmap/finunits.htm

Kooij, H. van der, & Goris, T. (2005b). *Insulation.* Lexington, COMAP, http://www.comap.com/highschool/projects/techmap/finunits.htm

Kooij, H. van der, & Goris, T. (2005c). *Sound.* Lexington, COMAP, http://www.comap.com/highschool/projects/techmap/finunits.htm

Kooij, H. van der, & Goris, T. (2005d). *Circular motion.* Lexington, COMAP, http://www.comap.com/highschool/projects/techmap/finunits.htm

Kooij, H. van der (Ed.), Goris, T., & Temme, C. (2003). *TWIN, beroepsgerichte wiskunde.* [TWIN, vocational mathematics.] Utrecht/Zutphen: ThiemeMeulenhoff.

McMohan, T.A., & Tyler Bonner, J. (1983). *On size and life*. New York: W.H. Freeman.

Noss, R. & Hoyles, C. (1996). *Windows on mathematical meaning.* Dordrecht, the Netherlands: Kluwer Academic Publishers.

Steen, L.A. (2001). Mathematics and numeracy: Two literacies, one language. *The Mathematics Educator, 6*(1), 10-16.

Steen, L.A. (2003). Data, shapes, symbols: Achieving balance in school mathematics. In B.L. Madison & L.A. Steen (Eds.), *Quantitative literacy: Why literacy matters for schools and colleges* (pp. 53-74). Washington, DC: The Mathematical Association of America.

Tennekes, H. (1992). *De wetten van de vliegkunst.* [The laws of flying.] Haarlem: Aramith.

Themerson, S. (1974). *Logic, labels and flesh*. London: Gaberbocchus Press.

INDEX

INDEX

40, 41, 49-53, 63-66, 70, 79, 82, 84-
86, 89-98, 100, 119-124, 126-129,
132, 133, 138, 141-143, 149, 151,
152, 157-159, 162, 164-170, 173,
175, 176, 186, 187, 189, 190, 194-
198, 203, 205, 207-209, 211, 212,
214, 215, 217-221, 224
word formula 84, 93, 133
function 7, 9, 10, 14-16, 19, 25, 41, 63,
66, 92, 101, 106, 119-129, 132-134,
180, 182, 184-186, 188, 189, 194-
198, 204, 207, 208, 211, 212, 215,
221, 225

G

generalization 8-10, 12, 18, 20, 39, 69,
70, 76, 81, 91, 95-98, 101, 119, 166,
184, 187, 198
overgeneralization 18, 20
geometry 7, 13-17, 27, 28, 52-56, 58-
62, 64-68, 73, 78, 127, 141, 142,
149, 169, 173, 215
graph 7, 8, 10, 16, 25, 28, 63-65, 67,
106, 107, 119, 122, 124, 127, 129-
133, 139, 150, 167, 181, 182, 185,
186, 189, 191, 194-199, 203, 205-
207, 209, 211-214, 220, 224
graphing calculator 63, 64, 123, 128,
137, 167, 170, 181, 182, 190, 191,
195, 196, 199, 224

I

inequality 12-14, 80, 105-107, 116

L

language 9, 10, 16, 17, 40, 41, 50, 70,
76, 79, 89, 90, 93, 99, 106, 138, 149,
155, 164, 217
longitudinal learning trajectory 69, 73,
75, 76, 78, 79, 86, 87, 133

M

math war 5, 26

Mathematics in Context 10, 26, 78, 87,
100, 106, 114, 133
mathematization 70, 124
horizontal mathematization 89, 93,
97, 98
vertical mathematization 20, 89, 93,
97, 98
mental model 70, 71, 96, 184, 191

N

notation 7, 16, 17, 25, 27-29, 34-36, 38-
47, 90, 94, 96, 99-111, 113, 120,
123, 124, 126, 127, 131, 153, 159,
177, 181, 191, 198, 223
notebook notation 114-116
reverse Polish notation 51

O

own production 78, 99, 147, 166, 170-
172, 173, 176

P

paper-and-pencil 183, 190, 191, 193,
194, 198-200
pattern 8, 10-12, 20, 24, 25, 39, 44, 70,
72, 73, 81, 84-86, 89-99, 101, 109,
110, 115, 120-122, 126, 128, 133,
148, 156-158, 162, 172, 176, 177,
186-188, 197, 198
permanence principle 9, 20
physics 9, 13, 23, 24, 25, 131, 148, 149,
160, 169, 223
practice 21, 72, 73, 102, 128, 133, 134,
137, 138, 146, 147, 152, 159, 165,
170, 175, 182, 183, 185, 191, 198,
200, 209
productive practice 25
precision 206, 215
pre-formal 79, 85, 107-109, 111, 113-
116
problem solving 5, 10, 12, 123, 132,
133, 143, 181, 183, 193, 200, 203
procedure 5, 7, 8, 21, 23, 24, 75, 76,

Lightning Source UK Ltd.
Milton Keynes UK
UKOW07f0729160216

268430UK00001B/114/P